War Widow

Other Books by Ziva Bakman-Flamhaft

Israel on the Road to Peace: Accepting the Unacceptable

War Widow

HOW THE SIX DAY WAR CHANGED MY LIFE A MEMOIR

Ziva Bakman-Flamhaft

ISBN-13: 9781539848776
ISBN-10: 1539848779
Library of Congress Control Number: 2016918256
CreateSpace Independent Publishing Platform
North Charleston, South Carolina

Dedicated with love to Steve, Odellia, and Ricky, who knew all yet not enough.

To Gabriella and Jacob: This is your grandmother.
And to the memory of my sister Miriam (Mickie) Schmeltzer
And my friend Amy Rubinstein.

I hope that my story will inspire women and men everywhere, especially those who have suffered through war, personal bereavement, and other challenges.

Acknowledgments

It had been years since I first thought about writing this book. But it was not until 2005 that I etched its first lines on paper. The occasion for which I wrote those words was the naming ceremony of my granddaughter, Gabriella. The passage I read was about my mother Khaya, which is Gabriella's Hebrew name (she is also named after her paternal great grandmother, Sarah). Hence the beginning of my fascinating journey into my family's past, and my own.

This book would not have been written without the help of a number of people. First, I wish to thank Marion Landew, a retired memoir-writing instructor at NYU's School of Professional Studies, for her encouragement when writing this book was a mere thought. I also wish to thank my friends who have waited for me patiently, hoping they will do the same when I assume my next writing projects.

Additional thanks are due to my editors who helped me through the different stages of writing this memoir: Beth Lieberman, Linda Sperling, Amy Hughes, and Stephen Brewer. I would also like to express my gratitude to Esti Cohn, my dedicated Israeli editor, who helped with the Hebrew version of my book.

My deepest thanks belong to my beloved daughter, Odellia, who, as a mother of two young children, must have felt neglected during the first years I devoted to writing this book; to my son-in-law, Ricky, who understood her pain and supported us both; and to my husband, Steve, a nobleman, for his patience, understanding, and support, but mostly for honoring my privacy and giving me the space I needed while undertaking this intimate endeavor.

Last but not least, to my grandma Brakha, without whose courage I might not have been born to tell the story of three generations of a typical Israeli family. To all with gratitude.

Table of Contents

Preface

Among the rewards that came with this writing was the rediscovering of my paternal family. As a child I had few memories of this family, the warmest being the gatherings of all thirty or forty of us in my grandparents' home for the Jewish holidays. By contrast, I practically grew up with my maternal cousins, enjoying the warmth that my mother's sisters showered upon me when I was a child. But while writing my story, I realized that my father's family had always been by my side in times of need. They appeared time and again in my life during crises—reliable, dependable, and comforting.

Other rewards that were part of writing this book were my visits to the Eastern European countries and towns where my parents were born and raised and to the homes in which they lived. In 2008, with five of my maternal cousins and our spouses I traveled to Lithuania. Walking in Vilnius, the country's capital, where in 1932 my mother had gotten her immigration certificate to Palestine, I could imagine her arriving there with anticipation, and that turning into joy once she obtained the desired document. I felt close to her there, but closer yet in the city of Klaipeda, where she spent a year preparing for her Palestine endeavor. But I felt closest to her standing in what was her family's small backyard in the village of Plunge, feet away from the park she remembered and admired all of her life.

I felt connected to her father when I found his gravestone, one among eighty-nine that were preserved from what was once the old Jewish cemetery in Plunge and placed on a nearby site. There, my cousin Itze sang in his baritone voice El Male Rahamim (a God filled with Mercy), the somber prayer for the dead, shivering the silence under the blue skies of springtime Plunge. I had heard this heart-piercing prayer many times before. But to hear my cousin solemnly singing that prayer in my mother's hometown, near our grandfather's gravestone, was an extraordinarily moving experience.

I was overwhelmed standing by the Koshan Memorial at the outskirts of Plunge, where we recited the Kaddish prayer. The shrine is named for the Koshan forest, which in the summer of 1941 was the killing field of 1,800 Plunge Jews, including my grandmother, aunts, uncle, an unborn cousin, and many other relatives.

In the summer of 2010 I traveled to Poland with my cousin Anat to trace our family's roots. My heart skipped a beat when we entered Przytyk, the birth town of my father, Anat's mother, and all but one of their five siblings. On a Sunday afternoon in July, none other than the mayor of Kielce, the district where Przytyk is situated, took Anat and me on a tour of the town, where we were searching for remnants of our family's flour mill.

Yet I felt closer to my father in Radom, to where his family escaped from anti-Semitic attacks. When I touched the old staircase banister in the apartment building where my father and his family once lived, its patina still rich in color, I felt as if I was touching my father's hands. When a kind elderly woman invited Anat and me to see her apartment, I could smell my grandmother's cooking. Later, in the town's Jewish ghetto I thought of my great-grandfather, who died there.

But it was in the death camps of Auschwitz and Birkenau that I broke into pieces. Nothing I have studied, read, seen, not Yad Vashem, not even my previous visit to Terezienstadt, prepared me for the camps' enormity and for the efficiency with which the Nazis ran their death-oiled industry.

What shocked me most was that not even the minutest detail was left to chance: not the place where the trains would stop, where victims would be "selected," where they undressed, where they were first disinfected and shaved, their hair used by the Nazis to manufacture fabric, not where they were disinfected for the second time, where their clothing was first fumigated, then fumigated for the second time, where their belongings were collected, sorted, and stored, where they would die by Zyclon B poisoning gas, where their corpses would be burned.

It took 25 minutes from the time the human cargo arrived at Birkenau for those "selected" to become ash. Many of those who survived that selection were sent to the hell of Auschwitz, where members of my father's family were murdered.

Throughout this book, the scenes and events I depict in my story are told exactly as I remember them, or as they were told to me. Because memories are subjective, I would not be surprised if events and occurrences that have registered in my consciousness in a certain way were remembered differently by family members and other individuals who appear in my book.

The title of this memoir suggests a particular experience that occurred at a specific time. But the narrative goes back three generations, beginning in Poland, and moving to Lithuania, Palestine, Israel, and the United States, covering a hundred years of family history. I took the liberty to elaborate different periods of my life, whether it is my childhood or my military service. Not only do these embellishments reveal how we as a society lived and played, but looking back, I realize that those were the years I began to develop into the woman I have become.

I have changed the names of various people and hidden or altered some facets of their lives in order to conceal their identities and protect their privacy or the privacy of their surviving family members. The names I substituted belong to no one I know personally. I have kept the real names of my own family members and the names of other characters for historical accuracy.

CHAPTER 1
A First Memory

Imma's glimmering green eyes are draped in fog again. She is staring at the window with a hollow look. Only a few weeks ago, when the sun shone with radiating brilliance, my mother was full of life. Only weeks ago, when summer's days lingered with light and the bathing season was still on, Imma took my sister Miriam and me to the beach. We went there daily.

"The beach does us good," Imma would say to us in a voice that made me think of gentle waves breaking on the shore.

Only a few weeks ago she was still wearing her bright summer dresses. But today she is wrapped in an old, colorless robe.

It seems it was only yesterday that she made me laugh when she hid behind the living-room curtain, then pushed it aside and made funny faces at me. But today her pretty face is graying like the bleak day that signals the arrival of winter—the season without laughter.

I am a little girl, not yet four. Still, I sense that the days are shorter and that my beautiful mother, whom I love so much, is sinking into an abyss of sadness and pain. The raindrops are hitting the windowpane, and I am scared of the coming winter because in winter Imma gets ill.

In my innocence I do not understand what a "nerve doctor" is, but I hear that Imma goes to one. I do not understand what electric shocks are, but I hear that Imma gets them when she goes to her doctor. I know that Imma will stay in bed in the coming days, that she will cry, and that I will be alone at home with her.

Miriam, who is ten, is going to school, but I am at home with Imma because there is no one to take me to nursery school. My father, who I call Abba, goes to work early, and my aunts have children of their own. Only my grandmother comes. When Imma is incapacitated she and I move to my grandparents' apartment, or sometimes stay with one of my aunts.

———

On the day I was born, in Israel, then Palestine, the moon eclipsed Jupiter, the planet associated with luck and good fortune. Its blackness may have been a sign of things yet to come my way. On earth, too, darkness outshone sunlight, for World War II was raging.

On that day, even as Allied forces relentlessly pounded Axis positions, and in spite of the losses it had suffered, Germany vowed to continue its war efforts. As hundreds of American bombers destroyed the Reich's aircraft factories, President Franklin D. Roosevelt presented to the United States Congress a budget of nearly one hundred billion dollars, anticipating that the war would last eighteen months longer.

Meanwhile, activists led by the anthropologist Margaret Mead and the playwright Rachel Crothers protested the declining status of women as a result of the prolonged war and demanded their advancement to policy-making positions. A quarter of a century later, I, too, would become an activist, preoccupied with the status of women affected by war.

In the Middle East, on the day I was born, Arab states signed an agreement to further their common interests, the most important of which was the prevention of the establishment of a Jewish state in Palestine. There, David Ben Gurion, head of the semiautonomous Jewish government, gave a moving speech, reaffirming the existence of a sole Jewish nation in spite of the dispersion of its people the world over, and called for national renewal in its native homeland.

It would take four years and three months longer for Ben Gurion to realize his vision and proclaim the creation of the State of Israel. The announcement, on May 14, 1948, came after a long underground war against Britain, and after fighting between Arab and Jewish factions had escalated into bloody, all-out war.

I do not know whether the darkness cast over Jupiter on the day I was born truly influenced the course of my life. But what transpired on that day affected the lives of everyone in my country, leading up to the day of its birth and continuing to the day of this writing.

———◆———

I entered this life in the winter of 1944, in the future Jewish state. Britain, ruler of the seas, had controlled the area by a League of Nations mandate since the defeat of the Ottoman Empire in the First World War. I have occasionally wondered how much joy my birth brought our family, for it was in wintertime, when the cold paints everything gray and the winds hums with gloom, that my mother suffered from her recurring depressions.

I am thankful that since that winter day I have been able to build a full and satisfying life. Yet I yearn for more. I want to uncover hidden layers of my inner self and let the artist in me flourish, as my teachers, long ago, had promised me it could. I want to write novels about elders' love, about intense passion, about women who refuse to end their lives gracefully. I want to never stop yearning.

Perhaps this yearning, for colorful moments that turned the blackness away, is what helped me endure those dark grinding days when I coped with my mother's illness and my father's inability to handle it.

In the past I viewed myself as a fragile child, a frail girl, and a weak young woman. But the picture that emerged while I was writing my story revealed a different self. I discovered that an inner strength I had not been aware of emerged any time I found myself in the midst of a personal tragedy or difficulty. In contrast to that frail person I held myself to be, I discovered a strong child who endured hardship from a young age, a smart child who knew how to protect herself when others could not, an observant teenager who found it hard to accept the innate gender inequality I saw around me, and a young woman who came into her own.

———◆———

I never asked my parents why they had chosen to have me in a faraway hospital rather than the alternative close to their home in central Tel Aviv. Maybe it was my mother's illness that led them to choose a bigger and more modern hospital, or perhaps it was based on a superstition she had about the old hospital's back-entrance morgue.

I remember well that back entrance, which I passed every day on my way to and from school. The sight of a figure wrapped in black being carried on a black stretcher out to a large black hearse used to curdle my blood. If only I could walk by with my eyes closed, I would think. I still recall the horror I felt, at age eight or so, when I saw two men bearing a small stretcher that carried a tiny body to that horrible black vehicle, which was far too big for that little person who once was. I wanted to flee, but in the grip of fear my legs slowed down, as if they had a will of their own. It was the day I learned that children, too, could die.

Six weeks before my mother's due date, my parents endured the long taxi ride to the new hospital only to be confronted by nurses who did not believe my mother when she screamed, "My baby is coming!" They scolded her for exaggerating her condition and demanded that she exercise self-control. They soon had no choice but to believe her: I pushed my way out then and there.

"You did what you wanted already then," my mother often told me, with both admiration and irritation. "You would have fallen to the floor if I hadn't caught you!"

4

She had caught me in her hands, in winter, her dark season. It was with a measure of gratitude that I listened to that story and to a similar one: When I was eighteen months old she brought me to the hospital, dehydrated because I could not keep food down.

"Why did you bring us a dead baby?" the nurses demanded of her.

"She's alive!" my mother insisted.

When one of the nurses moved her finger back and forth in front of my eyes to prove my mother wrong, I followed her hand, showing that I was indeed alive.

"You doubted me," my mother scolded. "Now treat her."

"Take her home and nurse her the way only a mother can," a different nurse whispered in my mother's ear. And so she did. Using a small spoon, throughout the night, she poured ten cups of sweetened tea into my small body.

"I did what no nurse would have done," she told me. And she did it even though she did not want me. She told me that, too, as she did about her desire to end her life.

"If it weren't for your sister and you, I would have committed suicide a long time ago," she told me when I was a child, a teenager, and an adult. I do not know whether she chose life because we cast a ray of hope into her existence, or because she felt responsible for us. Either way, I was glad she chose life, though I did not like to carry the burden of being responsible for her living in misery.

———◆———

Old memories may fade away. Some may be erased. Others remain sharp and clear, as if the events have just happened, and so it is with the memories I have of my mother's bouts of illness.

When my mother was unable to care for my sister and me, I moved with her to my paternal grandparents' house. Miriam moved in with our Aunt Tovah, my mother's older sister, who lived closer to her school.

My father, at the time working for a leading newspaper, alternated visits to both households.

I was two and some. My mother was in bed in an adjacent room while my grandmother dressed me. When she finished putting on my clothes, she presented me with a new pair of shoes, which she or my father had bought. Seeing them, I began to jump up and down on her bed, screaming with joy "I have new shoes!"

Having new shoes was not a small matter at that time of belt tightening, which began during World War II, continued through Israel's War of Independence, and lasted throughout a period of austerity that stretched into the 1950s. Though I was too young to understand those circumstances, I must have sensed the value of new shoes.

Unable to put them on my feet because I would not stop bouncing, my grandmother snapped, "No wonder your mother is so sick, with a wicked child like you."

Each word she uttered in her steady, deliberate tone landed on me like a blow; each word of the momentary scolding that must have been my grandmother's intention seared like a burn. And in my young mind the link between my mischief and my mother's illness was sealed; my grandmother's words echoed, repeatedly, multiplying as if to punish me incessantly.

I do not remember whether I stopped jumping then. But I have never forgotten the shiny redness of the laced shoes, the whiteness of the duvet cover on my grandmother's bed, or the pale tones of the yellow and white stenciled walls in the room. The walls, caressing with their soft colors, swallowed my grandmother's words and soothed my teary eyes.

Looking back at that moment, I want to protect the little girl that I was. Worse than the harshness of my grandmother's tone was her accusation that my behavior was the reason for my mother's recurring depressions, under the shadow of which my father, my sister, and I lived.

If that was not enough, in her bad moments throughout my childhood my mother called me horrible, offensive names that not even an adult should hear. Coupled with my grandmother's accusation, my mother's disdain made me believe I was the epitome of evil, worthy of punishment. I grew to believe I deserved every calamity that came my way, and each misfortune reinforced that belief, which engulfed me in dark fears for many years to come.

Even so, as time passed my mother got better, and so did my lot. By the time I grew to become a young woman, Jupiter has cleared, or so it seemed. With a promising outlook and a sense of calm, I felt blessed when, at the age of nineteen and a half, I met the most desirable bachelor in Tel Aviv.

CHAPTER 2
Love Is Painful

I met Yigal at my military base. I caught sight of him out of the corner of my eye. He smiled when he looked at me, but I did not smile back. I did not imagine that the striking young man I had just passed would be my husband. He, on the other hand, later told me that he knew I would be his wife the first moment he set his eyes on me.

"It was your innocent look as much as your beauty that captured my heart," he told me. "I saw you through the window of the officers' canteen. You were walking into the base looking like a delicate porcelain figurine dressed in a perfectly pressed uniform, wearing brown ballet slippers and white socks. Your green eyes were visible from afar; your black ponytail was revealed beneath a beret that did not quite fit on your head. You smiled at a guy and handed him money to buy you something. Watching you wait outside the canteen I said to myself, 'That's my future wife.'"

Romantic. Little wonder Yigal swept me away.

Yigal had come to the base as a transient officer, enrolled in an auxiliary training course. We first talked a month after he had seen me by the canteen, at the wedding of a young woman from the base. I had several suitors at the time, and one of them had invited me to be his date at the wedding. At first I had refused, as I had just ended a serious relationship with another man. That courtship had lasted a year, and I was not about to begin a new one. But my suitor was persistent, and I succumbed.

The minute I walked into the wedding hall I saw the attractive, dignified-looking young man who had smiled at me a few days earlier. He had strong facial features, blue eyes, and short, frizzy, reddish hair. Tall and muscular, he was self-assured, different than any of the men I dated. He kept looking at me, and I could not help but glance back. After a while he walked over and asked me to dance. I noticed his strong, beautiful hands.

He wore a crisp white shirt, black pants with sharp center creases, and fashionable black shoes. It was a slow dance. Moving gracefully, he held me close enough that I could feel his body's warmth, yet not so close as to anger my date.

"My name is Yigal," he said.

"My name is Ziva," I replied.

"I know," he acknowledged, and I felt a fluttering in my stomach.

The year was 1963. It was an enchanting summer night. He was twenty-four; I was nineteen. He made me forget all the young men I had dated with the magic of our first dance; by the time it was over we were in love.

On our first date we went dancing again, in the elegant ballroom of the Avia Hotel near Tel Aviv. I was wearing a white sleeveless dress embroidered with small pastel flowers that emphasized my tanned skin. Yigal was pleased.

"Let's get some fresh air," he suggested, and walked me out to a balcony. With our eyes locked together, he moved closer to me and I noticed how masculine his neck was. When he held me tight, I felt my pulse racing. We kissed, over flowing with excitement.

On our second date we saw the movie *Rome Adventure*, starring Troy Donahue and Suzanne Pleshette. We held hands when Emilio Pericoli sang "Al Di Là." We got closer.

After we had dated for several weeks, one night we babysat the children of Yigal's older brother, Moshe, and his wife, Gila. It was then that I first slept with Yigal, on a narrow couch in their living room. When it was over, naïve and inexperienced, I was not sure whether I had just lost my virginity. For one, I was not in much pain. Nor was I resting in a puddle of blood, or moaning with pleasure. Nothing seemed like the descriptions in the novels I had read.

I could not bring myself to reveal my ignorance to Yigal by asking him if we just had sex. Nor could I ask anyone else. My mother had even refused to talk to me about menstruation, until my father's cousin Bronca had pressed her to do so when I was thirteen. My married sister, who had a self-righteous streak, was unapproachable too, and my friends did not talk about sex, even if they had experienced it. Besides, I was afraid that if I were no longer a virgin, no one would marry me.

Yigal had not asked me whether I had had any previous sexual experiences before we had ours.

"She was a virgin," the veteran lover soon realized, pleased to discover a drop of blood on his underwear. "How large was the stain?" I wanted to know, needing more clues.

"Small, but unmistakable," he assured me. "Clearly you are no longer a virgin."

We began seeing each other almost every night. Capable and ambitious, Yigal was one of the youngest captains in the army. My parents and everyone else in my family adored him. By all accounts, he was a perfect marriage candidate. We rarely spent an evening apart, and when we did, I never questioned his whereabouts. In fact, I never questioned him at all, and not when, upon his return from a weeklong army retreat he showed me photographs of himself with other young men and women. One of the women appeared in all the photos. In some he had his arm thrown around her waist or resting nonchalantly on her shoulders. I put the photos down, saying nothing. Days passed and then, sounding as if he were insulted, he asked me, "Why don't you question me when I say I can't see you?"

"I shouldn't have to," I replied, saying nothing more. But I wondered when *would* I react if his insensitivity continued?

———————

By fall I had finished knitting Yigal a deep green sweater. He wore it with pride. In winter we broke up. It happened during an argument about his expectation of my parents' financial help if we were to marry. We were sitting in his military Land Rover across the street from my apartment house.

"If your parents cannot help us financially, perhaps we should not continue our courtship," he said.

"If that is your attitude, then consider our relationship over!" I replied, and got out of the car. My show of confidence did not reflect my love for him and the turmoil I felt in my heart. He sat there for a while, as if he was waiting for me to return, but I did not.

"I just broke up with Yigal," I told my parents when I entered our apartment.

They could not hide their disappointment.

"How could you break up with such a great guy?"

"There is something missing in our relationship," I said.

"This is not an answer," they insisted.

"I have no other answer. I cannot pinpoint what it is that bothers me." It was the truth.

"What is it that you want?" The sadness in their voices touched me. "You won't meet another guy like him!" they exclaimed.

Knowing they did not have the money, I dared not tell them about his presumption that they would help us buy an apartment if we were to get married. I was afraid my father would blame himself, and that my mother, unable to take the truth in stride, might berate him for his financial failures. Worse still, they might take out a loan, which they would have to pay off for years to come.

That night I could not sleep. The idea that Yigal was able to give me up because I would not ask my parents to help us buy an apartment was crushing. Over and over again I reenacted our conversation in the Land Rover, word for word. Suddenly, it hit me. Yigal was talking about marriage. *Our* marriage. And I had not even responded to his words, "If we get married."

Self-reproach flooded my head. But then I thought more about what bothered me about him. I did not like some of his friends. If the Hebrew proverb "show me your friend and I will tell you who you are" was correct, then Yigal was not the great guy everyone believed him to be. I was baffled, not sure whether I should trust my instincts. Still, I waited for his call. But he was silent.

Two weeks passed before he unexpectedly arrived at our home. He has come to make up, I thought, feeling euphoric. Instead, he returned the sweater I had knitted for him. I thanked him for bringing it back.

"What happened?" my parents inquired. Their voices echoed both hope and anxiety.

"We didn't get back together, if that's what you want to hear," I answered. My impatience was as obvious as their disappointment.

My twentieth birthday came and went, and still Yigal did not call. Two more weeks passed. Then he appeared, like a magician.

"I bought an apartment," he said. "I made the down payment today. I can pay the mortgage."

"Congratulations," I replied, then paused.

"I can't take it anymore," he said. "I can't live without you. I want you to be my wife!"

That was Yigal. He would not just come back. He had to have it all planned out, his intentions real, his abilities unquestioned. It was a pivotal moment.

"I am not the type of man to shower you with gifts and flowers," he announced. "But you will always have my true love."

And what about fidelity, will I always have that? I wondered. But my happiness exceeded my doubts. I was to marry the most admired young men I had met, becoming the object of envy among women in Yigal's social circle. I loved him intensely and he loved me.

The closer it got to our wedding day, set for July 22, 1964, the more excited we became. Among the most memorable occasions during that time was the evening Yigal's parents came to meet my family and have supper in our home. My grandparents were the guests of honor. Their elation was evident. Nothing could have made them happier than their granddaughter marrying the son of observant Jews—though not quite as Orthodox as they were. That he was a former yeshiva boy pleased them, too.

Yigal's father looked as if he felt privileged to shake the hand of my wise-looking grandfather, whose bright blue eyes were shining with delight. Their wives shook each other's hands with mutual respect, my stern grandmother smiling. Befitting the occasion, my parents were the most courteous of hosts. If they were concerned with the impression our small apartment would leave on their new relations, their fear was unfounded. Yigal's parents were gratified. For them, I was the best choice their son could have made.

When the wedding date was set, my mother and I began to look for a wedding dress. In the window of Englander Sisters, then the most stylish and expensive women's clothing store in Tel Aviv, was a beautiful knee-length, sleeveless dress made of white Swiss lace, with a flowing white chiffon coat to be worn over it. It took our seamstress nearly a week to sew an identical ensemble. Then she made elegant dresses for my mother and Miriam.

———◆———

Four months before our wedding, my period was late. I did not think much of it, since my menstruation hardly kept to a schedule, but Yigal worried that I was pregnant.

"If you are pregnant, we must do something about it," he said, sounding self-assured. "We have to think about our religious relatives, who would be devastated if you arrived pregnant to our wedding."

Though I could imagine the embarrassment of my grandparents and our own parents, I continued to confront him.

"Being late is not unusual for me."

"We can't waste time," Yigal argued.

While I had not worried about becoming pregnant, I thought about the bloodstain Yigal had mentioned after we first slept together. I was no longer a virgin. We had been in a sexual relationship ever since that night at his brother's home. Yigal was an experienced guy, and he took precautions every time we were intimate. I doubted that I could be pregnant. But even so, he could still be right.

Without further hesitation, I agreed to see a doctor Yigal knew at a small hospital in the Tel Aviv suburb of Herzliah. As usual, I did not ask questions. Who was the doctor? How did Yigal know him?

I had seen a gynecologist once before, when I was sixteen. My mother had taken me because my period was so irregular.

"Will you leave us alone?" the doctor had asked my mother then.

"Do you have something to hide?" he had asked me in a gentle, non-inquisitive voice, when she left the room. I did not, and the visit was not the bad experience I had dreaded. But this encounter was different. After a quick examination, the doctor determined that I was pregnant. I accepted his word, not knowing that a pregnancy test was required. Yigal and the doctor discussed an abortion, and I went along. Having no one to talk to about my diagnosed pregnancy, I relied on Yigal. Fearing the embarrassment we would cause our families and anxious about our parents' reactions, we did not consider moving up our wedding date.

I went to work the morning of the abortion as if it were an ordinary day and left the office early on the pretext that I had wedding arrangements to make. At midday, Yigal picked me up, and we drove to Herzliah.

He waited at the hospital while the procedure was done. I do not remember an operating room, only the doctor's office, where I was anesthetized. When it was over, Yigal drove me back to Tel Aviv, dropping me off at a busy intersection a safe distance from home. We spoke little, each of us caught up in our own thoughts.

The possibility of complications did not enter my mind as I walked home. And yet every step I took brought with it unsettling feelings. I was disappointed that Yigal had gone back to his headquarters in such a hurry. After all, unlike the other women who passed through his life, I was going to be his wife. He could have taken me to a quiet place, gotten me a cold drink, helped me shed my anxiety or shared his own emotions with me.

No wonder he is so admired in the army, he is a perfect strategist, I remember thinking. Or else he has done this before. Suddenly, I knew he had, and I suspected I knew the woman, too: She was a year or so my junior and happened to live on a street perpendicular to ours. Yigal had seen her occasionally before he met me.

After a twenty-minute walk, I stepped inside the door at home as if nothing had happened.

"Why are you home early?" my mother asked.

"I don't feel well. I got my period and have bad cramps," I explained.

There was no reason for her to doubt me, for severe menstrual cramps were the norm for me, and I did not show any signs of anguish, not outwardly, anyway.

I did not mourn our first unborn child then. If I felt pain where my maternal heart was beating, I was unable to identify it. A month afterward, I began to internalize my deed. I acted as if nothing had changed. Yet I felt as if I were living in a bad dream, caught in foggy hallucinations, with a heavy load crushing me. I wondered whether I had a split personality, with one side sensitive and emotional, the other cold and indifferent.

When six weeks after the abortion I had not menstruated, Yigal took me back to the doctor. Even now, extreme anxiety envelops me when I think about that time, and the intensity mystifies me after so many years. Perhaps it is the sense of danger I pinpointed even back then, without admitting it.

"You are pregnant again," the doctor said with confidence, and I went numb.

"We'll do what we have to," Yigal said. I heard his response as if I were in a deep sleep, listening to the conversation from afar. But then, my mind awoke, and I realized these two men were deciding what I should do with my body as if I were not even there. "But I am not doing it again. Not this time!"

I do not recall our conversation on the way back to Tel Aviv. I got my period the next day. I will never know whether I was pregnant the first time around, when the butcher from Herzliah performed the abortion on me.

———◆———

My father was proud to print our wedding invitations for the four hundred guests in his shop. Big wedding celebrations were rather common.

June was almost gone. The sun was brilliant, the days were long, the beaches were crowded, and in the open-air markets colorful fruits and bright summer flowers were on display. Our plans were moving along. The invitations had been sent. The dresses and the men's suits were ready, as were my bridal veil and my white lace shoes.

It was an ordinary Thursday, Yigal's usual free day, twenty-eight days before the wedding. As expected, my husband-to-be picked me up in the evening; his kisses were as passionate as ever, his hugs as reassuring, his smile that of a young man anticipating his marriage in a months time. Then the bombshell fell.

In a casual manner he told me that he had slept with another woman earlier in the day. He had been sunbathing on the beach, when an attractive French woman approached and sat nearby. She began talking to him and before the day was gone, she invited him to her apartment, where they made love. "The last fling before tying the knot," he said, with a smile. A sudden coldness rushed through my body. What a sorry cliché! But at least he did not plan it, I reasoned, trying to justify his behavior with an inane rationalization. It was not him I was trying to protect, but myself. I did not cry. I did not yell. I did not turn away from him. Composed and dignified I let my silence speak. I thought he understood.

The wedding arrangements went on.

The following Friday night we were strolling through the crowds on then-fashionable Dizengoff Street with Miriam and her husband Gershon. I was wearing a blue silk dress with white polka dots. Its low neckline was trimmed with a white silk collar and a big white flower. Our seamstress had sewn it, together with my extravagant bridal dress.

Yigal was as proud as a peacock. "Everyone is turning his head after my stunning-looking bride. Your big eyes are so green against your tan skin, you look like a cat on a hot tin roof, as pretty as Elizabeth Taylor."

"How about Ava Gardner? I prefer her mysterious look," I replied jokingly.

But nothing seemed humorous when minutes later he grabbed my elbow, directing my attention to a blonde woman who was passing by.

"That's her. The French woman from the beach," he said.

I stopped breathing, thoughts flashing through my mind: What am I doing? How can I marry this man?

They did not nod to each other. They did not matter to each other. They merely shared a fleeting sexual episode, the knowledge of which Yigal felt compelled to share with me. Worse yet, he needed to show her to me moments after praising the way I looked. But the invitations had been sent, the preparations were completed, and I was in love. So I went on with my marriage plans.

The day before my wedding, my sixteen-year-old cousin Yehudit, who still refers to me as the sister she never had, paid me a visit on her way to pick up the dress she had bought for the occasion.

"Today is my last day as a single woman," I said to her. "And I am taking you out to pay tribute to this day."

I took her to Zion, a popular Middle Eastern restaurant in the Carmel market. The meal was luscious. We then went to pick up Yehudit's sleeveless cocktail dress, made of yellow silk with a print of large orange roses. I called it a happy dress, one that reflected optimism, befitting the beautiful day my cousin and I had spent together before I began a new chapter in my life.

That evening, the last before my wedding, a new tumult began.

"What time are you going to the *mikveh?*" my mother asked me. She referred to the ritual bath in which brides purify themselves the day before their marriage, one of the many immersion requirements that observant Jews follow according to biblical laws.

"I have no intention of going."

"If there is no mikveh, I will not be at the wedding tomorrow," my mother proclaimed. Like many secular brides, I considered the ritual outdated and unnecessary. Many rabbis performing a wedding ceremony refrained from asking the bride for the mikveh certificate, though some brides bought fake ones just in case. Bridegrooms have never been required to show such documentation, even though Orthodox men perform the ritual, too.

My chance to persuade my mother disappeared when my grandmother showed up. Unable to conceal their satisfaction, the two women escorted me to the neighborhood mikveh.

Proper dipping requires that a woman's entire body be submerged all at once, with no barriers between her skin and the water. The attendant made sure she removed any possible remnants of polish from my nails, for even that would be considered a barrier. She then guided me to the stairs leading to the wide pool. Once I was in the water she instructed me to dunk ten times, reciting a prayer with each submersion. The first time, during which I closed my nostrils with my thumb and my index finger so as to stop water from flowing into my nose, did not count, for if the hand touches any part of the body it, too, is considered a barrier.

——•——

I looked pure and angelic in my white wedding dress and my delicate veil; my bridal portrait adorned the window of the most prestigious photography studio in town for months. No bridegroom could have been more proud as Yigal seemed to be.

A military chaplain performed the ceremony, which was prolonged by the added service of a rabbi from my mother's hometown. As a courtesy, he officiated at the wedding ceremonies of all the children of their hometown, and Yigal and I did not wish to be the first couple to break that tradition. Bad omen, we feared.

We were led to our wedding canopy by our parents: the bride by two elegantly dressed, serious-looking mothers, the groom by two smiling fathers. I was even kissed by my grandmother. It was a joyous ceremony.

Our traditional kiss was long and sensuous. We danced through the night to the tunes of a jubilant band and the romantic serenading of a singer named Don Julio. I was twenty and a half; Yigal was a month shy of his twenty-fifth birthday. We were in heaven.

Me, as a bride at age twenty. This portrait adorned the window of
the most prestigious photography studio in Tel Aviv for months;
family members often passing by to see the picture

Yigal and I having the first dance at our wedding in July 1964. I will always think of Yigal as the emblematic Israeli man, with his brusqueness and gentleness, his frivolity and utter sense of responsibility

CHAPTER 3

A Child Bride

We spent our wedding night in our new, one-and-a-half bedroom apartment in Ramat Gan, a small but growing city near Tel Aviv. By the 1960s it had become a desirable spot for young couples set on building new families. The move there was hard for me, and in my five years of residency I never developed a sense of belonging. The one thing that eased my departure from Tel Aviv was the fact that Ramat Gan was home to my sister, Miriam, my brother-in-law Gershon, and their two young children, Orit and Gil, whom I adored. Four years later their twin sisters, Michal and Yael, were born.

When I left home for the last time as an unmarried woman I forgot my things, arriving at our new home only with the wedding dress I wore. A Freudian slip? Perhaps.

A long time had passed since I had seen my parents laugh as heartily when Yigal and I, still in my wedding dress and high-heeled shoes, showed up at their home the morning after the wedding to collect my honeymoon clothes. My father looked jubilant, while my mother, who still had not talked to me about intimacy, looked at me with questioning eyes, curious about the night she believed I lost my virginity. How did it go? Her expressive green eyes inquired, and I enjoyed keeping her guessing.

We honeymooned at the seashore of Netanya, then a desirable vacation spot. Upon our return we carefully arranged the new furniture my parents had given us as a wedding gift. Today I see identical pieces in high-end vintage furniture stores.

On summer nights, when the skies sparkled with stars and the moon shed its gentle light, we sat on our terrace, often with family and friends who arrived unannounced for casual visits. While the refreshing Mediterranean air softly caressed us, I served lush fruits, light summer cakes, pastel-colored ice creams, and sweetened ice coffee. It was a promising beginning for our new life

Yigal soon left the military in quest of a civilian position to suit his qualifications. He would often talk about enrolling in the engineering program at Technion, the Israel Institute of Technology, in Haifa. In the meantime, he was trying to earn enough money to pay off our mortgage and build our financial future. An opportunity arose when a contemporary of his offered him a partnership in a driving school he planned to open.

Accepting the offer, Yigal passed the necessary qualifying exams and became a full partner. With a newly acquired white Studebaker Lark, equipped for teaching, he quickly earned a reputation as the best driving instructor in the area. Yigal did everything well, sometimes as if by magic.

His alluring magnetism was in full evidence on a late summer afternoon that I remember as if it were today. On her way to visit me, with her two young children in the back of her car, my sister had an accident. After her frantic call I hurried to the accident site, leaving a note for Yigal about the crash. The scene was chaotic, as onlookers gathered around the cars, shouting their unwanted advice and arguing about whose fault it was. That the owner of the other car was a well-known entertainer only added to the tumult. Suddenly, Yigal appeared at the scene, and all turned quiet. It was because the authority he displayed, calm and self-assured, that people listened.

I adjusted to the demands married life imposed on me, sometimes not too successfully. One evening, instead of going straight home from my job as a secretary in the Tel Aviv office of the prime minister, I had paid a visit to my friend Dalia, whom I had not seen for a while. I had not considered that my husband, who was waiting for me at home, had no idea where I was. When I got home, hours late, I learned that Yigal, worried that something had happened to me, had been searching for me. This story circulated among my aunts and uncles. "A child bride," they would chuckle, when they repeated the story.

On another occasion I took the wrong bus home. The bus I rode had two routes, and I got on the one that went to a town adjacent to mine. When I realized the mistake, the driver, who happened to live in my neighborhood, offered to take me home at the end of his route. It was not unusual for bus drivers to park buses overnight near their homes. Calculating that it would take me longer to take a returning bus back and then get on the right bus, or wait for a taxi, I accepted the offer. When I arrived home, Yigal was not there. Worried, he had gone looking for me at my sister's, and then driven to Tel Aviv to my parents' home. In a matter of two hours, my whole family, aunts and uncles included, was alerted. When Yigal came home, relieved to find me there, I did not tell him the truth, fearful that my harmless ride with a kind stranger would be misunderstood. Instead, I told him that I had to take two additional buses because of the mistake I had made. In those early days, I felt that my freedom was dissipating. And yet, that innocent bus story with its bitter taste taught me a lesson. I accepted the responsibility I had toward my partner in life, realizing his love and concern for me.

I became a respectful, caring daughter-in-law, though my utmost affection went to Yigal's father, especially after I saw him driving his horse-drawn wagon pulling a kerosene tank. In one hand he held the reins, while in the other he held a bell, which he shook, signaling the kerosene man's arrival in the neighborhood.

In the ultra-Orthodox neighborhoods of Bnei Brak, where my new husband's parents lived, kerosene was used for Sabbath cooking and for heating. I was stunned when I saw him on his horse, for Yigal had told me that his father was a gasoline merchant. Humble as the profession was, I had great respect for this man, who earned his living with honor and dignity.

——◆——

Yigal became a devoted and loving husband. Not only did he spend much of his free time with me, but from time to time he dropped by my office to say a quick hello. He would not tell me he missed me; he came just to spend a precious moment together, or just to wave to me, and I enjoyed his attention. My nagging uncertainties began later.

Yigal also became a dedicated son-in-law, worthy of my parents' love for him, a caring brother-in-law, and an adoring uncle to my niece and nephew. He had close relationships with my aunts and uncles, and my grandparents appreciated him too.

We visited our relatives often, mainly my family, for most of his had perished in the Holocaust. We became fond of visits on the Sabbath and holidays, but in summers we preferred to spend those days on the beach with my sister's family and friends. At the end of those beach days, we ended up having supper at our parents' homes, as we did in wintertime.

Our lovemaking was frequent and gratifying, although I remember few instances during intimate moments when I felt as if we were from two different planets. That sensation would sharpen when Yigal would comment, however humorously, on his manliness.

"Lucky you," he uttered once, with a smile on his face.

"What are you talking about?"

"See for yourself," he said, admiring his impressive erection. Holding his hand parallel to it, he extended his index finger and folded his other fingers, as if his hand were a pointed gun. However humorous he intended such a comparison to be, to me it seemed arrogant and sexist. Yigal was not a vulgar man, and the vulgarity offended me. Today, it is more as a woman than as a wife that I find this act to be an affront. That gesture, made so many years ago by a young man, still signifies the difference in the mindsets of women and men the world over. It is no wonder that feminists make the connection between power, the gun, and the penis.

I am certain that if the same episode had occurred in a later period of my life, I would have turned my back to him, gotten out of bed, and withdrawn to another room. But at the time, bright with hopes we had for our future, I was bedazzled enough to overlook those tiny blemishes—which was how I viewed such incidents.

Marriage seemed to suit us both. Like any other young couple, we had our disagreements; we fought and made up. But I could not escape the tormenting memories about the abortion doctor from Herzliah or the French woman from the beach and I became bothered by the fact that Yigal was the master of his timetable and was surrounded by adoring women, who were a large portion of his clientele. I became suspicions.

When power struggles emerged I stood my ground. A memory remains. An incident occurred on our terrace one summer evening. My sister had come for a short visit, Minutes later, two neighbor women joined Miriam and me. We talked and laughed, enjoying the fruit and ice cream I served. Then Yigal arrived. Greeting us, he saw the remnants of a juicy honeydew melon left in a bowl.

"How's your ice cream?" he asked me.

"Excellent."

"I would like some melon," he said.

"There is more in the fridge," I replied. "Help yourself."

"Why can't you do it?" he asked, his expression and body language implying that he deserved to be served.

"I'll be glad to," I responded, "if you'll wait a minute while I finish my ice cream before it melts."

The sweet summer air became thick with tension.

"I'll do it," Miriam announced, proceeding to the kitchen. I was upset with Yigal. Why couldn't he say, "When you finish your ice cream, would you please cut some more melon for me?" Better yet, why could he not leave us alone and do his own thing?

———◆———

I dreamed of having four children. But when I became pregnant at twenty-one I questioned whether I was ready for motherhood. It was a blasphemous thought in that society, where childbirth was a national mission. We were a people who had lost a million and a half children to the Holocaust and continued to lose young soldiers to a perpetual war with neighboring states. I tried to push away those creeping thoughts about my lack of readiness, relieved that I was able to conceive after the abortion.

My guilt turned into deep sorrow when I had a sudden miscarriage during my fifth month of pregnancy. We were at my parents' home on a Sabbath afternoon, enjoying my mother's cooking, when warm liquid began gushing down my legs. I stood there dripping, not comprehending what had just happened. Frantic, my mother grabbed her face. "Your water broke, she cried." Then she added, in horror, "Ziva, *mine kind*"—meaning "my child"—"it's a miscarriage."

We called my obstetrician, and upon her advice, Yigal and my mother rushed me to the private hospital in northern Tel Aviv where she worked. As she began to perform a dilation and curettage procedure, I started to hemorrhage, a development my doctor was not trained to handle. Worse, the hospital had no blood bank, and the country's central blood bank did not have my rare blood type, AB negative. My sister, brother-in-law, aunts, and uncles poured into the hospital to donate blood, but no match was found. I was close to death when my doctor managed to stop the bleeding. By late evening the national blood bank had found a single portion of my blood type and rushed it to the hospital.

My father later told me how horrified he had been when he saw me being wheeled out of the operating room, hours after I had been brought in, covered with blood-soaked sheets, my face as gray as that of a corpse. As a former volunteer in Tel Aviv's Magen David Adom—Israel's Red Crescent emergency services—he knew what a dead person looked like. He was unable to finish his sentence when he told me, "I saw my daughter being wheeled on a stretcher, not knowing if she was dead or alive…"

The baby I miscarried was a girl, too tiny to survive. I was heartbroken, but Yigal could think of nothing but my health. The main thing, he kept saying, was that I had survived; nothing else mattered. We became closer. Months later, on the occasion of our first anniversary, he surprised me with a small diamond ring, tenderly putting it on my finger. It would not make up for the loss, he knew, but it was a gesture nonetheless.

We listened to my obstetrician and tried again, and six months later I was pregnant. I stopped working. This time my doctor kept me off my feet till the danger passed at the fifth month of pregnancy, the time I had miscarried. I made it to the sixth. We were in the theater, when I felt the sudden onset of contractions. I was wearing a yellow maternity dress with a wide white collar I had bought days earlier. We rushed to the emergency room, this time to the large, modernized hospital where I had been born twenty-two years earlier.

The boy I gave birth to, after hours of agony and fear, weighed less than two pounds. I was in bed in the maternity ward when Yigal and Miriam returned from the preemie unit. They had seen the baby and knew he had no chance to survive. Though their faces told the story, I was still hopeful.

"Is he alive?"

"Yes," they said.

My tiny son struggled for thirty-six hours until he succumbed. There are times I sill wonder whether he was buried and where.

We were heartbroken. Difficult days engulfed us once again, sorrow hitting us in huge waves. My grief threatened to sweep me away to a ruinous eddy, but Yigal maintained a strong image, at least in my presence. Only with our neighbors did he mourn the loss of his son and express his fears about the effect the loss would have on me. He found solace in the fact that, unlike the last time, I came out of this miscarriage safely, physically, that is. That was the most important thing to him.

In those days he showed his true quality. He was sensitive, wise, warm, and loving. The more obstacles we faced in trying to enlarge our family, the closer we got. But I had not forgotten the abortion.

As understanding and devoted as Yigal was, his attempts to console me were futile after my second miscarriage. Unlike with my previous miscarriage, I had seen the baby that had been pulled out of me. He was alive and breathing, as tiny as he was. I cried most nights, and Yigal would hold me in his arms, his heart going out to me. I had other outbursts, coming out of anger and hopelessness. Once I blamed the loss of our children on the doctor from Herzliah, who had performed an abortion that might not have been necessary. But I blamed more than just the doctor. I remember the pain on Yigal's face when, sobbing, I put the blame on him.

"You took me to that butcher who destroyed my womb. You!"

His face ashen, he remained silent, for there was nothing he could have said. Struggling with his own sorrow, he must have regretted taking me there.

But we moved on. We switched doctors, choosing one of the better-known specialists in the field of obstetrics and gynecology at a major teaching hospital.

After a set of excruciating tests, my new doctor determined that my cervix needed corrective surgery. Soon I was pregnant again.

CHAPTER 4

From Przytyk to Palestine

My father never talked about his childhood in Poland. Perhaps he had forgotten his early memories by the time my sister and I were old enough to hear them, or maybe they were too painful to retell. What I know about his youth I learned from his sisters Sarah and Esther. Thanks to them I was able to reconstruct their family's life in Poland and Palestine.

The most dominant figure in my aunts' stories was their mother, my grandmother, that strict woman who had scolded me when I received my red shoes. It was she who shaped my father's personality and those of his siblings, and who influenced my own life perhaps more than I have been inclined to believe.

Even though my first memory of her was distressing, the older I became the more I realized what an exceptional woman she was. The more I learned about her and the family she headed, the more I admired and loved her. A woman ahead of her time, she epitomized feminism decades before the feminist revolution penetrated the Orthodox society to which she belonged. And though I did not inherit her coldness, which I recognize now as a protective cloak she wore against the malice of strangers, I have been blessed with many of her other traits. It could be from her that I got my feistiness, perseverance, and sense of justice, qualities that helped us both endure life's hardships and celebrate its accomplishments.

———◆———

One of six sisters, Brukha Wainryb was born in 1887, in Poland. She was sixteen when she married my grandfather, Menakhem Mendel Bakman, four years her senior. She saw him for the first time under the huppah. Like all marriages in religious Jewish communities during that time, theirs was arranged by their parents. I used to imagine my grandmother under the wedding canopy, a teenager dressed in a modest, white wedding dress, marveling through her lacy veil at her good-looking husband, who appeared handsome in his new *kapote*, the black-satin robe Orthodox Jews still wear on festive days. At that moment she determined that no matter what happened, she would be his equal, in spite of the traditional constraints her society imposed on women like her.

Rumor has it that my grandmother suffered numerous miscarriages and stillbirths before and after she gave birth to her eldest daughter, Sarah, who was born four years into her parents' marriage. It was not until 1911 that Brukha gave birth to the second of her seven children, my father, Tzvi.

———◆———

My grandparents lived in the village of Przytyk (pronounced *Pshi-tik*). Przytyk's Jews, like those of other Polish towns, suffered under a wave of anti-Semitism that had escalated after the Russian Revolution, when Jews were blamed for the spread of socialism. By the end of the First World War, incitement against them had turned into widespread violence.

Most of Przytyk's few thousand residents were Jewish. They lived mainly on two streets, in small houses, some wooden, some stone. As in most Jewish shtetls, cultural life centered on the synagogue and the *beit midrash*, where boys studied the Torah.

Shmuel Bakman, my great-grandfather, owned a flour mill, which operated on the bank of the Radomka, the river that runs through town. He was a tall, pious-looking, bearded man of medium weight, who wore an expression that radiated bewilderment and authority all at once. He died of hunger in the Radom ghetto in 1941 or 1942. His two sisters were sent with their families to Auschwitz. None survived.

In my possession I have a silver wine cup, engraved with the date 1878. My great-grandfather gave it to my grandfather, who passed it on to my father. I felt privileged when, in my twenties, my father handed it to me. He must have done so because he recognized my respect for our family's past.

Because sentimentality was a trait with which my paternal family was not blessed, I was surprised at the warm look in my father's eyes when he put the cup in my hands. Holding an item so perfect that had belonged to my ancestors moved me to tears.

"Why me, Abba?" I felt my chest expanding.

"Because I know it will be safe in your hands. You keep it," he said, in a steady, low voice, leaving no doubt that he meant it.

Though the cup had always been in our home, I studied it, as if seeing it for the first time. It measures two and a half inches long and is beautifully engraved, depicting European scenes of quaint homes on a lush riverbank. It is encircled by a crown of leaves and is decorated with elaborate flowers and diamond-shaped ornamentation. As I looked at it, an idea that seemed like a fantasy at the time flashed through my mind: that one day I would visit the places where my relatives—those modest, hardworking, God-fearing people from whom I descended—had lived. I fulfilled that dream years later.

I treasure the cup. Once a year, on Passover eve, I use it as Elijah's cup. Perhaps he will come for a sip of wine.

I do not know how many children Shmuel had. I knew only his three sons: Menakhem Mendel, my grandfather, and Moshe and Avigdor. My grandfather was a handsome man. Tall and fair-skinned, he had a high forehead, sparkling blue eyes, a straight nose, and a long gray beard that turned snowy white over the years. He had beautiful strong hands that looked as if a sculptor had carved them. I noticed his long fingers when I was a young girl. Because his religious beliefs forbade him to touch a female, whenever he saw me he would extend his fore and middle fingers to brush my hand. He looked regal in his black *kapote* and his large, black-velvet yarmulke. That is how God looks, I thought.

My great-grandfather's mill was a source of a steady income in spite of the heavy taxes he had to pay the Polish authorities. I do not know whether his other sons helped my great-grandfather run the mill. I know that my grandfather did, and that my grandmother managed its finances. Her position demanded frequent travel by rail from Poland to Germany and Russia.

Broadly educated and financially successful, the Bakman family was able to live in relative luxury in those days, enjoying a considerable measure of respect in town. It appeared too that real love developed between Brukha and Menakhem Mendel, this couple who saw each other for the first time at their own wedding. The "royal pair," as their neighbors called them, used to stroll together in the evening, passing by those neighbors, who stopped whatever they were doing in deference to the distinguished-looking couple. I can visualize my grandparents walking side by side, tastefully dressed, her arm folded in his, as they discussed the days' events at the mill, and the neighbors waiting, unable to take their eyes off them until they disappeared from sight.

History, however, had its own plans. When political instability over-took Europe on the eve of World War I, life for Przytyk's Jews became precarious. In my grandparents' household the growing hatred toward the Jews was expressed by their maid, whom they fired after they dis-covered that she had been abusing their two children, Sarah, who was seven, and Tzvi, who was three. With their parents out of the house working, and no one watching, the maid would yank hard on Sarah's braids, nearly pulling the child's hair out, and twist my father's nose and ears till tears ran down his face. She forbade them to cry and threatened them to be silent about her cruelty or they would suffer even more.

Such veiled anti-Semitism turned into widespread violence when the Cossacks began to attack Jewish communities in Eastern Europe. Some of those attacks were spontaneous; others were orga-nized and coordinated by the authorities. In the collective Jewish memory, the Cossacks are remembered as vicious militiamen who raped, maimed, killed, and looted from innocent Jews. "Hit the Jews and save Poland!"—or Russia, Ukraine, or any other country—they screamed, while astride their galloping horses, attacking their terri-fied victims.

Aunt Sarah described them as tall and erect warriors with soulless eyes. She remembered the sheepskin hats that covered their foreheads and ears from the frost. Their buttoned-down uniforms and tall black boots signaled unchallenged power. The way they wielded their long swords or guns indicated that they came to slaughter. Riding their fear-some horses, they trampled anyone who stood in their way. So real was her description that I could hear the sound of hoof beats clicking on the shtetl's streets as the masters spurred their horses to run faster and faster until they came to a halt, signifying trouble.

Clever and daring, my grandmother Brukha outsmarted the mighty Cossacks. When they stormed Przytyk, she would hide Sarah and my father in a safe refuge she had prepared under the beds. As the raids worsened, she became more resourceful. One day, when a rumor spread that the Cossacks were hours away from town, she prepared two large metal tubs. She filled one with apples, which were hard to come by; in the other she piled her freshly baked challah loaves, which the Cossacks could smell from a distance. She placed the tubs in front of each door of the mill's storage facility, intending to distract the invaders from looting the flour inside. When the Cossacks reached the warehouse, half-drunk, they consumed the food with such gluttony that they quickly forgot why they had come in the first place.

The neighbors were not as lucky. When the raid was over they arrived at my grandparents' home crying and howling. It was Brukha Bakman they came to address. One bearded man spoke for them all:

"You're the only one among us to have influence with the authorities, because of your business dealings. We heard you even know the governor himself. Please," he pleaded on their behalf, "go ask them to return what's left of our looted belongings."

Her hesitation lasted but a minute. Clothed in her best dress, made of blue brocade, and a matching hat, she went to the regional governor's headquarters.

She did not have to wait. Perhaps it was the respect he held for her, or else he thought she had access to powers higher than his own. She did not lower her eyes. She did not ingratiate herself. She did not hesitate. She stood erect, looked straight at him, and spoke in her typical direct manner.

"What do you think is expected of you after what has just happened?" she asked the governor, following the obligatory decorum. Her voice was low but sharp. "Think of the citizens in your district. What will they say when they hear that you permitted the looting of your own subjects? The same people who rely on your protection."

Within hours after she returned home, most of the looted belongings were returned to their owners.

When my aunts told me that story, I could envisage my assertive grandmother intimidating the governor. Perhaps her heart raced when she stood before the most powerful man in the district and brought serious allegations against him, but no one, not even he, could shake her belief in her mission.

It was not my grandmother's physique that gave her such authority—she was a narrowly built woman of average height. But she had powerful facial features. Underneath her elegant hats she wore a *sheitel*, the wig that is customary among married Orthodox Jewish women. Below horizontal brows, her light brown eyes were small and piercing. Her eagle nose conveyed intelligence, and her high cheekbones transmitted strength rather than beauty. She spoke with powerful hand motions that accentuated everything she said.

My grandmother was smart, clever, obstinate, and brave. But she was also cold. She hardly ever smiled. She never kissed or hugged her grandchildren. The only time I remember her kissing me was at my wedding, smelling as if she had just bathed with expensive soap or sprayed herself with a light fragrance, unbefitting of her unfeminine image.

———◆———

When the fighting during World War I moved closer to town, a worrisome rumor began to circulate that Przytyk's Jews were to be expelled. By that time my grandfather's brothers lived in Radom, a larger city located on the Mleczna River some twelve miles north of Przytyk. As soon as the expulsion news reached them, they rushed to the tiny village where their brother lived, empty carts harnessed to their horses, to remove the stored flour to Radom. They hurried their horses back and forth between the two towns, until all the flour had been transported. At nightfall, hidden by darkness, they gathered up the family and left Przytyk for the last time. Deep in the forest, my grandfather suddenly grabbed his brother's arm.

"Stop the horse!" he demanded, in a panic. "I must go back to Przytyk."

"What happened?"

"I forgot my *shtreimel*," he cried, referring to the round black hat trimmed with fur worn by ultra-Orthodox men on the Sabbath and other holy days.

I feel tense each time I reconstruct this scene the way my aunts had told it to me. I see the narrow, curving path in the treacherous black forest and hear the murmur emanating from the tall, wind-blown trees. I am awed by my grandfather's courage, as he decides to go back to Przytyk to retrieve his shtreimel.

"Continue without me," he directed his family. "I will meet you in Radom later."

"Don't go," his wife and children cried. "You know the Cossacks. Don't chance it!"

Without uttering another word, my grandfather disappeared into the forest, determined to salvage his shtreimel. Having no choice, my grandmother, her children, and their uncles continued the trip without him.

My aunts told me that my grandmother was certain she would never see her husband again, yet her expression revealed none of the turmoil she must have felt. I can imagine the efforts she made to look calm for the sake of her children.

To his family's joy, minutes before the beginning of the Sabbath, my grandfather arrived in Radom with the shtreimel in his hands. Years later my grandmother would have a reason to be grateful for her husband's decision. When her family was stricken with poverty, after they had lost all they had, she sold the expensive shtreimel. The money she received for it fed her children for three months.

My grandparents remained in Radom for ten years. During that time they had four more children: three boys, Simkha, Nehemiah, and Yaakov, and one girl, Esther. My grandfather studied the Torah, while his wife continued to work at the flour business and take care of her growing family.

I often wondered whether my grandmother imagined that a time would come when her worldview would clash with her husband's. For it did in Radom, where they disagreed on their children's education. When my grandfather insisted that their boys be sent to a yeshiva to study the Torah, my grandmother thought it was natural. But when he refused to send their daughter Sarah to high school because he believed girls needed no education, my grandmother rebelled. What gave her the courage to fight him was that old promise to be equal to her Menakhem Mendel, which I imagined she had made to herself under her wedding canopy. Having attended high school herself until she got married, in spite of being ultra-religious, she felt that what was good enough for her was indispensable for her daughter, especially at a time when the world around her was turning progressive. She won the fight and sent Sarah to school.

World War I was finally over, but times remained hard. When inflation skyrocketed in Poland (only Germany had it worse), Vladislav Grabski, both premier and finance minister, declared new steps to stabilize the economy. While his policies were not directed exclusively at the Jews, as merchants and artisans they were the first to suffer. And because Grabski was known for his ardent anti-Semitism, most Jews felt that they were burdened with heavier taxes than other Poles. Many sought to emigrate from Poland to the United States, but as America tightened its quotas of Jewish immigrants, Palestine became the desired choice. The British, who controlled the Jewish homeland, allowed only those who had vocation certificates or large sums of money, requirements my father's family was able to meet.

In 1926 the Bakmans arrived in Palestine with the fourth *aliyah*, or immigration wave. The immediate impetus for their emigration was an anti-Semitic incident that my grandmother witnessed on one of her business trips. She was traveling on a crowded train, when one of the passengers, a brutish Gentile, accompanied by a few friends, pushed off a Jewish passenger's hat. Amused by his roguish act, he proceeded to chop off the man's beard with a pocketknife. Without hesitation, my grandmother jumped from her seat and grabbed the young man's arm. With her usual cool, she commanded him to let go of the frightened man. The attacker recoiled, and the incident was over, but Brukha Bakman had made her decision.

When she arrived home she waited to talk to her husband without the children present. Only then did she tell him about the train episode. From the way she relayed her story, he sensed the conversation was leading elsewhere.

"What's on your mind, Brukha?" Her husband studied her face.

"We are starting a new chapter. We are going home to Palestine!"

We are going home. Within those four words she folded not only her family's saga but also a long and entwined Jewish history.

In February, on board the ship *Dacha*, my teenage father and his family arrived in the northern port city of Haifa, where they settled. There, by the Mediterranean Sea, my Aunt Tzipora was born, and Brukha became Brakha, the Hebrew derivation of her Yiddish name.

———•———

With a large family to feed and little time for reflection, my grandfather opened a store selling beds. But his prediction that the new wave of immigrants would create a strong demand for his merchandise did not work. He lost the business and the money he had invested in it. With my grandmother's encouragement, he looked for employment that did not require an additional investment. He ended up in construction, as a day laborer. Thrilled to find work, his face shone with delight when his fellow workers passed him a basket of bricks, which he carefully laid, one next to the other, with his elegant hands. When he wrote to his parents about the type of work he was doing, they demanded that he return with his family to Poland at once, an option my grandmother rejected.

Work was scarce, and food was meager. Still, my grandmother was too proud to ask anyone to lend her money to buy food for her hungry children. One day she heard a knock on the door. When she opened it she saw the neighborhood grocer, who was concerned that he had not seen her or her children for a few days. Making excuses, she did not let him into the apartment, refusing to permit anyone to see her children's swollen bellies.

If poverty did not create hardship enough, my grandfather was unable to accept the fact that in Haifa people worked and drove on the Sabbath. His children too struggled to adapt to the free mentality of the city, where men walked half-naked under the hot Mediterranean sun. It was hardest for Sarah to adapt. As the eldest child, she could remember the European customs (so different from the Levant ways) of men kissing women's hands and getting up from their seats when a woman entered a room or asking her permission to take off her coats.

After three years in that secular city, the Bakmans moved to Jerusalem. My grandfather was euphoric. The Sabbath was sacred in that golden City of David. Menakhem Mendel could pray to his God at the *Kotel*, the Wailing Wall, in spite of growing Arab opposition to the right of Jews to do so.

The children, however, were miserable. They viewed their father's demands that they live a strict Orthodox life befitting the divine city as a form of religious coercion. And because my grandfather preferred to speak Yiddish, they were thwarted in their efforts to master Hebrew, the spoken language in their new land, and they felt estranged. On top of all that, Jerusalem's holy aura, it turned out, did nothing to improve the family's financial situation.

When things could not get much worse, unexpected help arrived from my grandfather's niece, a former Radom beauty queen, who had immigrated to Brazil and become a respected member of the Jewish community in Rio de Janeiro. When she heard about her uncle's hardship in Palestine, she invited him to Rio, where she promised to help him find suitable work. The year was 1928. Desperate, he accepted the offer, planning to bring his family overseas as soon as he was settled.

———————

The older children breathed a sigh of relief when their father departed. His leaving meant the end of his religious obsession, which he had forced upon them, sometimes by physical means. By contrast, my aunts remembered their youngest sister, Tzipora, who was two when her father left, sitting in front of their house for hours each day, singing in Yiddish, "Papa come home...."

In Brazil my grandfather became a rabbi and a *shokhet*, performing the ritual slaughtering of animals and fowl in accordance with Jewish dietary laws. He fared well, able to send home fifteen pounds sterling each month, an immense sum at that time. The money improved his family's situation, allowing my grandmother to feed her children, furnish her home, give her daughter Sarah a large wedding, and save a considerable amount of money.

My grandmother continued to maintain a strict religious home, though she understood that her growing children needed a measure of freedom, in spite of the strict atmosphere in their Jerusalem neighborhood, where the smallest degree of individuality seemed rebellious. She was not afraid to be defiant in the sacred city and disobey the stern rabbis from nearby yeshivas who acted as modesty police. Feeling free to interfere in the lives of others, they took added liberties with households absent a male figurehead. They insisted that she send her children to ultra-Orthodox schools, while their younger disciples, who guarded the streets, tried to enforce modest wear on her daughters and ultra-Orthodox attire on her boys. She refused to obey their commands.

Two years after his departure, my grandfather commanded his wife and children to join him in Brazil. With his improved financial situation, he wrote to his wife, he was able to rent a large apartment and awaited their arrival. Conditions in Brazil in 1930 were volatile, after a coup d'état in October replaced one dictatorship with another. But Menakhem Mendel's situation was sound and stable.

My father, who was nineteen, refused to leave.

"I am not going!" he told his mother. She looked at him with empathy. She understood his attitude.

"Me, neither," seventeen-year-old Nehemiah chimed in. "I'm tired of all the moves. This is our home, and that's that!"

Sarah smiled. Newly wed, she was going to no new land.

My grandmother was sympathetic to her children, who had become attached to their new country, mastering its language as if it were their native tongue. In spite of the comfortable life she was assured to have in South America, she refused to go into a "second exile," as she called the Brazilian excursion. Her role as an Orthodox wife, decreed to remain by her husband's side, did not make my grandmother's choice easy. Tormented, she decided to seek the advice of a renowned Torah scholar.

No one could see Rabbi Avraham Yitzhak HaCohen Kook, then chief rabbi of Palestine, without a prearranged appointment. But my grandmother went to his court anyway. When she arrived, she came across the rabbi's *gabai*, or assistant. Unable to hold back her tears, she related her story. Rabbi Kook, who heard her through his open window, demanded that she be given an audience with him at once. He agreed with her that she should not uproot her children. To support her family, he advised her to relocate to Tel Aviv, the largest Jewish urban center in Palestine, which had begun to boom economically, and start working in commerce. But her children—the younger ones ranging between the ages of four and fourteen—should stay in Jerusalem. "The day will come," he predicted, "that Menakhem Mendel will return to the Holy Land, and the family will reunite."

I do not know why my grandmother needed to work. Perhaps my grandfather stopped sending her money because she had not joined him. What I do know is that following Rabbi Kook's advice, she entrusted Sarah to help with the Jerusalem household, and moved to Tel Aviv. There she shared an apartment with a woman who owned a haberdashery business, selling ties, ribbons, lace collars, buttons, and the like. To familiarize herself with the secrets of trade, my grandmother began to help her new friend, making the runs from suppliers to buyers, mastering the city's business world.

One day, tired and hungry, she entered a new restaurant. The owner, a German Jew by the name of Yutka, took an interest in my grandmother and shared her own success story with her. Yutka was a good baker. Before she opened her own restaurant, she trudged from one restaurant to another and offered their owners tastes of her baked goods. Before long, her products became so popular that she decided to open her own place.

"Come up with your own products," she suggested to my grandmother, "and do what I did."

Yutka's story encouraged my grandmother. But if she were to stay in Tel Aviv, she wanted her children with her. Her decision made, she began to look for a suitable apartment. While searching, she came across a store in the center of the city. On display were small jute bags filled with noodles and farfalle. Examining the products she thought they looked coarse and shapeless. "I can do much better," she concluded. "This will be my product. We are staying in Palestine!" She was steadfast.

She moved her children, except for Sarah, to Tel Aviv. With their help, my grandmother began producing and selling her thin noodles that became as popular as Yutka's creations. In due course she invented her own dough-rolling machine so she could make more noodles faster.

I used to love her thin Passover egg noodles, which I now make. I also remember her fried dough ribbons sprinkled with sugar, and her *kreplakh*, the small dumpling filled with ground meat that she used to make especially for me, since it was one of the few foods I liked. Coming from her, this was a tremendous show of love.

———◆———

In 1935, Rabbi Kook's prediction materialized. After seven and a half years in Brazil, my grandfather returned to his family. They awaited his arrival with joyful anticipation. But his reappearance in their lives revived a familiar problem. Having had to declare a Hasidic affiliation in Brazil, even though he had not been a Hasid, and now identified with the strict, ultra-Orthodox Gur sect, Menakhem Mendel returned home more pious than ever.

Clashes were unavoidable when his sons rejected their father's demands that they study the Torah, pray three times each day, and isolate themselves from the secular world to which they had assimilated. And though they tried to treat their father with the respect he deserved, the harsher he became, the less of his authority they accepted. Several of them were old enough to go their own way. Though they tried to reasonably follow the religious customs with which they were raised, in the end all of the sons developed an aversion to religion altogether.

Many years after my father left his father's home I witnessed his antipathy to the religious way of life Menakhem Mendel had tried to impose on him and his siblings. I was seven or eight when he brought *chspeck*, or fresh bacon, to our kosher home. What made his deed worse was the fact that he did so on the eve of Yom Kippur, the most somber day in the Jewish calendar. He hid the package, wrapped in white paper, in the back of our icebox, until the following day, when my mother was at the synagogue, spending the entire day praying. My sister was also there, with friends, and I was alone at home with my father. On that day of atoning and fasting, he fried the chspeck and prepared two sandwiches on challah bread, one for him, the other for me, and made me promise to keep to myself what had happened in our kitchen.

"Ziva," he warned, "you cannot tell anyone, especially Imma!"

I bit into the sandwich, and nodded in agreement, not just to placate my father, but also for the thrill of sharing a secret that was ours alone. I shared another secret, years later, as a young woman, when I caught my grandmother smoking a cigarette, a deed most uncommon among Orthodox women.

"Grandma!" I cried, my eyes wide with astonishment.

"I'll kill you if you tell anyone," she warned me. To her, as to my father, I remained a faithful ally.

My grandfather continued to work as a shokhet for a few more years, until he was employed by Tel Aviv's religious-community committee. On Friday nights, when the Sabbath arrived, my grandfather forced his boys to discuss the Torah lesson of the week. He forbade them to leave home on the Sabbath, except to go the neighborhood synagogue, and demanded that my grandmother enforce his strict rules as well.

Like Don Quixote, unable to face the real world around him, my grandfather could not accept his children's secular tendencies. He sent his two youngest sons to study in ultra-Orthodox schools: Simkha to a yeshiva in Jerusalem and Yaakov to one in Tel Aviv. They wore *peyot*, the sidelocks ultra-Orthodox Jews are required to wear. One day Simkha returned from Jerusalem without his sidelocks. My grandfather was furious.

When my grandmother's father arrived in Palestine on the eve of World War II, he tried to soften his son-in-law's attitude toward his children. Rather than adhering to his father-in-law's advice, my grandfather complained that the family had fallen apart in his absence, under his wife's care, and he needed to put it together again.

"I left Jews when I departed, to find goyim when I returned," he protested bitterly.

The near-fanatic portrayal of his personality I heard from my aunts contradicts the grandfather I knew. To me, he was warm and loving, particularly during the difficult periods of my childhood, when he was a source of security and balance, which I needed. He was the grandpa who visited every Friday with sweet candy in his pockets for his beloved granddaughter. When, as a high school student, I read with him Rashi's commentaries on the Bible and Talmud, his face shone with joy. He was the one who called me "Pipkalé," his blue eyes radiating warmth.

My grandmother never criticized Menakhem Mendel in front of their children. She kept her anger hidden and was careful not to confront him in their presence. Years later she revealed to her children the intensity of their fights concerning them. Sometimes she did not speak to him for weeks at a time.

———◆———

With her husband back home and the crisis his return produced, my grandmother stopped making her noodles. At the time, Osem, the Israeli food company that decades later developed into a conglomerate, sought to employ her and pay handsomely for her recipe, but she refused. Instead, she became an activist, advocating for the education of Orthodox girls, an issue she first championed when her eldest daughter was a teenager, and one to which she dedicated the rest of her life. She became a respected member of the national parent-teacher association, and was often away from home. She also cared for needy pupils and the elderly, and established a charity organization that supplied clothes to the poor. It was the first charity organization in Tel Aviv to expand nationwide.

Though different from one another, my grandparents not only managed to stay together—having little choice about that—they also, with their seven children and their many grandchildren, succeeded in building a united, dependable family. Now in its fifth generation, our clan numbers more than one hundred descendants.

As they grew old together, Brakha and Menakhem Mendel developed a mutual dependence and even a friendship. The proof of that is displayed in a photograph that was taken at my wedding. It shows the "royal couple" in an intimate moment, sitting close to one another. Her right arm rests on his left while she talks to him, and he, listening to her, is looking at her intently.

My grandmother passed away in June 1968. My grandfather lived ten months longer. They are buried side by side in a cemetery near Tel Aviv in a section that is allotted for *tzadikkim*, or righteous Jews. The engravings on nearby headstones commemorate the lives of the dead, telling of the demise of Eastern European Jewry; of rabbis who led their congregations for half a century; of parents, brothers and sisters, children, and children's children who were tortured and murdered in pogroms, in the ghettos of Lodz and Chelmno, in Auschwitz—of a fate that my father's family escaped because of my grandmother's vision.

My grandparents, here in 1964, and their young family arrived in Palestine in 1926. They decided to emigrate from Poland after my grandmother witnessed an anti-Semitic incident on a train. "We are starting a new chapter, "she told my grandfather. "We are going home"

CHAPTER 5

From Bravery to Despair

"Tell me Ziva, do you really think this garden is a *park?*"

The sixty-year-old woman who asked me that question, rather mockingly, was my mother, Khaya. We were strolling in Central Park, the verdant sanctuary in the heart of Manhattan.

We promenaded for some time before I took her to a spot that would afford her a panoramic view of the park's splendor. On our way I showed her the famous Bethesda Fountain, the band shell where prominent musicians perform, the twenty-two-acre lake that reflects Manhattan's high-rise buildings, the zoo, the Delacorte musical clock, all to no avail.

"Just another park," she insisted.

"It's not just any park, Imma," I rejoined. "It's one of the most famous parks in the world. To really see it you must come here a few times, and even then there will still be things to discover on yet another visit."

She shrugged her shoulders. "If you say so."

I thought our visit to the park would be one of the highlights of her first trip to New York.

"It's not such a small park, Imma," I said, in a last attempt to impress her. "It measures over four kilometers long and almost a kilometer wide!" I felt triumphant. Now she had to be convinced.

She smiled. Her bright green eyes expressed forgiveness for my fervor. Her face, I thought, still showed signs of her old beauty.

"If you had been to Plungyan, you would have seen a *real* park," she said, looking sentimental. She was silent for a moment, her mind, I imagined, drifting back to her hometown, which she had left more than four decades earlier.

We continued to walk until we reached my favorite spot, facing a stone bridge over one of the arms of the park's lakes. It was a beautiful landscape. The trees were starting to change their colors, nature's paintbrushes turning green leaves into gold and golden shades into a fiery orange that shimmered in the autumn sun. Nearby a great white egret stared at us as if offended by my mother's remarks.

I too believed that his magnificent home deserved more than a comparison to a park in a remote town in Lithuania. But at that moment I let my mother embellish on her childhood memories—not just for her, but for me as well, as I began to envision my own journey to her birthplace to trace my ancestral roots there. Little did I know then that thirty-five years later I would fulfill that wish, standing on my mother's old backyard, stepping down to the path that led me to the magnificent park she remembered.

———◆———

Unlike my father, who never talked about his hometown in Poland, my mother frequently mentioned the small Lithuanian town where she was born and raised. On bright sunny days my sister and I listened to her stories about her shtetl's colorful characters, such as Moishe the *muziker*, whose off-key tunes could be heard from afar; Motke the *ganef*, or thief; Tzipe the *pleplerke*, or babbler; Moishe the *kailiker*, or cripple; Yankel the *hoiker*, or hunchback; and Shmeel the *rizikant*, or gambler. Her tales laid out before us an array of people and events she remembered from a time gone by. But those cozy hours, when we sat together and listened to her enchanting stories, faded in winter, when my mother succumbed to her annual depression.

My mother talked neither of wealth nor of poverty. In Plunge—Plungyan was the Yiddish name—she and her family lived in a typical four-room house with a small backyard dotted with patches of flowers and vegetables; the yard has since been tiled over with red bricks, the old wood on the house's exterior replaced with coarse concrete. Its distinctive paned windows were removed to make room for large modern ones, which display dresses in what has become a women's clothing store. But the original wooden shed in the back of the house is still standing, just as it appears in old photos.

My mother, Khaya, was born to the Sher family on January 17, 1915. The park she longed for was but steps away from her family's house on 15 Darius Street. Though in reality the park is smaller than the one she had inscribed in memory, its pastoral beauty cannot be exaggerated. It has a regal-looking gateway, ornamented with wrought iron and classic white-arched masonry. A large mansion stands in the midst of its expansive gardens. The Babrungas River, a stream of which gleams in the park's luxurious meadows, waters rare trees and feeds many ponds.

Khaya was the fifth among eight siblings. Traditional rather than Orthodox, her family was open to the modern winds that swept across Europe. The girls were educated, and sons and daughters alike were allowed to join secular Zionist organizations if they so wished.

Among her siblings, my mother was the first to emigrate, journeying to Palestine in the early 1930s. Her sister Tovah followed her there a year before World War II broke out. Their brother Shimon, with his young wife, Hannah, immigrated to the United States, also in the early 1930s, becoming a respected rabbi at Congregation Keter Yisrael in Borough Park, Brooklyn. Of those who stayed in Lithuania, only Sorke and Eerle, the youngest sisters, survived the war. The Nazis and their Lithuanian collaborators murdered the rest of their immediate family, killing six in all.

In her youth, my mother's beauty was legendary among those who had known her. When I was a young woman, her old acquaintances would tell me, "If you want to know how pretty she was, look at pictures of Greta Garbo. No other woman was as beautiful as your mother."

I understood what they meant, though to me she looked more like Gloria Swanson. Hers was a classic beauty, and tales of her looks traveled beyond her hometown. When she approached the bank of the river that runs through town, men would whistle and stop to watch her crossing the bridge. "Here comes Khaya the beautiful, with her big green eyes," they would sing. Seventy-five years after my mother left Plunge I walked on that bridge. Though it was far smaller than I had envisioned, it registered as huge in my mind.

When my mother was seventeen, my Aunt Tovah told me, she was arrested on the bridge after she had bent to retie a loosened shoelace. Apparently the policeman who detained her suspected she was making a signal of some sort to members of the banned Communist party. Her brother Yitzhak bailed my mother out, vouching that she was not a Communist.

But she was a Zionist, planning her immigration to Palestine to take part in building the Jewish state that was yet to come. At the time of her arrest, my mother was a committed member of the Revisionist Zionist movement Beitar. Perhaps it was she who hung on the wall of her home in Plunge the famous photo of Theodor Herzl—the father of political Zionism, who envisioned the creation of a Jewish state in its homeland—next to a portrait of her father, Moshe Leib, who died of poor health in 1925. Those two images are visible in a photograph that shows my mother's mother and six of her eight children seated at a Seder table. Only my mother and her brother Shimon, who had left Lithuania five years earlier, do not appear in that picture. A calendar on the wall reveals the date the picture was taken: April 15, 1938. Sent to my family in Israel, with an inscription written in perfect Hebrew, it was the last photograph of the Sher family.

———•———

Jewish immigration to Lithuania began in the fourteenth century. Plunge was one of the first settlements the newcomers built. Their choice of location was not accidental. Plunge is situated on the road that leads to the harbor city of Klaipeda, also known as Memelburg, or Memel, the name my mother used. Throughout their generations, the Jews of Plunge developed a thriving commercial center and a rich cultural life; Jewish institutions of all sorts flourished.

In 1933, when she was eighteen, my mother left Lithuania for Palestine. Prior to her emigration aboard the ship *Martha Washington*, she spent a year on a farm, training for her future as a Palestinian pioneer. During that training, she experienced the strongest expression of anti-Semitism she had endured. After she proved to work much faster than the other farmhands—picking strawberries, as I recall from her stories—a group of non-Jewish workers ganged up on her, threatening to kill her if she did not slow down. I have often imagined her, dressed in a short-sleeved white blouse and an ankle-length floral skirt, moving quickly among the strawberry rows. Perhaps it was her beauty as much as her efficiency that irritated them.

Leaving home eight years before the Nazi occupation of Lithuania, my mother escaped the horrors the rest of her family experienced during the Second World War. Her mother, her brother, two sisters, one of them married and eight months pregnant, and most of her other relatives were murdered in that war. I have long suspected that my mother never forgave herself for escaping the same fate.

———◆———

During the time of my mother's immigration, the British controlled Palestine. Because Middle Eastern oil was already an important strategic asset, the British consented to Arab demands, and imposed stern restrictions on Jewish immigration, challenging Ben Gurion's idea that every Jew who arrived safely in Palestine enhanced the realization of a Jewish state in its homeland.

As part of their restrictions, the British refused to grant immigration permits to Jewish women unless they were married. The reasoning was that unmarried women were economically dependent, making it too costly to absorb them.

To get around the British policy, the Jewish leadership in Palestine arranged fictitious marriages between women who wanted to immigrate to Palestine and men who already lived there, or men who had been granted the coveted immigration certificate. Once the women arrived in Palestine, the temporary marriages were dissolved.

Problems arose when some of those "spouses" refused to grant the divorce. My mother found herself in such a bind, after receiving her certificate from the head of the Palestine office in Kovno, or Kaunas, Lithuania. I believe she and her designated "groom" sailed to Palestine on the same boat. Captivated by her beauty, he fell in love with her and when they arrived refused to grant her the annulment to which he had agreed. According to my mother's account, authenticated by my father, the man threatened to kill her if she left him. He yielded, giving in to the realization that my mother would never love him.

By my mother's side during that ordeal was her friend Blumma. They met on the boat en route to Palestine and became lifelong friends. Upon their arrival, along with other pioneers they joined a settlement in Upper Galilee, where they became admired cooks, preparing meals for their fellow immigrants. My mother assumed the additional role of seamstress, mending the groups' work clothes. When the two women left the settlement a year later, they were as hopeful and jovial as they had been when they had first arrived.

Blumma, a cheerful, heavyset woman whom I remember fondly, lost her laughter after one of her sons was killed in northern Israel. He was hit by Syrian shelling following the Six-Day War in 1967, and another son fell in the War of Attrition seven years later.

My mother, too, lost her laughter. Leaving her family behind in Lithuania at the age of eighteen took courage, determination, and a commitment to the Zionist cause. But in Palestine, her bravery and sense of purpose and resolve gave way to depression and despair. No one who had known my mother in her youth could have imagined how that stunning, energetic, blossoming young woman would fade like a wilted flower in the darkening chill of winter.

I cannot be sure of what triggered my mother's illness, except for the speculations I had heard about her exaggerated fear of cancer.

Anxious about her health, she visited doctors often. One day, complaining of stomachaches, she asked her doctor if it was possible that her symptoms were a sign of cancer. Without much thought, he referred her to a specialist, placing a letter in her hand. Once out of his office she opened the envelope. Her doctor had written, "suspicion of cancer." Supposedly, the shock of reading those words, which confirmed her fear, caused her depression.

Though I have never doubted the story, I have wondered how much it really had to do with her recurrent depression. Curious about the possible connection between shock (or posttraumatic syndrome) and mental disorder, I learned that trauma could be one among the multiple causes of depression, the others being genetic, biological, psychological, or environmental. Whether there had been a predisposition that might have exacerbated my mother's situation, I will never know.

Though my mother rose like a phoenix in the sun-warmed days of each summer, she fell into the abyss of depression each winter. In so doing she shattered not only her own life, but also the lives of those closest to her—my father, my sister, and me. Partners in her anguish, we loved her still when the sound of laughter was gone from our home. At times I wanted to be by her side and hug her tightly to show her that I loved her, to let her drink from the fountain of my youth and strengthen her broken spirit. At other times I wanted to scream in anger. But mostly I wanted to curl into a shell like a snail and hide until spring arrived. It was not until I was older that I grasped the meaning of depression and comprehended its destructive force.

———•———

I do not know how my parents met. A mutual friend may have introduced them, or else they met at a meeting of the Beitar movement, to which both were affiliated then, at the onset of their political lives. (They ended up dedicated to the Socialist Labor movement.)

I often imagined my father being overwhelmed by my mother's beauty when he first saw her. I wondered if he stared at her, if his heart plunged, or whether his voice trembled when he uttered his first words to her.

She was five feet two inches tall, slim and yet curvy, and had exquisite taste in clothes. Her skin was dark and smooth, her hair black and wavy, cut in a straight line just below her ears and combed back, revealing a high forehead and a widow's peak. Her slightly upturned nose was perfectly proportioned, her lips small but full, her eyebrows thin, long, and arching. Beneath them were the greenest of eyes, big and deep set, with a gaze direct and mysterious.

I also envisioned her seeing my father for the first time, impressed with his wiry, tall, erect figure, and his long-fingered hands, like his father's. I imagined her feeling dazed by his looks, lowering her eyes in a gesture of shyness.

He was intellectual looking, with wise amber-brown eyes and a high forehead, his reddish-brown hair receding on both sides. His nose was straight and powerful, and his lips were often curved into a cynical half smile.

By my calculation, my parents must have met in late 1934. In 1935, after months of courting, they announced their engagement on the occasion of my grandfather's return from Brazil. I do not know when they got married. Their wedding announcement and their marriage certificate have disappeared, perhaps with other irreplaceable family memorabilia that my mother tore to pieces a few years before her death. Her reasons for this act of destruction remain a mystery. She may have been depressed, or frustrated or angered by the memories invoked by the photographs and papers. I can only imagine the remorse she must have felt once she realized what she had done. My own shock at her deed remains. Among the items she shredded were precious fragments of my past that now exist in my memory only: three post-cards my husband had sent me from the battlefield. The last words he would ever write to me in his clear, small handwriting. Three simple, white postcards with blue script, some of it erased with black ink by the military censor. I can still visualize these postcards, but I can never touch or smell them.

———◆———

My mother died in 1993, at the same hospital where I was born. She had spent the last eight years of her life in assisted-living housing, sharing a small apartment with her neighbor of more than five decades. When Miriam and I went to collect our mother's belongings, we were stunned to find out what she had done.

"She did not answer me when I asked her why she was doing it. Instead, she continued to shred every piece of paper and every photo," her roommate told us, shrugging her shoulders.

In a somber mood, Miriam and I cleaned out our mother's closets and cleared the shelves. It took us less than two hours to make her space available for the next potential resident; when we were done, it was as if she had never existed, confirming one of her favorite sayings: "Life is a *poof*, and then it is over."

In addition to having no documents in my possession confirming my parents' marriage, I discovered that it is not recorded at the Rabbinate Bureau of the Israeli Ministry of Religious Affairs, where marriage registries go back to 1912. It is probable that they were wed by a private rabbi; such marriages, common at the time, were not publicly recorded before Israel was established in 1948.

Perhaps I would remember their wedding date if they had celebrated their anniversary, but they never did, as far as I can recall. They had no wedding pictures, either, though this was not unusual; in those years many couples opted to have formal portraits taken months after their weddings.

I do know that by September 1936 they were married. In my possession I have a handsome photograph of them, decorating a Jewish New Year greeting card that corresponds with that date. My mother is dressed in a white ensemble, and my father wears a white, collared shirt. They made an attractive couple. In November of the following year, Miriam was born.

My father was a gentle man, if authoritative and stubborn; my mother was submissive to him, but seemed bitter about the submissiveness marriage imposed. He liked things immaculate; she could be sloppy. He was pedantic and needed his books; she needed people. He was an unsuccessful if determined businessman; she was a woman of elegant tastes who could not afford the things she liked and felt trapped in a small apartment in an unfashionable neighborhood while her relatives enjoyed more luxuries. Yet my parents' life together was not a tiresome journey. They found mutual affection and even love on sunny days when my mother was well.

In spite of his gentleness and his determination to understand my mother's situation, my father would erupt at her complaints,

I don't know the exact date of my parents' marriage. They were probably wed by a private rabbi, before such unions were recorded. They were married by 1936, about the time this photograph was taken

The year they got married, 1936, they sent out this Jewish New Year card

sometimes getting angry enough to turn over a table, even one covered with dishes. Though such episodes were seldom, the memories of them and the mortification they caused me are still imprinted on my consciousness.

———◆———

On weekdays in the summer, my mother brought Miriam and me to the beach. We splashed and swam in the clear, warm Mediterranean water, played on the sand, and ate popsicles sold by vendors, who announced their merchandise in rhymes, each vendor more creative than the last.

When I was a child, summer looked to me like an eternal glory, colored in a blend of gold and blue. But its enchantment never lasted, its brilliance dimming in the twilight of fall. Year after year, when the air turned cool and the smell of damp earth and falling leaves spread in the air, I began to feel dread, fearing the times when she lay in bed in that sad season, popping pills and crying, unable to get up. And though we never talked about it, I suspect that my father and sister dreaded those things, too.

Years went by and seasons changed. I was a married woman and a mother myself. Her green eyes fixed on me, with sadness, she asked: "Tell me, Ziva. Was I a good mother?"

"Yes, you were," I answered, and in my heart I thought, "you did the best you could," remembering that when she was healthy, safe from the dark days of winter when her laughter sank in the despair that consumed her, she was a loving, devoted mother.

CHAPTER 6
Winter

Against the stark memories of my mother illness when I was a young child stands the sweetness of the period when my mother's two youngest sisters, Sorke and Eerle, lived with us.

My mother, her sister Tovah, and their brother Shimon were shocked when they learned that their two youngest sisters survived the war.

In July 1941 they endured the horrific massacre in the Koshan forests, where they had witnessed the murder of their mother, their two sisters, one of whom was eighth months pregnant, and the rest of their relatives.

No one had described what had happened in Koshan better than Jacob Bunka, the last remaining Jew in Plunge until his death in 2014 at the age of 91. Bunka dedicated his life to memorialize Jewish Plunge. He attained permission from the Soviet authorities (who controlled Lithuania from the second world war to 1991) to amass the eighty-nine gravestones from what was the old Jewish cemetery in Plunge, and place them in their current spot.

In his 2002 memoir *Plungian,* he graphically described how 1,800 of the town's Jews, men, women, and children, were rounded up by local Nazi collaborators and brought to the forest, where they were systematically killed.

Many of these Jews were forced to dig six huge pits for their own burial and that of those arriving after them. The murderers, often drunk, tore small children from their mothers' arms and cracked open their heads on trees or rocks, then tossed their tiny bodies into the pits along with their mothers. Layer-by-layer, the wounded were thrown into the pits to suffocate under the dead, the sound of their cries mixed with screams. That was the hell my two young aunts survived.

From Koshan Sorke and Eerle had been sent to the ghetto in nearby Telze, and then to the Shavli ghetto. They walked four miles each way daily, to and from a German aircraft factory where they worked as slave laborers.

In 1944, the Nazis moved them to the Stutthof concentration camp in Poland. They endured a death march, and at some point during their ordeal (the particulars are unknown to me) found refuge in a barn. The farmer sent them away with a loaf of bread and an enamel cup. The sisters filled the cup with snow to melt into drinking water, using their body heat. In the Polish forests they met up with Jewish partisans, and so they survived. When the war ended, Sorke and Eerle arrived in the Center of the Diaspora in Milan, Italy. It had been established by the Jewish Brigade, a unit of Jewish fighters from Mandatory Palestine, incorporated into the British army in World War II, to shelter Jewish refugees on their way to Palestine. As the two sisters mingled among the refugees and their rescuers, they started a conversation with a Jewish soldier from Palestine.

"Do you happen to know a family named Bakman?" they asked him.

The soldier could not hide his surprise. "*My* last name is Bakman!" he answered.

I can always envision the sisters, hardly able to remain standing, when they heard the soldier's last name. Holding onto each other, they continued, "Then, do you know a Tzvi Bakman?"

"What is he to you?" the soldier asked. I can imagine his heart pumping furiously.

"He is married to our sister Khaya."

"And I am Nehemiah, Tzvi's younger brother," he said, overwhelmed by the sheer coincidence to emerge in this unexpected conversation.

Hugging each other, the sisters began to cry, and the soldier joined them, just as emotional.

Nehemiah cabled his brother and sister-in-law, my parents, with the good news. But there was bad news as well. It was then that my parents learned that my mother's brother Yitzhak, a teacher who had been living in Telze during the Koshan extermination, had been killed there.

On the twenty-fifth of December, 1945, my aunts arrived in the northern coastal town of Naharia, Palestine, on board the ship *Hannah Senes*. The ship, named after a young Jewish paratrooper from Palestine who in 1944 had been executed by the Nazis for her attempt to rescue Hungarian Jews, had started its journey eleven days earlier from the port city of Savona, Italy, carrying 252 Holocaust survivors. It was the first vessel to sail from Europe to Palestine since the British had sealed off the harbors, in order to prevent Jewish refugees from arriving. Under dark skies on Christmas night—chosen by the ship's operators because they expected the British soldiers guarding the shores to be celebrating rather than paying heed to the blockade—the refugees were dispersed in area settlements, with the aid of local residents. The following day my father found Sorke and Eerle in Kibbutz Yagur and brought them to our home, which seemed to expand in order to accommodate them.

Nehemiah was killed two years later during Israel's War of Independence. My only memory of my uncle is the way he laughed at my mischievous behavior as I stuck my chewing gum to his chair before he sat on it when he visited our home.

———◆———

Sorke and Eerle lived with us for months. They must have showered me, a year-old toddler, with love the way they always did. In time Sorke married Yisrael, a partisan from the legendary Bielski group. She may have met him as she and Eerle took refuge in the forests.

Led by Tuvia Bielski and his three brothers, the group rescued Jews from the ghettos where they had been rounded up for annihilation to fight the Nazis in occupied Poland. Hiding and operating in the forests of what is now Belarus, from 1942 to the end of the war they set up a community of more than 1,200 Jewish fighters and survivors. The 2008 film *Defiance* tells their story of bravery and endurance.

Eerle married Ephraim, a fellow refugee she met on the boat that carried them to Palestine. The two couples moved to small apartments, one above the other, in a new neighborhood on the outskirts of Tel Aviv.

Unable to separate from us, they visited us often. I remember fondly how, bad eater that I was, Sorke tried to make me like food. She would sit me on the thick banister of our ground-floor balcony and feed me banana slices that she had cut into different sizes and shapes, pretending they were cakes made by the most famous *conditorie* in Tel Aviv.

After the sisters settled in their own apartments it was only natural that the next time my mother was too ill to take care of Miriam and me, she and I would live with them. My sweet aunts never scolded or blamed, only loved.

Perhaps my mother should have been hospitalized rather than treated by private doctors. The electroshock therapy and various medications they prescribed were not always effective. But my father preferred that my mother continue with those treatments, even though they were pricy, rather than be separated from my sister and me, especially since she suffered only in wintertime. When that season's gray turned golden so did her mood; when the chill surrendered to the cuddling warmth of a new spring, she recovered and even thrived.

In good health she became a loving mother who sheltered her daughters. A fragile child, I felt loved and secure when she wrapped me with tenderness and watched me as if I were the precious apple of her eye.

This was the mother who took me to my favorite restaurant—a rare outing in the semi-socialist society in which I grew up—and watched me eat the food I liked, ordering nothing for herself. She fought to place me in a better grammar school than the one in which I was enrolled, and she went to school to defend me when necessary. She made me the most beautiful Purim costumes, for most of which I won first prizes. She was the mother who arrived by cab at midnight at the home of my Uncle Yaakov and his wife, Esther, when I was seven or so, because she presumed that I would cry that first night I slept away from home. She was the mother who took me for my first bra, even though, at fourteen, I did not yet need one, because she wanted me to have pretty breasts when I grew up. She was the mother who took me to the dermatologist to prevent acne and to the gynecologist when my menstruation was irregular. She was the mother who made sure that my sister and I wore the finest clothes and ate the best food available. She did all that in her good days, and sometimes even when she was ill.

I was six in the winter of 1950, not yet enrolled in first grade. Because of her illness, my mother and I had moved in with Eerle and her husband, Ephraim. I was standing alone on their terrace looking inside the apartment when I saw my mother suddenly begin to disrobe. My father had arrived a short while earlier after visiting Miriam at Aunt Tovah's. My mother's upper body was naked, her breasts and back completely exposed. My father and aunts begged her to stop undressing, while my uncles stood nearby, embarrassed and helpless. First they pleaded, then they reprimanded, to no avail.

My beautiful mother had a crazed look and seemed in the midst of a trance. Her big green eyes, which could sparkle like precious stones, turned black. Their expression, one I had never seen before, horrified me. Standing among those who loved her she seemed alone, detached from her surroundings, floating in her own sphere. My distraught father, part of the same surreal scenario, continued his attempts to bring her to her senses.

"Khaya, that's enough," he begged her over and over again, trying to grab her hands. But she fought him off, readying to strip off the rest of her clothes. Suddenly he began to sob and then to hit her naked back with both his hands. "Khaya, stop, Khaya, stop," he pleaded, weeping. She scrunched her back and protected her face with her hands.

"Abba is trying to get Imma out of her bad spell," I told myself. "That's why he is hitting her." My beautiful mother was caught in a tormenting delirium, going through something horrific I could not understand, and my father was unable to calm her.

I had never been so frightened. I wanted one of the adults in the apartment to come out to the terrace and hold me, comfort me. I wanted them to tell me that my mother and father would be fine. But at that horrible moment I had a keen understanding that I should stay on the terrace and remain as quiet as I could be. I knew enough not to cry or make a sound. I understood that no one inside that room could attend to me, no matter how terrified I was.

I stood there frozen. Suddenly, I saw my mother changing back, as if reacting at last to my father's desperation. She became calm, returned to her senses, her eyes turning green again, as if a magic wand touched her.

Does she know what just happened? I wondered. I still do. But the question that floods my mind when I recall that episode is: how did I cope with what I had just seen? For many years I believed that I had acquired strength much later in life, when I needed it most. It never occurred to me until I was writing these lines that it could have happened in those moments, when I was standing alone on the darkened terrace witnessing that scene with the people I loved and trusted most falling apart.

———◆———

Later that evening someone compared the weather to the frosty European winters they remembered. The following morning the city was covered in a thick carpet of snow, and white flakes still swirled in the air. It was the first snowfall in the Israeli's coastal plain that anyone could recall. It seemed to cleanse the air and erase the darkness that had befallen my aunt's home the day before.

I was alone on the street that morning. Standing near my aunts' apartment house I gaped at the spectacular sight. The street and the sidewalks, the trees and the bushes, all were submerged in a blinding white powder I had never seen before. Mesmerized by the beauty spread before me, I stood in the middle of the street and let my imagination wander. I pictured my mother being happy in the winter, wearing a long woolen coat, an elegant hat and gloves, looking as she had in her old pictures. She was walking by my father's side. He wore a suit and tie, as he always did on outings. I was running in front of them, the three of us marveling at the white miracle that surrounded us. In the midst of my fantasy, a taxi appeared next to me. The driver stretched his arm out and put his hand on my shoulder.

"Little girl," he asked, "didn't you hear my horn? I've been beeping for a long time, but you haven't moved." He drove away, and I still did not move.

———◆———

The summer when I was four-and-a-half, my parents decided to spend a week at a health resort in the Judean hills of Jerusalem. They had been gone but a day or two, and I already missed them, even though Miriam was with me. I was standing with her on Eerle's terrace, when two sparrows flew toward us and rested on the railing.

"Little birds, little birds," I pleaded, "would you please fly and bring my parents back home?" Scared by my motion, the birds flew away. At that moment the doorbell rang. As I turned my head I saw my parents at the door. Missing us, they said, they had cut short their retreat.

"The little birds listened to me," I yelped, and ran into their arms.

"What birds?" they asked laughing.

"The ones that brought you home."

That summer, like all summers, my mother's melancholy disappeared. Once again I felt secure, in the season's warmth, its smells, and its brightness.

CHAPTER 7

Miriam

My sister looked thin to me when she picked me up at the Tel Aviv airport in the summer of 2004. Though concerned, I waited until we stopped at a café to mention it.

"You've lost weight since I was here in the winter," I said, as if complimenting her, though she had always been slim. "Are you dieting?"

"No," she replied, and I felt my heart skip a beat.

"How did you lose the weight, then?" I tried to sound envious. "Your thinness suits you."

"We changed our eating habits after Danny's bypass surgery."

Danny had been her boyfriend for six years, and they had been living together for the past eighteen months. Her answer reassured me, until I picked her up at work a few days later—Miriam was the director of an insurance company branch office—to go out for lunch.

"Make sure she eats," her assistant urged me. "She has stopped eating."

"I will make certain of it," I said in a tone that meant to hide my renewed anxiety. We ate at an outdoor restaurant in Tel Aviv's port. The blue Mediterranean glittered in front of us, and the bright June light gave Miriam a healthy appearance. To my delight she ordered plenty of food. The aromas of olive oil, lemon, and garlic must have increased her appetite. Devouring every bit, she showed no sign of illness, and my mind eased once more.

When she was hospitalized three months later and I told her I was coming back to Israel to be with her, she told me not to worry.

"You would do the same for me," I argued.

"True," she whispered. "In that case, I can't wait for you to arrive."

I mumbled a silly joke about getting a manicure so I would look good for her, hoping she could not detect that I was choking back tears.

The following day, when I went to the hospital straight from the airport, I saw how much she had deteriorated. Like other gravely ill patients, she was preoccupied with herself. There was no hugging, no kissing, and no tears, as if it had not been three months since we had seen each other.

To my surprise, Miriam was released from the hospital the day I arrived. Suffering from a severe shortness of breath, she was yet to be diagnosed, pending analysis of an array of tests. But her doctor suspected there was no hope. The best he could do for her was to let her go home to be in familiar surroundings.

"Connect me to the oxygen tank, I can't breathe!" she gasped on the way out, looking as scared as a wounded animal. Within a few days the tests confirmed that she suffered from an inoperable lung cancer. Fifty years of heavy smoking had destroyed her lungs beyond repair.

I nursed her, careful that her sudden dependency did not humiliate her. Most of the time we were alone, talking, laughing, or simply being, two sisters connected as if we were one.

Miriam's four children clung to hope. To my relief, she never understood how ill she was. I realized she was dying but I did not expect that she would be gone so soon. A week after I had arrived to be by her side, I returned to New York, to begin teaching the fall semester. Four days passed, and she was back in the hospital.

Her son-in-law, Neri, called me. "Speak to your sister. I'll hold the receiver close to her ear."

"Can she still hear me?" I asked, my voice cracking. I knew she would not last. She was in a twilight zone—not one between dawn and sunrise or daylight and dusk—but that which arrives when life meets death.

"Every word," Neri assured me.

"Hi, Mickie. I love you," I said, using her nickname. For her sake I tried to sound cheerful.

Thousands of miles away, I longed to touch her. I wanted to say something encouraging, something that implied a future—that I would see her on my next visit, when I had time off from teaching. By then, I wanted to tell her, she would have recovered, responding to the chemotherapy she was supposed to begin the day of our conversation. But I could not lie to her, not even in her last hours.

"There will be no other chance," I said to myself. "Just say it. Wish her good luck with the treatment. Inspire her. Lie!"

But the words would not come out. "Say good-bye, then," I told myself. But I could not do that either—she might still believe she could be saved.

"I love you, Mickie," was all I could utter. Hours later I was on an airplane on my way to her funeral.

———◆———

Like most siblings, Miriam and I fought as girls. Yet no one could have been more proud of her older sister than I was of mine. In grammar school, during the two years we overlapped there, I flaunted my status as her younger sister. In high school, too, I was proud to affirm that I was her sibling when teachers recognized our last name. Her army service was another source of pride for me, especially when her picture in military uniform appeared on the cover of a popular army magazine. She was among the few nonprofessional soldiers of her time who had earned the rank of staff sergeant. During the 1956 Sinai Campaign, Israel attacked Egypt in retaliation for the murderous activities of the *Fedayeen* (Arab guerillas), and France and Britain joined in to punish Egypt's president, Abdel Nasser, for his nationalization of the Suez Canal. I felt important, as Miriam was stationed in the Chief of General Staff bureau of the Israeli Defense Forces, where she was the proofreader of the bureau's ordinances. One day in the corridor she bumped into the chief of staff himself, the legendary Moshe Dayan. She was so flustered by seeing him in person that instead of saluting him, she smacked her face in disbelief. He laughed. Soon Miriam became our neighborhood heroine when she was the one to discover the fate of our neighbors' son, alive and well, after his parents had not heard from him for weeks. Even my mother, who did not like the soldier's mother, sent her a bouquet of flowers to congratulate her on the good news.

———————

My first memories of Miriam are of those ordinary rivalries that arise between sisters. I did not understand as a child that she and I saw the world from different angles. The six-year age difference between us was significant, and we had different personalities. Our parents considered Miriam the talented, studious, and obedient daughter, while I was spoiled, careless, rebellious, lacking discipline. She listened to our parents, was the better student, excelled as a soldier, and studied law. I questioned authority, barely finished high school, and as a soldier narrowly escaped military jail. "This is Miriam, my angel," my mother used to say when introducing her to acquaintances. "This is Ziva, my Satan, her father's daughter," she would say to introduce me. Ironically, as the two of us became older, my sister looked like my father and I was the spitting image of my mother.

But Miriam was no angel. Among my earliest childhood recollections, one involving Miriam passes before me like a horror movie. Not yet three, I was sitting on the wooden cabinet that housed my mother's

Singer sewing machine. It stood under an open window that faced the street. Helpless and scared, I cried as rocks kept flying at me, somehow missing my small body.

Two people who used to pass through our neighborhood terrified me. They were Holocaust survivors, perhaps, each left alone in the world, abandoned and desperate. One was a man, who used to yell to me that I had a human face but the eyes of a cat, while making scratching gestures with his hands and howling like an angry feline. The other was a woman, known in our neighborhood as the Madwoman with the Yellow Hair, who ran after kids, threatening to hit them with a long wooden stick she always carried.

That day, my nine-year-old sister and her friends had decided to have fun by taunting the poor woman from the window of our apartment. When she began screaming and hurling rocks, one of them placed me on the cabinet as a human shield, hoping perhaps that, seeing a toddler, the woman would halt her attack. Except they ran out to the street and continued to agitate her, and she resumed hurling rocks at me. To this day I do not know how I was not hurt.

There were other incidents, mostly when our mother left me under my sister's care. Miriam "accidentally" burning me with a hot iron. Miriam commanding me to do certain things, forbidding me from doing others, and always terrifying me with the price I would pay if I did not obey her. Once she smacked my face as hard as she could, demonstrating the consequences of daring to defy her.

One day she "trimmed" my long hair in a straight line to a length that reached the center of my ears. My hair formed a triangle, jutting out at the bottom on both sides. Even the best-known hairdresser in Tel Aviv could do nothing to improve the grotesque look. "What do you expect me to do with this head?" he asked my mother. In fourth grade at the time, I refused to go to school for a week.

I was no angel either. One reprisal sticks in my mind, less for the payback than for the occasion associated with it. I was five when

Theodor Herzl's remains, which had been interred in Vienna since 1904, were brought to Israel for reburial. My parents, my sister, and I were among the thousands who rushed to view the casket that held the father of political Zionism. The coffin was placed in front of the first Israeli *Knesset*, the Israeli parliament, which then met in Tel Aviv, before its journey to Jerusalem for its final interment.

It was a momentous event in the life of the new nation to which I belonged, but I started the day with my own plans. We were all in a festive mood when we sat down to eat before leaving our house. I waited for the precise moment when Miriam began eating her sunny-side up egg to pour my sweet hot cocoa over her mashed yolk.

My misbehavior did not end there. When she was a teenager listening to American songs on the radio, I would tattle on her to my father, knowing that he would make her turn to a Hebrew station. Those were the days when our age difference was still meaningful and we fought over unimportant things. But later we became the closest of sisters. As adults we were by each other's side in happy times and in tragedy, in health and in sickness, until she died, three months shy of her sixty-seventh birthday. In 1939, when Miriam was two, our mother planned to take her to Plunge, to introduce her to the family she had left behind six years earlier. The travel documents were ready, the gifts prepared. Among those was a prayer book that my parents bought for our grandmother, Rachel-Leah. The prayer book's cover was made of brown leather, adorned with gold trim and a copper bas-relief depicting the tomb of Rachel, the biblical matriarch.

On the book's first page, in his neat handwriting, my father wrote an inscription: "To my grandmother from Miriam." It was the prayer book my mother used every Jewish high holiday. It had never arrived in Plunge, for the trip was canceled after a telegram from my grandmother instructed my mother not to come.

In March of that year, thousands of Jews began to flee Plunge and its surrounding region, after Lithuania had succumbed to Hitler's threats and surrendered to Germany its industrial port city Klaipeda. It was not the time for a young Jewish mother from Palestine and her two-year-old daughter to visit.

———◆———

Miriam grew up to be slender and attractive, and had countless admirers and many suitors by the time she joined the army. Five feet five inches tall, she had short, brown, curly hair, a small, turned-up nose, and big light brown eyes framed by thick and perfectly arched eyebrows like those of Elizabeth Taylor. For her prom, Miriam wore a long, light blue gown that our Aunt Hannah had sent her from America. Its top, which had a wide décolleté and drop shoulders, was made of taffeta; its long skirt was tulle. To me, she looked like a fairy princess.

I was twelve when Miriam started to go out with boys. One Friday afternoon I heard her and my parents whispering. Suspicious that their evening plans were the subject of the conversation, I begged my parents not to leave me alone in the house at night. They promised they would not and were home when I went to bed. But when I woke up to go to the bathroom later, I found myself alone, locked in a dark apartment. My parents were out and so was Miriam, on her first Friday night date. On her way out, after my parents had already left, to keep me "safe" she had locked the door to our apartment and taken the key.

Unable to find the light switch, I returned to my bed screaming with terror. When no one came, I began to bang on the walls with my feet. Our neighbors and landlords the Warshawskys finally heard me, but they could not open the door to our apartment. The Rubins, who lived above us, heard my cries and banging, too. After the neighbors consulted with each other, the Rubins broke one of our shutters, and brought me to the Warshawskys' apartment.

"Ziva has been kidnapped!" I heard Miriam's distressed cry when she returned home. She made that assumption because two similar crimes that occurred not far from where we lived had been well publicized in the newspapers a week or two earlier. One was the rape of an eleven-year-old girl; the other was the murder of a ten-year-old girl. I remember their names still. When my parents returned home they were horrified to hear about the commotion I had made. My father was so upset about my behavior he did not talk to me for days. From then on I had to stay home alone every Friday night, except those times when it was my parents' turn to host an evening.

After completing her national service, Miriam enrolled in the law program at Tel Aviv University. Studying law in Israel does not require an undergraduate degree, as it does in America, but upon completing law studies and passing the equivalent of the bar exams, graduates are required to enroll in a two-year apprentice program. Miriam never completed that final requirement, as marriage and childbirth interrupted her studies.

At the university Miriam met Gershon, who fell in love with her at first sight. But someone else had taken an interest in my sister: Every night after Gershon dropped her off at home, an intruder climbed onto our terrace and peeped through the shutters to see Miriam changing into her sleepwear. Though the intruder was not interested in me, I felt terror when I heard him land on the terrace while I was left home alone on Friday nights. I covered my head with my blanket and stopped breathing until I heard him jump out.

The prowler stopped stalking Miriam after my father and Gershon ambushed him when he was hiding in a front yard across the street from us. Because he was not caught on our terrace, the police released him for lack of evidence.

———◆———

Gershon was twenty-two; Miriam was twenty. She made a pretty bride, dressed in a one-of-a-kind gown sewn by Sarah, our talented seamstress.

I wore a light blue dress that Sarah made from fabric recycled from a dress of Miriam's. The black-and-white photo from her wedding adorns a cabinet in my living-room.

Gershon died of melanoma when he was thirty-six, leaving behind my sister and their four young children. Nine months before his death I arrived in Israel on a flight that I had impulsively arranged a day earlier. I did not know that Gershon was ill or that he would be operated on the next day. His cancer had just been diagnosed, and Miriam had decided to keep it a secret until after the surgery, so that I would not worry while I was so far away. At the airport I was greeted not by my sister, who would ordinarily have picked me up, but by my cousin Moshe, who drove me straight to Hadassah Hospital in Jerusalem.

"Why did you come today, of all days?" my sister asked me with relief.

"Because I knew that you needed me," I answered. Such was our relationship.

CHAPTER 8

Wartime and Illness: My Childhood Years

I was the only child among my friends who had a pair of grandparents. At the age of seven, unaware of the scourge that had swept Europe, I believed that all parents died when their children marry. That was how I explained to myself the mysterious absence of grandparents among my friends. Looking at my parents, I would vow never to marry, intending in that way to save them. How my paternal grandparents had survived my parents' wedding was a mystery to me.

There was something else that mystified me about my grandparents. I do not remember seeing them cry over the loss of their son Nehemiah, who died in the midst of Israel's 1948 War of Independence. Nor do I recall seeing my father or his other siblings grieve over their fallen brother. Many years later I learned the hard way that tears and sorrows hide in different ways in the folds of a broken heart. I can assume they mourned in their own way, lonesome in their anguish, unable to demonstrate emotions. What I do know is that every summer on the anniversary of Nehemiah's death, my grandmother and her daughters attended his grave.

Nehemiah had been wounded once before in the Arab-Zionist struggle, in 1936, in Jaffa, during the Great Arab Revolt, orchestrated in opposition to the British control of Palestine on the one side and to the purchase of land by Jews on the other. I was not yet born when

Nehemiah was first wounded, but war remained a constant in my country in the years leading up to independence and beyond.

As a young child, I was probably involved in some secret activity that took place in my own neighborhood during Israel's pre-independence period. When I grew older, I understood why the name of our neighbor Mr. Kohelet was spoken in our home with admiration, and only then did I realize why my parents sent me to bring cakes to neighborhood meetings he attended. He was in all likelihood the head of a local Haganah cell, running clandestine meetings in the homes of our neighbors.

I was four the first time I carried the tall yellow sponge cake my mother had baked for the men attending the secret meetings. Knowing that I had been given a grown-up task, I walked slowly, holding the plate with the uncovered cake in both hands, taking careful steps so I would not trip or drop it. I remember the pride I felt when the men in the meeting complimented me for a job well done. To this day I have no idea whether the cakes I carried were just to be eaten, or whether there were hidden messages in them.

Haganah was a mainstream underground Jewish defense organization created in 1920. Together with Irgun and Lehi, its two radical splinter groups, it was integrated into the Israeli military post-independence, but not without a fierce struggle. I recall going with my parents and sister to see the ship *Altalena* burning on the shores of Tel Aviv. It was loaded with a thousand tons of weapons and an equal number of Irgun fighters. When Irgun's leader, Menachem Begin, refused to yield control of the ship to the government, Prime Minster David Ben Gurion decided to seize it by force. One month after independence, while Israel savored the first ceasefire in its war against the invading Arabs, it was a seminal moment in the life of our new state. At four and a half I could not understand what the adults were talking about, but I sensed both the shock and admiration my parents felt toward Ben

Gurion when he refused to allow the existence of a separate army in the new state.

Almost every family had relatives or friends who belonged to each of the clandestine defense movements. That was the face of the nation before independence, and my family was no exception: My Aunt Sarah's first husband was one of Lehi's founders. In 1944 he died of a gunshot to his head, leaving Sarah with two young children. Until her dying day, in 2005, at the age of ninety-six, my aunt claimed that she did not know whether his death was the result of a suicide, an accident, or an assassination.

My Uncle Yaakov and his wife, Esther, were also members of Lehi. Yaakov was imprisoned, first in Eritrea, then in Kenya; Esther was sentenced to life imprisonment in Bethlehem for her participation in the bombing of Haifa's railway factories. They met in a detention camp near Haifa on the eve of independence.

Yaakov was freed before his fellow prisoners because of my grandmother. As she had done in Przytyk years earlier, with stubbornness, perseverance, and a regard for justice, she fought the authorities—this time the British—and succeeded in securing the release of her son. When the remaining Kenya prisoners arrived on Israeli shores after the British had left Palestine, Yaakov was waiting for them in a military Jeep that displayed two machine guns. When they saw him waving to them from afar, they understood that the state they had been fighting for had been established.

I have vivid recollections of those days. Some are my own; others are woven with stories the grown-ups told and knowledge I acquired. I was not four yet when on November 29, 1947, the United Nations General Assembly recommended the partition of Palestine into one Arab and one Jewish state, with Jerusalem to become an international city. I was too young to understand the vote, but I comprehended the sacredness of the moment.

Like everyone else in Palestine, my family was glued to the radio when the roll call was announced. I have never forgotten the huge roar thundered by a nation overjoyed with the prospect of becoming an independent state after 2,000 years of exile. But the thrill turned overnight into a war for survival, when the Arabs, who rejected the UN's Partition Plan, began to attack the Jewish communities in Palestine.

———◆———

Nearly six months passed between the UN vote and May 14, 1948, the day Israel became independent. The following day Egyptian Spitfires began to bomb Tel Aviv every three hours. To this day I can feel my young heart racing when the warning sirens wailed, and we rushed to the bomb shelter at the end of our street, about three hundred feet from our house.

"Grab my hand, quick," my mother would hasten Miriam. "Tzvi, be careful," she would then instruct my father, who ran as fast as he could, holding me in his arms, my mother and sister dashing behind. Though I remember feeling safe in my father's arms, I shiver when I recall the terrifying up-and-down wail of the air-raid sirens. Within minutes the street filled with neighbors, some carrying their toddlers in hammock-like baskets, all hurrying to the relative safety the bomb shelter provided.

We remained in the shelter, sometimes for hours at a time, until we heard the steady sirens alerting us that the immediate danger had passed. I remember the nights. Some neighbors were engaged in mundane conversations, their voices low whispers; others, their nerves shattered, fought over frivolous matters. Though far away from our shelter, the recurrent explosions sounded to me as threatening as if they blasted nearby.

The dangers of war did not emanate from the skies only but from land and sea as well. From the beginning of the Arab revolt throughout the War of Independence, the Arabs commandeered tall structures from which snipers shot into Jewish neighborhoods. Our house was targeted from Hassan Beck, an imposing mosque with a tall minaret, located north of Jaffa. The mosque is still standing tall and active, but the bullet holes in our apartment house have long since been patched.

My father did not fear the snipers. Each day at dawn, even when shooting was ongoing, he collected the morning paper from our terrace. British soldiers, pointing their Sten submachine guns at him, warned him to go back into the house; the same soldiers pointed their guns at my mother and me, when I was not yet four, because we were walking on the wrong side of the street when a curfew was in effect.

———

Until 1950 or so, when he opened his first printing press, my father worked for *HaBoker*, or "The Morning," a major newspaper that concentrated on the arts and politics. Regarded as the best typesetter in the country, he earned what was considered a huge salary, and we had the finest clothes and foods money could buy.

Even during Israel's austerity regime, which lasted for the first decade of the state's existence, when food was rationed, my mother found ways of buying restricted foodstuff. We consumed plump chickens, plenty of eggs, and thick homemade sour cream. My mother bought those items from a farmwoman who came to the city once a week to sell her goods. One morning, while standing on our terrace, I saw her walking by.

"Imma," I yelled. "Here is the woman who sells you eggs and..." Before I was able to complete my sentence my mother pulled me into the apartment.

"I heard you. That's enough!" she said, and rushed to the door to let the woman in. Although many of our neighbors probably did the same type of dealing themselves, it was only whispered about, for fear of the rationing inspectors. I suspect that my father, honest man that he was, and never involved in household matters, did not know about the "trade" relation between my mother and the farmwoman.

———◆———

My early school years were marked not only by conflict and war but also by my mother's illness, which was acute then. I attended kindergarten sporadically, my memory of it shaped more by the times I was absent than by the time I spent in the classroom. On her good days, when she could function with the help of a variety of medications, my mother walked me to school. On bad days she stayed in bed, and I stayed home with her—not only because there was no one else to bring me to school but also because I must have wanted to stay with her.

The kindergarten was housed in a simple, single-story structure with a yard facing the street. I remember my teacher, Tzipora, a nurturing, full-figured woman in her forties, with long graying hair twisted into a bun and secured with hairpins. She had a pleasant, round, fair-skinned face. Her blue eyes were young and kind; her smile was warm and reassuring; and she spoke softly.

I have an enduring memory of an afternoon when my mother failed to pick me up from kindergarten. Long after the other kids had gone, I was still waiting for her to arrive. I felt frightened and abandoned, but mostly ashamed. Even Tzipora's tight hold of my small, sweaty hand did not comfort me. I noticed the glances that Tzipora and her younger aide exchanged, and overheard my teacher whisper, "What shall we do with Ziva?" In those days before telephones, there was no way for them to find out whether someone was picking me up.

"We'll wait a little longer, and then I will walk her home," I heard the aide reply.

Then I saw, coming up the street, walking as fast as his frail, thin legs could manage, our elderly landlord, Mr. Warshawsky. He was a regular feature in my childhood, to whom I never gave much thought, but that day I could not have been happier to see him. He did not need to explain why he was there.

We walked home in silence. My mother was in bed, sobbing, her dark skin and disheveled black hair contrasting with the whiteness of the big European pillows she rested on and the blanket that covered her. Remorseful, she cried her heart out to me, trying to find forgiveness for having forgotten her little girl.

At my mother's insistence, for grammar school I was enrolled in the prestigious Balfour Public School, located in the center of Tel Aviv. The school's several hundred students, from six-year-olds to teenagers, who made up twenty-odd classes, formed a double line every morning in the schoolyard, as we did after our lunch break and during school plays and ceremonies. The most somber ceremony took place every year on Israel's Memorial Day, Yom Hazikaron. Dressed in blue and white, the colors of the Israeli flag, we stood and listened to the principal's heartfelt speech and to the senior pupils who read famous poems about fallen soldiers. The school choir sang melancholic war and remembrance songs, and the list of fallen graduates was read, as memorial candles were lit.

My first-grade teacher was Miriam Goldstein. She was tall and thin, her stern-looking face framed by short, wavy gray hair. Her narrow, clever eyes were always moving left and right, right and left, scanning the forty faces before her, until they settled on one student. Most of us wanted to avoid her attention; she ridiculed students who gave the wrong answers, and if we misbehaved she pulled and twisted our ears or hit our hands with her wooden ruler.

My fear of her was mixed with admiration and even fondness. She never singled me out for derision, and sometimes, whether it was real or imagined, I detected warmth when her otherwise icy glare fell on me. Her attention fostered in me a sense of worth. I felt smart in her classroom, and I loved going to school because of her.

In first and second grades I formed many friendships, several of which have been lifelong. But it was Ella who was my best friend in those early school years, and it was she who first made me aware of my sexuality. When we were seven we were playing at my home, alone on the terrace.

"Do you want to see my pootie?" she suddenly asked me.

"Why?" I was barely aware of my own body, let alone hers.

"I'll show you mine if you show me yours," she said. And so we did, sitting on the terrace floor, hidden behind its parapet. Though I was not impressed, I knew that what we did had to be kept a secret.

Ella and I were friends throughout our grammar school years, until at fourteen she began to run around with a fast crowd, and my father forbade me from seeing her again. I obeyed, though she and I continued to meet in school, parting ways when we went to different high schools. By sixteen Ella was pregnant and engaged to marry her child's father, a handsome air force pilot. Before her wedding she brought her fiancé to our home to introduce him to my parents and me. I was astounded at how mature she looked and how she talked when she was in his company, addressing him as "my love," "my dear," "my darling," as if she were the heroine in one of the novels we had both read. At seventeen she was mother to a boy, but she and her first husband divorced within ten years. She remarried, gave birth to a girl, and died of brain cancer just a few years later.

———◆———

Until I was eight, my mother walked me to school every day. In those days, children walked to school unescorted, and it was unusual for a child my age to be accompanied by a parent for the twenty-minute walk. But my mother insisted, as if she wanted to make up for the times when she was ill.

On the day my mother permitted me to walk to school alone, I wished she were with me. Stepping along by myself, I suddenly came upon two women so strange I was convinced they were creatures from outer space. Of the same height and walking in fast small steps, they wore full, long cream-colored skirts, tops with puffy long sleeves, and odd-looking head covers that curved in narrowly on both sides before flaring outward. Never having seen such a sight before, I ran to school as fast as I could, my heart racing with fear. Breathless, I told my teacher what I had seen. She explained that the women I saw must have been nuns dressed in their habits.

There was one other child who was escorted by his mother every day, not only to school but also to the classroom. His name was Dov. His mother looked much older than the others. She was small, her figure bent and her hair all gray. Her face was wrinkled, but it brightened with love and pride when she looked at her precious child. When he turned nine, she granted him more independence and permitted him at last to walk alone to school.

I understand Dov's mother's caution. She and her husband were Holocaust survivors, and Dov was their only child. Rumor had it that they had lost their older children in Nazi concentration camps. On the first day he walked alone to school, a toppling construction crane landed on Dov's head, killing him. The enormity of that loss made me aware, at a young age, of life's frailty, and caused me to question the existence of God.

———— •— ————

"I wish you would die!"

It is not hard to imagine how I felt when my mother flung such words at me.

"Khaya, how can you talk like that?" Our neighbor, who had come to visit, was aghast.

"She is driving me crazy," my mother cried, trying to defend herself.

It was winter, but I still was unable to understand how a mother could speak like that to her child so soon after Dov's death. I had been sick with scarlet fever for six weeks, and I had angered her by opening the window above my bed.

My mother must have been frustrated at having been cooped up at home with me for such a long time. But all I wanted was to have a peek outside after being stuck in bed for a month and a half. Although she never said so, I am certain that she regretted her words as soon as she uttered them, as she was so protective of me. Perhaps she was unable to find the right words to express her remorse.

Often her overprotectiveness was a source of embarrassment for me, especially when she would come to feed me in the middle of a play date at a friend's home. In the winter my mother dressed me in layers so that I would not catch a cold, or worse, pneumonia. The overdressing caused me a humiliating moment when I was in fourth grade. The school nurse had come to our classroom to immunize us against tuberculosis. We formed a single line next to our teacher's desk to get the shots, on our upper arm, close to the shoulder. The process went without interruption until it was my turn. The nurse could not pull high enough all the layers of sleeves I wore. After a long struggle she gave up and administered the shot in the middle of my arm. I remember the glances the nurse and my teacher exchanged when they tried, together, to pull up all my sleeves, not to mention the giggles that passed through the classroom.

How Miriam and I explained to ourselves our mother's seasonal transformation, I do not know. Though the varierty of medications her doctors had prescribed my mother were adictive—she was dependent on them for the rest of her life—they did help her. Perhaps some of the drugs she was given had been newly introduced in the mental health field. Whatbever the case was, by the time I reached fourth grade my mother's illness was under control, winters and summers alike.

While I did not stop dreading winters, few things made me more proud than my mother's involvement in the Parent Teacher Association. Her appearing in school well dressed and looking as beautiful as she had in our summers outings, being loved and admired by teachers and fellow parents alike, meant she was healthy. The best sign yet for the change in her condition arrived soon: She was going to have another child.

But the child did not survive.

———— ◆ ————

I was nine and home alone with my mother when an official from the hospital came to notify her that my little brother, born two weeks earlier and whom I had never seen, had died of infant jaundice. She howled and cried, nearly losing her mind with grief, while I did my best to take care of her.

We never talked at home about that terrible loss or the way it affected us all. It was as though it had never happened, or as if mentioning it would make my mother ill again.

I do not remember seeing my mother cry after that horrible day when I was alone with her, nor did I see my father cry over his baby boy. But I have never forgotten my mother's radiance during her pregnancy, and how she looked in the maternity dresses that our seamstress had made, particularly the black summer dress dotted with a pink and green leaf-like pattern. Nor will I forget the constant smile on my father's face during my mother's pregnancy and how proud he looked walking by her side.

I do not know if the pregnancy was planned or whether my parents meant to move to a more spacious apartment after the birth of their third child. I do recall questioning where they would put a crib in our cramped apartment. Afterward, I wondered how the boy's death affected my father and whether he had ever gotten over losing his son.

Because of the baby's illness, his bris, normally conducted on the eighth day after birth, was delayed, and he had not been named. When writing this story I traveled to the hospital where my brother had been born to try to find out where he was buried and whether he had been named before his burial. But the process of recovering this information was legally complicated, as well as emotionally haunting, and I gave up my search. But in my mind I named him Shmuel, after my father's grandfather.

Some of my fondest childhood memories are of summertime family outings. My father and I often made excursions on Sabbath mornings, he in suit and tie, me in my best dress. Here we are in Tel Aviv's Independence Park, in 1953

CHAPTER 9

Sabbath Day Outings

In spite of war, illness, and loss, my childhood had it charms. Chief among them were our summertime family outings.

On Sabbath mornings in summer, my father took Miriam and me rowing in the Yarkon River, which flows through Tel Aviv to the port. An outing by the river was a favorite activity for city folks, who enjoyed cruises on small tourist boats, or took out rowboats for a river run. The highlight of those excursions was the waterfalls of Sheva Tahanot, or Seven Mills, named after the mills that had operated there from Ottoman times until the 1930s. It was a lovely spot, the view of the cascade adorned with eucalyptus, palm, and citrus trees and thick river greenery, including the yellow oxalis flowers from which we kids loved to slurp the tangy juices.

My mother disliked rowing. On the occasions when she joined us on those summer days, when she was healthy and blooming, we strolled along the lush green banks of the river until we arrived at the water-falls. Family photos show us well dressed against the backdrop. When we went without her, my father and Miriam liked to pretend that we were sinking. My father would row to a dark wooded corner, where the tangled tree branches hung over us like scary limbs. He would tell me they were kidding only when I cried.

On some Saturdays, dressed in our best clothes, we visited my Aunt Tovah's family in the country, traveling there by shuttle taxis, since public transportation was not available on the Sabbath. We passed the green cornfields, now given way to estates of spacious villas, until we reached their house, in a community built for Lithuanian immigrants. I loved their large yard with its fruit trees and chicken coop, though I was frightened by the turkeys. The big porch on the house continued to serve as a meeting place for us cousins many years past our childhoods, until Tovah's death in 2006.

My aunt and uncle tried hard to convince my parents to follow them there. "One day the small investment will pay off," they argued. But my father refused, not wanting to commute to his printing house in Tel Aviv and back.

On many afternoons we went to Ginati Yam, a long-gone historic café on the city's seashore promenade. Outdoors, my parents used to dance in perfect coordination to the music of a live band, while Miriam and I sat at a table on big wicker chairs, eating ice cream scooped into silver goblets and adorned with wafer triangles. We munched on white almonds that had been soaked, peeled, and sprinkled with salt, and were served on small squares of parchment. I can still taste that rare combination of the salted almonds and the sweet ice cream.

These outings, so different from the scary winter days, seem to me now so enchanting that I want to hold on to them and not let go.

———•———

When Miriam thought she was too old to join us on our family jaunts, I spent many Sabbath mornings alone with my father. One Sabbath, when I was seven, I was walking with him on Allenby Street, then the Champs-Elysées of Tel Aviv, my left hand holding his right. Suddenly, he noticed that I held peanuts in my right palm.

"Where are these peanuts from?" he asked.

"I grabbed them from the street vendor when we passed by," I admitted, not realizing that what I had done was stealing.

"Then we must go back, and you must return them to the vendor, but not before you tell him that you took those peanuts from him." And so I did. The vendor forgave me, smiling widely, and I never forgot the lesson my father taught me that day.

Occasionally we went to the old zoo, located in northern Tel Aviv, where the city's municipal building now stands. Among the young people of my generation, the zoo was better known for its heavyset guard—himself a Tel Aviv institution—than for its animals and birds or its impressive aquarium.

Sometimes my father took me to soccer games. In one game one of the players lost his shorts and stood in his underwear in the middle of the field. Amused, the crowd roared with laughter. But I did not laugh—my sense of his embarrassment brought me to tears.

At other times we went to the city's old Luna Park or the newly built Independence Park. My father always dressed in a suit and tie, and I wore my best dresses. I loved those outings alone with my father. To me they were a silent expression of his love, conveyed when he held my hand or wrapped his arm around my shoulder. Unlike my mother, he found it hard to express his love with words.

———◆———

My father and I also shared a love of reading. My friend Ella was an avid reader, and my father often set her up as an example for me. So great was his love for literature that he had to rent a cellar in our small building to house the hundreds of books he owned, which ranged from Balzac to Plutarch, to Chekhov and Dostoyevsky, to Hayim Nahman Bialik, Shaul Tchernichovsky, and Sholem Aleichem.

When I was growing up, my father would bring me every book in print that was age appropriate. At twelve I read Louisa May Alcott's *Little Women* and Betty Smith's *A Tree Grows in Brooklyn*; at fourteen I read Ayn

Rand's *The Fountainhead*, Daphne du Maurier's *Rebecca*, and my favorite, Annemarie Selinko's *Désirée*, all in their Hebrew translations. I loved traveling to the faraway places the stories took me. I felt as if I personally knew all their characters: Jo, Meg, Beth, and Amy; Mary Frances, who, like me, lived in a modest city apartment; and Dominique, with her tormented soul. I loathed Mrs. Danvers and pitied the new Mrs. De Winter. And, oh, how I loved Désirée for her defiance of the strongman of Europe.

It would have made my father extremely happy to know that I too have joined the family of writers.

My mother often preferred to skip our family Sabbath outings and stay home. Perhaps she needed time for herself, pleased with the quiet around her when she was getting ready for the guests who came for the Sabbath meal. On most Saturdays they included my Uncle Simkha, who was divorced, his daughter Dalia, and Yossef, who was married to my Aunt Tzipora, my father's beautiful youngest sister. Yossef, looking like a movie star, with his shiny black hair and his stylish sunglasses, would arrive on a motorcycle, thrilling Miriam and Dalia. I was shy, however, and spoke to neither him nor Simkha. Yossef gave up trying, but Simkha always attempted to trick me into talking to him. I did not succumb, except to accuse him, to my parents' amusement, of flattery.

After the Sabbath meal, the men—usually joined by one of my father's friends—played cards. Ironically, their card playing, an activity forbidden on the Sabbath, would get underway against the background of cantorial music emanating from the radio. Standing on our terrace one Saturday afternoon, I was surprised to see my grandmother approaching. I ran into the apartment as fast as I could to warn my parents and uncles. Grandma Brakha never visited us on the Sabbath, but that day she came to prove wrong our new Orthodox neighbor across the street. Apparently he knew my grandfather and had complained to him about his agnostic son, who was sinning on the Sabbath.

In a frenzy, the men collected the cards and quickly hid them in the closet, and Miriam and I gathered up the small change and hid it under the bed. We fanned the air with our hands, attempting to disperse the cigarette smoke—as smoking too is forbidden on the Sabbath—while my mother sprayed her perfume all over the apartment. My grandmother was not fooled, but she did not say a word. That our neighbor saw her was enough.

———◆———

Our Sabbath preparations began on Thursday. In those days before supermarkets, food products were weighed on old-fashioned scales and wrapped in newspapers. Fish were not scaled, cleaned, and cut for customers, and my mother would bring home live carps from the market and place them in our bathtub until Friday, when she prepared them for the Sabbath meal. I could never eat them, seeing their transformation from the creatures I had played with only a day earlier to gefilte fish patties. But I do now, and I cook them the way my mother did—though without having to kill and dissect the fish myself.

Of all the dishes my mother prepared for the Sabbath, my favorite was her famous cholent, a traditional stew cooked in winter because of its heaviness. It is made of beef and potatoes, barley, a variety of beans, and a homemade stuffed derma or kishke, all cooked for twenty-four hours. I loved the aroma that emanated from the small stove and filled our apartment. It signified that my mother was well.

But my most cherished memories of my mother's cholents are those that preceded our acquisition of a stove. On Friday, before the Sabbath, I would go with her to Bella's "bakery" to deliver the cholent, secured in a tightly closed pot covered with newspapers and tied with cotton rope. Bella, a kind, elderly woman, homely and obese, with hair growing out of her chin, always sat outside the bakery in her floral dress. She would take the pot, and with her long, large wooden spatula, slide it into her deep brick oven, where the stew would be left to simmer until we collected it just before the Sabbath meal. My cousin Dalia often joined us on the walk to the bakery to pick up the pot. We could barely wait to open it and smell its intoxicating scent.

The cholent my mother cooked at home tasted as good, but it lacked the ritual of the trip to the bakery, which Dalia and I still reminisce about. My mother's stuffed derma, with beef intestine (or occasionally turkey or chicken neck skins) providing the pouch for the stuffing, was my favorite food of all. She sewed both ends of the pouch to secure the stuffing, removing the thread before serving it. Cooked in the cholent, the stuffed derma's skin turned dark brown—it was the prize of the dish. Because I loved the crispy ends, my parents always saved them for me. When my father wanted to tease me, he would tell me that he had snuck into the kitchen and eaten the ends before the meal was served. One day I choked on the thread, which my mother had forgotten to remove. My parents laid me on my bed, opened my mouth wide, and extracted the thread. I stopped eating the ends, and my father's teasing came to an end. In wintertime, I make the same cholent my mother made, preparing the stuffing without the intestine skin, and it tastes just as good.

On many afternoons we went to Ginati Yam on the city's seashore
promenade, where my parents would dance to the tune of a live
band, while Miriam and I ate ice cream from silver goblets

More Sabbath outings. A favorite spot for us city folks was the Yarkon
River, which flows through Tel Aviv to the port and is lined with
eucalyptus, palm, and citrus trees. Though my mother sometimes joined
me, my father, and sister, Miriam, she preferred to stay home, enjoying
the quiet as she prepared for the guests who came for the Sabbath meal

CHAPTER 10
Home

Until the eve of World War II, my parents and Miriam had lived in a spacious apartment in the more fashionable northern part of Tel Aviv. But preferring to live closer to the Mediterranean shore and to my father's place of work, they moved to a smaller apartment in the heart of the city, the way most small families lived.

As the years went by, all of our relatives had moved upward. Some moved more than once to newer and larger apartments, in more desirable neighborhoods, mostly in the northern parts of the expanding city, while we remained in our old apartment. At times, during my high school years our home caused me embarrassment when my friends from those northern districts visited. We never talked about it, but I often wondered whether Miriam felt the same way. I know my father did, and I have little doubt that our living situation frustrated my mother, though I never heard her complain about it.

Things could have been different. In the early 1950s, during Israel's austerity period, there was a severe shortage of paper, resulting in a lucrative black market. Because my father was in the printing business, some schemers approached him with a plot to take advantage of the situation. But their plan repulsed him, and he refused to participate, despite the wealth it might have brought to our family. I have always been proud of his honesty, which guided me even before the day he made me return the peanuts I had swiped from the street vendor on Allenby Street.

In an earlier period, months before Israel was created, the founder of a new evening paper, *Maariv*, had asked my father to join his endeavor. But my father was reluctant to invest his money in a new publication that would have to compete with the popular *Yediot Aharonot*. The new paper succeeded, and my father, realizing the opportunity he had missed, established a new Yiddish daily.

After that venture failed he created a weekly magazine for men, which changed to a neutral weekly called *The Universe*. It failed too. My father did all this while owning his printing house, his dream come true, for which he had left his high-paying job. He had three successive printeries. A fire destroyed the first. His partners, two brothers who emptied the business's coffers and fled the country, ruined the second. The third printing house was successful, but then my father suffered his first massive heart attack, which prevented him from working full time. Until he became ill, the paper he had worked for pleaded with my father to return to his old job, offering him a handsome salary and an attractive pension, but he wanted to be independent. And so, we remained in our modest apartment in an aging neighborhood, while my father's stellar reputation as a typesetter remained intact.

———

Our apartment, though small, was tastefully furnished. The mahogany furniture, the brass chandeliers, and the elegant lacy curtains that covered our windows reflected my mother's good taste. When necessary, we opened the white double wooden doors that divided our two rooms. One served as the living room, and at night became my parents' bedroom; the second was our dining room, which by night turned into Miriam's and my bedroom. Those two rooms never felt too cramped, even when relatives came to stay with us, regardless of how long they remained.

My parents bought their apartment through an arrangement called "key money," which was a combination of part ownership and low-cost rental that provided people of moderate means the ability to buy an apartment. An elderly couple, Sarah and Yitzhak Warshawsky, owned the white, Bauhaus-style, two-story building in which we lived. It had curved terraces; ours were hugged by a narrow yard along the front of the house, where I planted green vegetables and yellow sunflowers in summertime. My blooming garden was a lovely adornment to our two terraces, where my father used to cool off after a long workday, happy to swap the summer's heavy heat with the breeze that emanated from the Mediterranean Sea.

In the autumn of 1957, from one of the terraces, with my family, I used to watch Sputnik, the Soviet satellite, orbiting earth. From the distance of hundreds of miles, it looked like any other shiny star.

We shared the first floor with the Warshawskys, to whom I owe my fluency in Yiddish. Their apartment door, like ours, was always open until bedtime. On many evenings, Mr. Warshawsky would enter our living room and listen with my parents to the news on the radio. Night after night he marveled at the miracle of a human sound coming from a wooden box.

"How did the people become so small to be able to live in that box?" he wondered. "And how did they get in there?"

Until his death in 1960, Mr. Warshawsky joined us for our traditional toast at the conclusion of the Jewish New Year and at the end of Yom Kippur, enjoying my mother's sugar cookies.

"*L'Chaim*," my parents, my sister, Mr. Warshawsky, and I would say at once, raising our crystal wineglasses, wishing each other a peaceful, prosperous, and sweet New Year. Each year, on Sukkot, the harvest festival, I used to decorate the tiny sukkah hut our landlord had built in our yard, and it became the prettiest of our neighborhood sukkahs.

Mrs. Warshawsky never joined her husband when he ate in his sukkah; so that he would not be alone, I would join him there for meals during the holiday.

———————

A thin wall, half made of glass, separated our small kitchen from the Warshawsky's kitchen, which had a terrace. Tucked between them was a small toilet room we all shared. A little, narrow window aired it of the heavy cigarette smoke my father would leave behind. In that tiny toilet room, Mrs. Warshawsky ate green apples she hid from her husband, when apples were a luxury few Israelis could afford.

A nail on the wall held a roll of toilet paper. During Israel's paper shortage, when toilet tissue could not be found, families were forced to use alternatives. In our toilet, small squares of cut newspaper hung on the nail. One day my grandmother, who had come for a visit, angrily stormed out of the toilet.

"How dare you do such a thing?" she shouted. I had never seen her so angry.

"What are you taking about?" my mother asked, her fright visible.

"It's a blasphemy," my grandmother shouted, waving her fists. "Blasphemy!"

Her rage had been ignited by those pieces of paper with Hebrew writing on them. Orthodox Jewish law forbade the use of paper with Hebrew letters for hygiene purposes, because it could potentially spell the word God and its synonyms, insulting the Almighty. The paper shortage was soon over, and once again we could pamper ourselves with the real thing.

As I grew older, the nail on the wall became a source of embarrassment to me. It reminded me not only of the hard times we endured during the period of austerity, but also of my father's bad business decisions, which prevented us from living in a more modern apartment.

The old landlord couple did not care about that minute detail, and my parents never mentioned it. I carried my discomfiture deep within me, never speaking out, for fear of insulting my father.

Next to that room stood a bathroom, which we also shared with the Warshawskys. On Friday afternoons, after she finished cooking, baking, and cleaning house, my mother would bring in wood from our backyard and place it in the small stove under the water boiler, ignite it, close the stove's tiny iron door, and secure it with its small latch. We found great pleasure in bathing in hot water on Fridays before the Sabbath, after sponge bathing during the week, especially in wintertime. Only my father showered in cold water, summer and winter alike.

I loved the smell of the burning wood, but the ritual came to an end when my parents replaced the old stove with an electric water heater. In the toilet, however, the nail on the wall remained intact.

———————

A steady feature in our home was my mother's "landsman," a businessman from her hometown who made sure we could buy whatever we desired, even though we could not pay for it in one lump sum. Years before charge cards were introduced to the world, the landsman's credit system worked smoothly between him and his clients. He would give them checks for a certain amount of money, which they could use in a list of stores. After buying products with his money, they would pay him over time, with interest. When my sister and I got married, we each received an impressive array of household necessities, including thick down blankets, towels, and bedding my mother had collected with this credit.

Our home was also often frequented by our talented dressmaker, whom we believed to be the best in town. Her magical fingers produced the most gorgeous dresses from the simplest to the richest fabrics. Sarah the seamstress—we never referred to her as just Sarah—was a chubby woman of medium height, with long black hair, dark eyes dotting her round face, and lips she carefully widened with red lipstick. She was capricious and of good appetite, and her arrival at our house created a big commotion. She was hired for two or three days at a time, in springtime or fall, to sew our dresses. In those days our Singer sewing machine, with its monotonous hum, would become the centerpiece. On our dining table, her working space, Sarah the seamstress would spread her unique patterns and cut the fabrics accordingly. I will always remember her most magnificent creation, Miriam's wedding dress.

In between sewing seasons, the seamstress visited us to enjoy my mother's cooking. One evening, when I was twelve, I walked out our front door, which led to a dim stairway. Before I was able to reach the light switch, I saw a moonlike face floating in the air and screamed as loudly as I could. The face, afraid of my screams, started to shout as well. But it soon recovered and yelled, "It's me, Sarah the seamstress!" It was a rainy night and she was wearing a black raincoat with a hood, which was invisible against the evening darkness. The incident, which circulated among my entire family, remains a source of great laughter among my cousins to this day.

I anticipated our seamstress's arrival with both trepidation and excitement. Single, in her late thirties or early forties when she first began to work for us, she was well dressed and heavily made up, though not a pretty woman. I was a young girl, not well acquainted with relationships between the sexes, but I understood that Sarah the seamstress yearned to meet a man, and I was protective of my father. I was afraid she would grab him away from my mother. But I also knew that my mother would look stunning wearing the dresses Sarah the seamstress would make, and that my father would walk proudly by her side.

When I was growing up, the Friday night card game was a popular form of entertainment. Like many secular men and women of their generation, in the 1950s and '60s, on Friday evenings my parents played cards with a group consisting of six couples, rotating among households each week. The game was a social occasion I anticipated eagerly.

The men played poker, for mere pennies, while the women played a variation of gin rummy, for pennies as well. The men sat in the dining room, in the back of our apartment, the women in the living room, in the front.

The group was a colorful collection of people that epitomized the society in which I was raised. Some were happy and optimistic; others seemed burdened with harsh memories. I liked some of them more than others. Edith was one I disliked, not because of her faults but because she was pretty, cheerful, and sensual looking, and I detected glances between her and my father.

Another woman, Betty, I resented for a mean-spiritedness she displayed one night when I was about fifteen. Coffee and sweets were served mid-evening during a break in the card game. My mother was a fabulous baker, most celebrated for her tall and fluffy sponge cake. That night she served her famous cake with coffee presented in a new set of cups and saucers made of a "miracle" product, a thick, unbreakable material in a soft cream and pastel yellow pattern resembling a fabric fit for a light summer dress.

I was sitting with the women in the living room, when my mother emerged from the kitchen, holding a tray with the new cups filled with hot coffee. I saw the lipstick stain on one of the cups as soon as she entered the room. Embarrassed, I stood up, intending to remove the cup and alert my mother. I suspected that she had tasted the coffee before she brought it in the living room to make sure it was sweet or hot enough, and left the smudge. But I was too slow. Betty grabbed the cup and saucer and began to hum to get everyone's attention. She moved her eyes from the women to the cup, directing their attention to it. She slowly turned the cup for everyone to see. At that point I took it from her hands to bring it back to the kitchen.

Betty ended up having a sad life, losing her husband and her beloved only daughter, and I forgave her for her deliberate attempt to humiliate my mother—but I have never forgotten it.

My mother ensured that our sheets and towels were thoroughly washed and ironed and meticulously arranged in our closet. It was she who taught me how to clean a home. But she did not always follow suit, and her housekeeping habits sometimes ran to the slovenly. Inheriting my father's high sense of hygiene, I became pedantic about cleanliness, and the dirty cup incident humiliated me deeply. More than that, however, Betty's deliberate attempt to insult her hostess aroused my strong sense of duty to protect my mother.

CHAPTER 11

The Fig and the Mulberry Trees

"Lift your leg," the children of my neighborhood commanded the poor horse that stood on our street, harnessed to an ice cart, while its owner dozed off after he had finished his rounds of selling ice to the neighbors.

"Lift your leg, leg, leg!" we demanded, impatient, while the bold among us stroked one of the horse's fetlocks. The animal would then raise its leg and flick its tail, not because it obeyed us, but because it was tired of standing still on the hot asphalt or it was shaking off flies. We kids would burst into delighted laughter, believing that our attempts to train the stubborn animal were finally paying off.

With his piercer the iceman cut the blocks into quarters, thirds, or halves, depending on the wishes of his customers, who carried home the frozen chunks in iron prongs made for that purpose. When the cart departed it left behind slivers of ice that shone like diamonds. But they melted too soon.

Only a handful of households had electric refrigerators. The rest of us kept food fresh in white enamel iceboxes. The water from the melting ice accumulated in a metal drawer at the bottom, requiring real skill to empty it without flooding the kitchen.

The donkey that pulled the bread wagon on its way to our corner grocery store was not as popular as the iceman's horse, but we welcomed its arrival nonetheless. So aromatic was the scent of the freshly baked bread that when I smelled it I would run to the grocer to buy a loaf. Not too many foods tasted as good to me as a hand-cut slice of warm rye bread, spread with butter, its crust rubbed with fresh garlic. At times, instead of butter we used olive oil that my mother's friend Blumma had home-pressed.

We were so used to eating fresh bread that every day we discarded the unused portion. When my Aunt Tovah's family moved to the suburbs, we collected the day-old bread and brought it to the country once a week, as feed for the chickens and turkeys my aunt raised. An unpleasant odor that I can still smell emanated from the bread when my aunt mixed it with water to feed to her birds. When chicken feed became available, we stopped collecting the bread.

At the curve of our building, next to its white-cement parapet, our milkman stopped each day to pour fresh-smelling unpasteurized milk from large aluminum jugs into a measuring container, then into the pots handed to him by his customers. He and his family lived in a house at the end of our small street. The sleeveless white cotton undershirt he wore revealed arms that had long lost their youth. In time, a younger milkman took his place, leaving pasteurized milk bottles in front of our doors. I missed the old milkman's morning ritual, which I had so loved even though milk was not among my favorite drinks.

Next to the milkman's house stood an old fig tree so abundant with fruits that the neighbors could enjoy them from summer to the Jewish high holidays in the fall. So sweet were those green figs they left little wonder why the Bible described the fig as one of the seven species of fruit and grain with which the land of Israel was blessed.

A fish vendor was another regular on our street. Each Thursday he made his rounds, pushing his carts, selling tiny fresh flounders the size of sardines called *Moshe Rabbenu*, or Moses our Rabbi. No one else sold those small flounders, which my mother dipped in flour and fried in sizzling golden oil. Legend has it that these fish have a flat body because they were sliced in half when Moses parted the Red Sea. How

I wish I could find Moshe Rabbenu nowadays and repeat my mother's recipe.

The fish vendor's call when he arrived in our street used to remind me of earlier days still, when men passing by sold fresh charred beans (my sister's favorite snack) that had a distinctive smell; and others, wearing red Turkish turbans, sold a sweet syrupy drink made of tamarind fruit. On their backs they carried their large ewers made of copper and decorated with colorful stringed beads. From those ewers they poured the drink into small glasses, which they balanced on a copper tray held in one hand. All of this, a world of its own, was within reach of the street where we lived. And if we children wished to gorge ourselves with the sweetest treat of all—purple, almost black, ripe mulberries— all we had to do was to cross the street to Mr. Berman's yard, where the tallest mulberry tree reached toward the sky.

In summer, when the mulberries ripened, we kids used to gather around the tree to collect the abundance of fruit that had fallen to the ground, our teeth and fingers blackened from the luscious oval berries. When Mr. Berman heard us, he would come out of his house, smiling generously.

"Good day, children," he would say, in his thick German accent.

"Good day, Mr. Berman," we would reply, in a cheerful chorus.

"You ought to eat fresh mulberries only," he would say, and then he would climb the tree in his short khaki pants, accidentally revealing body parts we should not have seen, and shake the branches until a purple rain of fresh berries fell to the ground just for us. His gentle wife would stand on their small balcony and watch her husband until he climbed down from the tree. She then smiled at him, adoring the way he was with us. They had no children.

Mr. Berman's generosity extended into winter, when he helped us kids feed the silkworms we bought every year in our neighborhood stationery store with the mulberry tree's green leaves, which we layered in a shoe box, its cover dotted with holes to provide air. The silkworms' life cycle fascinated me. I watched them grow fat and then weave their silken cocoons, and when they became small gray moths, I let them go.

———◆———

In those faraway, long summer days, as children we searched for things to do. When we did not assemble around the ice-carrying horse, we jumped rope and played hopscotch, marbles, and knucklebones. We collected stamps, old English decals, and colorful silver wrappings from chocolate boxes. We looked for illustrated Camel and Nelson cigarette boxes, and used bottle caps to cut out the pictures we liked. We sat on the sidewalk and rubbed apricot pits against the cement until we had worn a hole on each side. Then we emptied the white kernels from the pit's inside, and blew air through the holes, creating perfect whistles. We also made whistles out of ficus leaves, rolling each into a precise tube, neither too wide nor too narrow.

———◆———

Within walking distance from our home, on the western end of Yaavetz Street, stretched the vibrant Carmel market. This colorful, noisy souk is as energetic today as it was in the years when rationing was over. There was nothing one could not find there: luscious fruits and vegetables, fresh fish displayed on beds of ice, poultry and meats hanging on metal hooks, aromatic cheeses, herrings, olives and pickles, cakes and breads, ethnic foods and spices, flowers, and clothing. All items were loudly advertised by the sellers, their competing yells becoming an unsynchronized choir. The customers of the market were and are people from all walks of life, rich and poor, who come to buy the freshest and best produce and other items. Though there are other markets of its kind, such as those in Jerusalem and Marrakesh, to me there is no market like the Carmel anywhere.

Its smells ranged from the intoxicating perfume of the flowers my sister and I bought every Friday on the eve of the Sabbath to the distinctive aroma of falafel balls frying in oil to the foul stench of discarded chicken parts. The market's maze of small streets emanating from the main market artery, with their tiny restaurants and charming renovated old homes next to dilapidated ones, attracts me still.

I remember well the moments when my mother bargained with this or that vendor for a better price for his merchandise. I would cringe, wishing to disappear, not understanding the routine game that took place between seller and customer. Bargaining in the food market was not, or so I thought, an acceptable practice for refined people. Once back home, the sweet tastes of honeydew, watermelon, persimmon, and *Annona* fruits (custard-apple) made up for my embarrassment.

The joy I found in these episodes of daily life was disrupted by tragic events that shook our close-knit neighborhood. There were deaths, divorces, accidents, and suicides, and the neighbors always stepped up to care for one another in hard times.

Across from our house stood a four-story building owned by the Sapirs, the parents of two daughters: Liora and the younger Yarkona, who was my sister's age and spent much time in our home. After Mrs. Sapir's untimely death, Mr. Sapir remarried and was often abusive to his daughters. When Liora was seventeen or so, and Yarkona was twelve, he threw the girls out of his home and made plans to sell the building. Families on our street took the girls in, and my father and our next-door neighbor attained power of attorney and fought for their interests in court. As a result, Mr. Sapir was forced to give his daughters two apartments in the building, which they still own. Their father was not seen or heard from in our neighborhood again.

One evening when I was twelve and Yarkona was eighteen, her boyfriend Danny brought her to our home. They arrived there from a Kibbutz where she spent her military service. She was acting strangely that night, letting out awful screams. Her eyes were glazed, and she seemed to be in a state of bewilderment, recognizing no one around her. An ambulance was called, and two attendants tied Yarkona to a stretcher, covered her with a white sheet, and took her to a mental institution, where she remained for months. The scene frightened me, stirring up memories of my mother's breakdown at my Aunt Eerle's apartment six years earlier.

After her release, Yarkona married Danny and had two children, but some years later Danny left her. With little income, Yarkona became a domestic helper, working for my Aunt Eerle, among other people, and occasionally helping with my sister's children.

After my mother's death in 1993, I had lost any knowledge of the Sapir sisters, until the summer of 2008, when I located Liora. Gracious about my call, she remained discreet about her sister's whereabouts. She only told me that Yarkona was alive.

Then there was my friend Zahava Cooper. She was seventeen the first time she tried to end her life. I was home from the army, helping my mother prepare for the Sabbath, when I heard Mrs. Cooper screaming in horror upon finding her daughter unconscious from an overdose of pills. Perhaps it was the pressure that brilliant and gifted student put on herself to excel in her high school matriculation exams that pushed her over the edge. Zahava repeated her suicide attempt at least once more before she was institutionalized. She eventually succeeded, jumping from a fourth-floor window of the hospital where she was a patient.

Israel's wars too brought bereavement and sorrow to our neighborhood. We were shocked by the death of nineteen-year-old Yossi, one of 172 soldiers who died in the 1956 Sinai Campaign. He was the son of Holocaust survivors who had immigrated to Israel ten years earlier. His mother's shrieks of agony and despair when she was notified of the loss still reverberate in my ears.

I cannot think of these unhappy events in my neighborhood without conjuring the heartrending image of a severely disabled teenager who lived across from Bella's bakery. His mother locked the destitute boy inside their cellar-like apartment, never permitting him to leave their home. The only connection he had with the outside world was through a tiny barred window, from which he looked out at passersby, communicating in a language no one else could understand. I saw his face through that window many times and once I looked straight into his eyes. I felt pity for that boy. Had he lived on our street, I thought, he would not have been caged; he might even have enjoyed the heavenly fruits that grew on the fig and mulberry trees.

CHAPTER 12

A Fighting Spirit: My Teenage Years

At the outbreak of World War II, for the purpose of minimizing the danger to schoolchildren in the classroom during air raids, students attended school in shifts, either in morning or afternoon. Tel Aviv was bombed sporadically during that war, and again during Israel's War of Independence. The most damaging attack had occurred in September 1940, when Italian bombers killed 137 people and wounded hundreds, including young children.

The Balfour school, when I began classes there in 1950, still had morning and afternoon shifts, because the school was overcrowded and unable to accommodate all its pupils in a single sitting. After a successful protest by our parents—my mother was one of the organizers—those of us who attended the second shift moved to a separate building, where our classes were held during regular hours.

Our new school was intimate and warm, and we loved our fifth-grade teacher, who, while stern, made every subject interesting. Our sixth-grade teacher, however, was not well liked. It was said—falsely, as it turned out—that her father was the commander of Palmach (the elite force of Haganah during the British Mandate) and one of the founders of the Israeli Defense Forces. And because she had a limp, we believed that she was a brave fighter who had been injured in the War of Independence. She was respected more for the rumors than for her skills as a teacher.

One day I passed around the classroom two photographs of our class taken in first grade. Seeing what "babies" we had been humored us, but our joy was short-lived. Furious at the commotion, our teacher confiscated the pictures—the only copies—and, working herself into a tantrum, tore them to pieces.

Furious in return, I organized my classmates to strike, demanding we get our fifth-grade teacher back. Arguing my case at the principal's office, I took responsibility for my deed. I reasoned that our teacher should have exercised self-control rather than lose her temper. She was correct to confiscate the photos, I told the principal, but rather than shredding them to pieces, she should have kept them till the end of the school year and then returned them to me.

We organized a mutiny, sitting around the water tower on the grounds, boycotting classes until our demands were met. After two days the principal offered us a compromise: We were to continue the sixth grade with our current teacher, and we would have our fifth-grade teacher back the following year. We agreed.

Weeks after the strike, I had my bat mitzvah. As was the custom, I had a simple and modest party, held at home, and the guests were primarily classmates. My party was somewhat fancier than the norm, however, because I had printed invitations, which my father had produced in his shop. Our teacher, Nira, had accepted my invitation, and because it was the only bat mitzvah she agreed to attend, I took it to be her offer of a truce.

When we reached eighth grade, the separate school closed, and we moved back to the Balfour campus. It soon became clear that we had fallen behind our peers in the established institution. I was part of a group of six pupils placed in the most advanced of the three eighth-grade classes to which we were absorbed. Though I found school to be stimulating, I kept falling behind, feeling overwhelmed.

One day I gathered enough courage to participate in English class. Our teacher asked for volunteers to read aloud parts of Abraham

Lincoln's "Gettysburg Address." Since he was known for his mean-spiritedness, it was no small step for me to volunteer to read in front of my class, from which I felt estranged to begin with. When the teacher saw my raised hand, he said to the class, with unmistakable sarcasm: "Oh, look whose hand is up." Locking my knees together and choking back a wave of humiliation, I slowly read the paragraph, terrified to make a mistake. I read well, but I never raised my hand again in my English class.

One day some boys decided to pay our teacher back for his cruelty and placed a live frog under a stack of papers on his desk. There was no end to our delight when the frog leaped at our reviled teacher when he lifted the papers; his round, fat face became red with rage. As a punishment, all the pupils in the class had to copy Hans Christian Andersen's "The Nightingale" three times. It was our teacher's favorite punishment, imposed for an offense as small as a whisper.

<hr />

When my Uncle Nehemiah died in 1948 during Israel's War of Independence, Rachel, his eccentric wife, was left behind with two daughters and two sons, the youngest born four months after his father's death. Since the day I knew her, Nehemiah's widow appeared and acted like a lost soul. Her clothing was always disheveled, and her long dark hair was uncombed and wild looking. Because she was hardly capable of raising her children, let alone maintaining a relationship with her husband's family, I rarely saw my cousins, who were cared for by their maternal uncle, with the help of my grandmother and her daughter, my aunt Esther.

Eight years after Nehemiah's death, his eldest daughter, whom I will refer to as Tamar, had to leave her uncle's home. Since my sister was serving in the military, my grandmother asked my parents to take seventeen-year-old Tamar into our home, a proposition that my father must have felt pressured to accept.

A restrained man, my father was not disposed to showing affection. But when Tamar came to live with us, he appeared to be a changed man. She was a demonstrative person, and when she caressed him, he responded in kind. When she kissed him, he returned her kisses. When she hugged him, he hugged her back. I have no idea what all this kissing and caressing was about, and it seemed strange if not inappropriate. Perhaps my father felt obligated to compensate his niece for having lost her father.

At age twelve, not realizing how deeply my father loved me, I watched him and Tamar with envy. I do not remember relating my jealousy to my mother—though I did complain that Tamar had used my hairbrush, which not even my sister was allowed to do. But my mother must have chastised my father for the deep fondness he showed his niece, while neglecting to show the same affection to his own daughters and possibly his wife. After Tamar had stayed with us for two months, she left our home. I do not know why Tamar left us. What I do know from my Aunt Sarah is that my mother made a point of warning my grandmother that unless Tamar was removed from our home, a catastrophe would occur. Her leaving exacerbated the fights my parents were having during that time. My father must have blamed my mother for sending Tamar away, and his conscience must have bothered him for his failure to care for his fallen brother's child.

During the worst of these fights I was standing near the door that separated our two rooms, and I saw my father pull the tie he wore around his neck with such strength that his face changed color. As he tried to strangle himself my mother scuffled with him and managed to pull his hands away from his neck. I was paralyzed by fear, unable to move or utter a sound. I watched my parents wrestle as if they were two strangers, unaware of me standing near them. My father then stormed out of the house, slamming the door with such force that I thought he would never come back. Agitated, my mother dragged herself to the kitchen. My legs followed her there as if they did not belong to me. She was swallowing pills.

"No! Don't kill yourself. Not you too!" I screamed. Somehow my mother found the strength to calm me. She showed me that the pills she was taking were prescribed. It was a Saturday. Miriam was away for the weekend, visiting her boyfriend's family in Jerusalem, and I was alone with my parents. I wanted to blame someone for what had happened, but I was numb.

Unlike my own memories of the period she stayed with us, Tamar recalls not the mutual affection she shared with my father, but a spoiled cousin who had a home and two parents. She also remembers my father sobbing when she left our home, something I do not. She married at eighteen and moved with her husband to the southern part of the country. After having two children, she got divorced and moved back to her mother's old house near Tel Aviv. She lives there still. When I have met Tamar at our family gatherings, I have never mentioned the time she stayed in our home, or acknowledged the difficult life she had had since childhood. At one of those gatherings she gave me a silver necklace with a note attached expressing her love for me. When I look at it I see not only a small pomegranate medallion hanging on a silver chain but a drama all of its own, involving a family touched by tragedy and a scene I could never forget.

Many years later my Uncle Simkha's ex-wife, who had been close to my mother, told me that my mother had wanted to flee with Miriam and me to her brother's home in America when we were young. My father too was thinking about leaving the marriage at some point but remained as well. Apparently, neither knew about the other's intention.

When I think of my parents' fights and their periods of disaffection, I wonder what had happened to the attractive young man and woman who fell in love so completely; to the man who had marveled at his wife's beauty and the woman who had once so admired her husband's intelligence; to the man who used to wink at my mother when we sat at the dining table and the woman who responded with a suggestive smile. In spite of their rifts, that they stayed together tells me they shared a mutual dependency and love that far exceeded their mutual sense of responsibility for Miriam and me.

———————

A short while after the tie incident, the Sinai Campaign began. It started on October 29, 1956, when Israel, alongside Britain and France, attacked Egyptian forces in the Sinai Peninsula. For its part, Israel was retaliating for repeated cross-border raids against its civilians, organized by Egypt, and for Egyptian president Gamal Abdel Nasser's blockade of the Straits of Tiran, which closed off trade routes from Israel to Asia and Africa. Britain and France retaliated against Nasser's nationalization of the Suez Canal, which provided a link between the two great powers and their past and present colonies.

Patriotism ran deep in Israel in the time of the Sinai war, as it had in other stressful times, and even children my age contributed to the national security efforts. My friends and I collected empty bottles and old newspapers, sold them to grocery stores, and then donated the proceeds to the national defense fund.

As we had during the War of Independence eight years earlier, we made runs to the neighborhood shelter when the sirens warned us of air raids, except this time our parents did not have to carry us. On the first night in the shelter, terrorized by the sounds of distant explosions I could not control my violent shaking. A neighbor put valerian drops under my nose, and I inhaled the potion until my trembling subsided. Years later this memory evokes my deep empathy for today's children who suffer the consequences of war in the Middle East and elsewhere.

———————

I had neither a high school graduation nor a celebration. I did not graduate from high school when all my friends did. In those years most high schools were expensive private institutions. My grammar school grades had been poor, and I applied to only one high school, Shalva, from which my sister, a good student, had graduated two years earlier. By entering Shalva, which was popular but not known for academic excellence, I lived up to the prophecy of one of my eighth-grade substitute teachers, a nervous, vociferous elderly man. On an occasion when I had misbehaved, he yelled at me in front of the class: "One day I'll drop dead in the classroom, and when it happens, it will be your fault. Only Shalva will accept you."

Shalva, meaning tranquility, was located in old northern Tel Aviv, on a residential street around the corner from the modish Ben-Yehuda Street. Mordechai and Genya Vilensky were the school's owners and principals. Old-school Europeans, they were rigid pedagogues. Mr. Vilensky was an energetic man in his fifties. His trademarks were his bushy snow-white hair and the small pair of gold-rimmed glasses he wore over his blue eyes. At his wife's urging, he was trying to catch us doing something wrong, in the classroom or out. He once stopped me in the hallway to check my fingernails.

"Hmm…," he murmured, while examining my hands.

"Is anything wrong, Principal?" My nails were not long, but after inspecting them a while longer, he summoned me to his office and clipped them. Convinced by his wife, he believed that long nails were meant to sexually arouse boys, as were belts, which female students were not allowed to wear. A psychologist with a tendency to self-aggrandizement, Mrs. Vilensky, a petite woman with searching brown eyes and short salt-and-pepper hair, had a habit of inventing odd guidelines and designating her husband to implement them.

But these regulations alone did not satisfy the Vilenskys, who were obsessed with teen sexuality. In the name of modesty, Mrs. Vilensky designed dowdy new school uniforms when I was in the tenth grade: Girls donned brown skirts, white cotton blouses with small brown polka dots, and a beige woolen V-neck sweater for winter, worn over the blouse; boys wore brown pants, white shirts, and brown cardigans.

Every year our class went on a three-day trip. In the tenth grade we went to Mount Carmel. A popular tourist attraction, it contains a monastery believed to stand on the spot where the Prophet Elijah battled with the false prophets who worshiped the idol Ba'al, as is described in the Bible (First Kings, 18:9–40). The tall statue of Elijah's triumphant attack is the highlight of the trip.

The school nurse decreed that I was too skinny to withstand the difficult hike to the top of Mount Carmel.

"I am not missing the trip tomorrow!" I announced to my parents. I was so determined, they had little choice but to let me go.

I arrived at school equipped with a duffel bag and dressed for the journey, except for my shoes. Having planned my mutiny at the last minute, I had not had time to get hiking shoes and wore a pair of beige flats instead. None of the school administrators noticed me in the tumult of students readying for departure.

The trip went well until the climb to the historic spot on Mount Carmel. My shoes were inadequate for the terrain, and I slipped and began rolling down the mountainside. Luckily, I tumbled into a tree, which stopped my fall. When I looked up high above me, against the backdrop of a clear blue sky I saw my classmates and the two teachers who had accompanied us looking down with horror. Pulling myself up with the trees' branches, I climbed my way back. Somehow, I emerged from the fall with only a bruised back.

When I was safe, my French teacher hugged me tight, her eyes expressing fright. She wanted to take me to an emergency room, but I refused to go.

"I wasn't supposed to be on this trip," I told her. "If you take me to a hospital, I would be in trouble, perhaps thrown out of school."

After a short hesitation, she smiled. "The main thing is that you survived this horrible fall," she said. "I'll agree to keep your secret on one condition: When we arrive in Zefad [the highest city in Israel] you have to go with me to a synagogue to recite *Birkat HaGomel*." This prayer is offered upon surviving a dangerous encounter. I agreed.

———◆———

The curriculum in our high school was split into two basic divisions. Students in the humanities concentrated on literature and languages, history, Bible and Talmud studies, and world geography. Students in the sciences focused on mathematics, physics, chemistry, biology, and natural science. As we approached the eleventh grade, we chose our division.

I was not bad in geometry, but I was awful in other types of math, even though I had tutors. I was also weak in the other subjects in the science division, so it was natural that I chose humanities. I enjoyed my classes in Hebrew and English literature, French, and, most of all, Talmud studies, especially the classroom debates, which often turned into invigorating dialogues between our teacher and me. But after one month, Genya Vilensky took me out of humanities and placed me in the science division.

She had based this decision on the result of a "psychometric" test she had devised in order to place students in the "right" course of study. My poor grades in math and sciences and the lack of interest I had in those subjects were irrelevant. Why she waited a month remained a mystery, though I believe it had something to do with class-size regulations enacted at the time by the Ministry of Education. Both she and her husband rejected my pleas to stay in humanities, which was overcrowded.

"Math is too difficult for me," I protested in their office.

"Your sister excelled in math when she was a student here. She will help you," her husband insisted.

"She is married and eight months pregnant," I objected. I was adamant.

"Leave these premises at once!" Mr. Vilensky cried. "You are spitting in a well from which you once drank," he scolded my sister, heavily pregnant, when she came to school to plead with him on my behalf. His refusal, and his rudeness to Miriam, sealed my decision. Although I was sad to part with my friends, I chose to leave Shalva and look for an alternative rather than spend the following two years struggling with subjects I could not comprehend.

———

Thus began a battle with my father, who valued education above all else. For him, dropping out of school without having been accepted at a new one was tantamount to committing a crime. As far as he was concerned I should have stuck it out and endured the hardship of my remaining high school years, no matter how unbearable they might become.

"You need to learn to cope with situations that are not what you wish them to be," he said. His disappointment was evident. He did not speak to me for two weeks, softening only when I criticized him for lack of support for the decision I had made.

"You didn't back me," I told him, but he did not accept my accusation.

"What did you expect?"

"Something. Anything." I was so hurt by his reaction that I could not find the right words at first. Then they gushed out. I told him that if I were in his place, having contacts with major newspapers, there would not be one newspaper I would not have contacted to publicize the unfairness committed by an institution against a sixteen-year-old. Reluctantly, he made peace with my decision. I even suspected that my steadfastness made him proud.

Searching for a new high school three months into the academic year, was no easy task, but I had luck with Dvir, a school in Ramat Gan that was still in the experimental stage, waiting for formal recognition by the Ministry of Education. Dvir agreed to accept me at midyear on the condition that within a month I raise my barely passing grades in physics and physical education. I pleaded with Shalva to retest me, but Genya Vilensky refused to accommodate me within the time frame acceptable to Dvir. That was my last dealing with my former high school.

A few days later my father returned home from work unexpectedly early. There was a proud gleam in his eyes that he did not try to hide.

"I managed to have you accepted in the jewel of all high schools," my father told me. My eyes widened with disbelief. Before I was able to ask him any questions, he named the school: Herzliah. My father, who knew its principal through his book-printing business, had gone to speak with him.

It was indeed a venerable institution. Its history and its high academic standards had made it the most important learning institution in Tel Aviv and among the most esteemed in the country. Named after Theodor Herzl, it had been founded in 1909 as the first Hebrew high school in the country. It was less than a ten-minute walk from our home, and I had passed by its majestic building, mixing Mediterranean and European architecture, whenever I walked to my Aunt Tovah's house. Magnificent and palatial, its original building was made of stone and glass, it had pillars and arches and two tower-like configurations adorning its front. I used to touch the wrought-iron gate that surrounded its garden with awe. Because of its growing student population in 1959 the high school was relocated to a fashionable neighborhood of northern Tel Aviv.

Overwhelmed with emotion, I said nothing. It was the first time that my unassuming father had used his connections, and he had done so for me. And now I would refuse to embrace the opportunity. My eyes filled with tears.

"I am very sorry, Abba. But I can't go there."

"What do you mean?" He clenched his jaw.

"I do not belong there."

"From what aspect?" he asked me.

"Academically," I said. My voice was quiet. "I have no confidence in my academic abilities. The gap between Shalva and Herzliah is huge. It will be too overwhelming for me."

My response was hard for him to accept, but I meant what I said. I did not add that I did not feel I belonged in a school with a student body composed of wealthy teenagers from prosperous families. I did not want to hurt my father more than I already had, after the effort he had made. But I could not accept the opportunity he gave me. My fear of failure was too strong.

"You are selfish and ungrateful," my father responded. His tone deepened with anger. "You don't know how to appreciate things that are done for you."

I said nothing. I knew I saddened him.

———◆———

I enrolled in a two-year program in Mishlav, a night school that prepared students outside the mainstream system to complete their studies for the rigorous matriculation exams Israelis take at the end of high school. Except for homework, my days were fairly free—until April 2, 1961.

That was the first day of the historic trial of Adolf Eichmann, the Nazi mastermind of the Final Solution. Nearly a year earlier, the Israeli Mossad had abducted him from a Buenos Aires suburb. The drama of his capture has been well documented. He was seized on May 11, 1960, and smuggled into Israel on May 22. The next day, Prime Minister David Ben Gurion announced to the Knesset that Eichmann was in Israeli hands and that his trial would soon start.

The country was jubilant. Newspaper hawkers were running in the streets, screaming the news from the top of their lungs. I remember the whole front page of the evening paper *Yediot Aharonot* contained a single headline in huge letters announcing Eichmann's capture. At the dinner table I asked my father who Eichmann was, and he replied, "Hitler's right-hand man."

Until the 1970s, the history of the Holocaust was not taught in schools. Pupils learned about that calamity through commemorating ceremonies that schools were mandated to hold after a 1959 law endorsed Yom Ha'shoah ve'Hagvura, or Holocaust Remembrance Day.

We read *The Diary of Anne Frank*, and saw the tattooed numbers on our surviving relatives' arms. But we were still kept in the dark about that disastrous part of Jewish history. I, like many Israeli youths, knew little about the Holocaust. Most of what we knew was gleaned from our relatives' whispers about what happened "there," in *lager*, or camps. We knew we had lost relatives, but as it was with cancer, which in my youth was often referred to as "that disease," the Holocaust was rarely mentioned by name, and its details were not revealed. That changed with the Eichmann trial, which became a turning point in the world's understanding of the Holocaust and in the way Israelis themselves viewed the survivors. At once, their image shifted from victims who had gone to their slaughter like sheep to heroes who had survived the unimaginable. Israel became the mouthpiece of Jews the world over.

Because television had not yet been introduced in Israel, the trial was broadcast on live radio from morning to late afternoon. For seven and a half gripping, shocking months I was glued to our radio, as from its familiar, comforting, dark-wood frame came the horrific accounts voiced by surviving witnesses. For those seven and a half months, my days at home were starkly different from any days I had spent before. My struggle with Genya and Mordechai Vilensky and my search for an appropriate high school became trivial. The trial was education at its best. I grew up instantly.

I tried to imagine the overnight loss of one's status in society, the loss of home, possessions, and income. That was bad enough but far less harrowing than envisioning the unfathomable atrocities described by the shattered voices of the witnesses: Toddlers tossed alive by Nazi soldiers into flames. Babies thrown in the air like rag dolls to be caught on the swords or shot by the guns of thrilled SS guards. Children crying in the arms of their mothers while taking their last poisonous breaths in the gas chambers. Subjects of the cruel medical experiments of Josef Mengele suffering indescribable pain. I was infuriated by the bestiality of the Germans and the wholesale murder of families, including my own. I raged against Hitler and his systematic attempt to eradicate my people. That rage has never left me.

The commanding voice of Gideon Hausner, the Israeli attorney general who acted as chief prosecutor, the plainness of Eichmann's voice speaking in his own defense, the heartrending whispers and cries of the witnesses, and the images portrayed in the trial were forever etched in my mind and in the collective memory of Israelis and Jews the world over.

The trial was over on December 11. On December 15, Eichmann was sentenced to death. On May 29, the Israeli Supreme Court rejected his appeal, and on June 1, 1962, just after midnight, Eichmann was executed. His ashes were scattered over international waters in the Mediterranean Sea so there would be no physical remnants of his being. Life returned to its normal routines.

Mishlav seemed the right decision. I took my studies seriously and met students of different ages from diverse walks of life. Some of us met in small study groups, and I formed new friendships. I even had a crush on a good-looking young man with blue eyes and blonde hair who had already completed his army duty.

In the late fall of 1962 I took the high school matriculation exams, not without a struggle. Because I was a few months shy of eighteen, I had to get special permission to take the exams, which was granted one month before they began. I studied day and night, often with my mother's prescription stimulants helping me to stay awake into the early morning hours. I did fair in some subjects, better in others, but I knew I was not going to pass math. To avoid failing, I got conveniently sick, leaving that battle for another time in the future. The next big step in my life, as for most eighteen year olds in Israel, was enlisting in the army.

CHAPTER 13

Wasted in the Army

There are few gloriously happy days in one's life. They often mark events, such as marriage, the birth of a child or a grandchild, or recognition for a great achievement. I am fortunate to have had those. But there is another day I count among my happiest: the bright spring day in 1964 when I left my military base for the final time.

After two years of mandatory service, marked by numerous infractions and summary courts-martial, I was honorably discharged from the army. I remember the great sense of liberation I felt as I was leaving the base behind me. I walked slowly and deliberately, taking great pleasure in each stride, invisible shackles melting into thin air. Every step brought me closer to freedom. The familiar asphalt road on which I walked seemed to me softer than usual, the skies above more brilliant, the horizon wider. My uniform was as crisp as ever, my shirt carefully buttoned, pockets included. My beret was placed properly on my head. No one could fault me for the slightest offense. Not that day. After two long years I would never have to see that place again. I walked taller than ever, my selfhood intact. I did not break!

I have nothing against the army—quite the contrary. It is a necessary and admired organization in many nations, but is particularly so in Israel, a country that has been surrounded by enemies from the days before its inception. But I was wasted in the army. Not because it did not recognize my abilities; it actually did. But, as with the opportunity my father afforded me when he had arranged for my acceptance in Herzlia High School, I did not have the self-confidence to realize my talent.

The army did not need many of us females, who came out of high school with no skills, but it used us nonetheless. Most did not complain, as I did, in my own childish, insignificant way.

Like many young recruits, I sought wisdom and meaning and fulfillment in my military service. But my inability to accept authority prevented me from achieving what I was seeking. It was not that I had a problem with the structure of military hierarchy. Rather, it was rebelling against blind and senseless authority that got me into trouble.

———◆———

I could have avoided serving in the army. But I opted to do what was expected of me as a member of the collectivity in which I existed. At the age of seventeen, any Israeli who is eligible for military service gets the much-anticipated notice of enlistment. Its arrival is often a family affair, greeted with a mixture of joy, pride, and anxiety.

When my notice arrived, I went to the enlistment bureau in Jaffa, where the conscripted go through a series of physical, psychological, and psychometric tests. I felt proud taking the number ten bus to the bureau. It was the same bus I used to take with my mother to the beach when I was a child. It was also the same bus we had taken to the hospital to visit my father after he had suffered heart attacks when I was a teenager.

I'll soon be like them, I thought, with satisfaction, when I first saw the soldiers in that bureau. But to my dismay, I was rejected from military service for being borderline underweight—the same reason I had been barred from my high school trip several years earlier. At five feet two inches tall, I weighed 102 pounds.

Since birth, being underweight has been a major issue in my life. I was born six weeks prematurely, weighing four pounds, and had to spend six weeks in an incubator. As a baby and a toddler I hardly kept food down. As a child I was often sick. As an adolescent I appeared emaciated. Relatives loved to feed me, and friends joked about filling my pockets with rocks so I would not fly away with the wind. Overnight class trips and sleepovers were often forbidden. And then the army confirmed it: I was too skinny to serve my country. I was miserable. I was not coming of age. I would have no rite of passage. I would be an outcast. So I protested, and pleaded, and promised to gain weight, and I got in.

And so, at the age of eighteen, I was able to ride on a bus with other female recruits traveling to the military absorption base in Tzrifin, in central Israel. I was still wearing civilian clothes: a pair of brown pants and a beige and brown argyle sweater my sister had knitted for my eighteenth birthday a month earlier. I was carrying a beautiful letter she had written to me, her younger sister, who had come of age. For years I cherished that letter, which disappeared with the other documents and pictures my mother later destroyed.

At the absorption base we were divided into different groups and dispatched to training bases, where we rigorously trained for six weeks. We were then assigned to permanent bases for the remainder of our military service.

In spite of its grueling nature, basic training was the only good experience I had in the army. On sandy hills I learned target shooting with the heavy Czech-made M-16 that shook my whole body with each shot. I learned to take apart and clean my rifle. I learned to throw hand grenades, to crawl with a heavy kit bag filled with military gear, to watch for the enemy on my left and the enemy on my right, and to hide in ditches and camouflage myself. I built tents, peeled potatoes, washed aluminum pots ten times my size, dusted my barracks, shined my boots, and pressed my uniform to perfection. But in the end, basic training did not mean much: In my time in the military in the early 1960s, women—officers included—filled administrative positions mostly. Many lower-ranking female soldiers saw their abilities wasted while they served coffee to their male superiors and did other mundane chores.

During the training period my barrack mates and I, like all soldiers, loved getting care packages from home. The parcels were distributed to us on a certain day of the week, and on that evening, after training had ended, opening our packages became a ritual. Most of us shared the goodies we had received, but one soldier, a tall blonde who looked older than the rest of us, did not. One night after we had switched the lights off, thinking we were asleep, she bit into a fresh, juicy apple. The luscious crunch of each bite pierced the silence of the barracks. Fresh and juicy apples were not yet in abundance in Israel, and each of us began speculating how many apples she had received.

I do not recall our exact number, but I do recall the two symmetrical lines of cots covered with itchy, woolen blankets. Each morning when we were called to order, we stood at attention by our cots, dressed in our formal winter uniforms, our right hands outstretched, holding our guns with the base evenly resting on the floor.

I recall the long line of stained white-porcelain sinks attached to a wall outside the barracks, and how we used to dash each morning to catch one before someone else did. In the large washing room, showers were open. The only privacy we had was in the toilets, which were a row of simple wooden stalls over deep, open pits.

On my first night's watch duty I was alone, guarding an empty spot that had but a small lone bench. The night was pitch black, the air sweet, the quiet piercing. All I could see were the shining stars; all I could hear was the fading sound of barking dogs in the distance. I was humming familiar songs in my mind so I would stop thinking about how scared I was. Suddenly, I heard gunshots from afar. Shaking like a leaf, my lips trembling with terror, I dropped my gun and ran as fast as I could to find shelter, an act punishable with a jail term. When all turned quiet I went back to my spot and completed my shift. Because it made little sense for me to stand guard there alone, I began to question the absurdity of blindly obeying senseless orders, an issue that followed me throughout my service.

After completing basic training I was assigned to the air force, where I was to be enrolled in a prestigious meteorology and air-trafficking course. Only a few qualified recruits were selected, I was told. But instead of embracing the opportunity, once again I became overwhelmed with fear about failing the math and science I presumed would be required. I was crying when I asked my parents to speak with the son of our old neighborhood milkman, who was a lieutenant colonel in the General Staff. Perhaps he had enough influence to get me out of the course.

"Are you sure, Ziva?" The lieutenant colonel thought my request was strange. He seemed concerned I was about to make a bad mistake. I remember the meeting. I was seated with my parents on the living-room sofa; the lieutenant colonel was on an armchair to my left. He was leaning towards me and looking into my eyes trying to convince me to remain in the course. "Only a small number of new recruits get this opportunity," he said. "You must be very talented, otherwise the air force would not have selected you." But what he must have seen in my eyes was panic and exasperation.

My parents did not try to change my mind, though afterward I wished they had. I still wonder whether my life would have been different—not better or worse, just different—had I had the confidence the army had in me.

I got out of the course but, as a reprimand, I suppose, I was stationed in the training base of the supply corps, one of the least-desired bases to which a soldier could be stationed. When I arrived, my superior, who was the base's adjutant officer, had no idea what to do with me. Right then he recalled that the paymaster was being discharged in less than a month, and decided that I would replace her.

An ironic twist, I thought. But though I was bad in math, I was always good with numbers. I calmed myself. I would manage.

He walked me over to a small office with an iron-barred window, where I met Rachel, a tall Argentinean with curly dark hair. The warmth with which she greeted me before proceeding to teach me my new job was reassuring. Less than three weeks later she was discharged. Soon my superior officer was gone too, replaced by a new captain, with whom I did not get along. Managing my new job would not be as easy as I thought it would be.

Most nights I slept at my parents' home and commuted three hours to and from my base, which was about fifty miles south of Tel Aviv. I slept there only when I had to: the nights before our once-weekly early-morning roll call; when I was on night-watch duty once a months, manning the phones and alerting the officer in charge when necessary; and when I was confined to my barrack after being summary court-martialed, which was not infrequent.

I lasted as a paymaster for a year, until I discovered that a transient soldier had been using a fictitious name to be paid twice. I reported the incident to my superior. But instead of investigating the theft, he accused me of fabricating the story to cover up missing money, and demanded that I pay the seventeen Israeli liras (the shekel replaced the lira in 1980) from my own pocket. If I did not have the money, my parents surely did, he said. In today's terms I would have to lay down between $400 to $500.

Once again I went to my neighbor, lieutenant colonel Matz, the milkman's son. This time I sought his help to find out the proper procedure in such cases. On his advice I demanded that my superior report the incident at once to the Military Investigation Police (MIP), who started an elaborate inquiry. The MIP found the cheating soldier but also uncovered several irregularities regarding my position. It was illegal for a paymaster to operate without formal training in a designated course and at no time was a paymaster allowed to operate on paydays without an overseeing officer, as I had done. Unable to forgive the insult, my superior replaced me with a shy, obedient young man.

Still a private—a rank that was quite unusual after a year in the army—I became the base's noncommissioned cultural and welfare "commander," a position that is unrelated to one's rank. My new boss was the base's drill sergeant. My job was to counsel soldiers with psychological or welfare problems, visiting their homes when needed, and reporting my impressions to the city-major. I was also responsible for providing soldiers with free tickets to cultural events.

The city-major is the urban or regional liaison between the military and individual soldiers and their families. His or her responsibilities include treating soldiers under psychological duress, supplying free welfare and legal services to soldiers and their families, caring for the families of incarcerated soldiers, offering soldiers free entertainment, and the most dreaded of duties, contacting the families of military casualties, injured or dead.

Tel Aviv's city-major, with whom I worked, was a short, skinny, puffed-up junior officer, with narrow, mean-looking eyes and a screeching voice. Ironically, four years later he would knock on my own door at two o'clock in the morning, bearing dreadful news, his eyes softened, his voice a mellow whisper.

———◆———

By the time I took up my new position I had gained the reputation of being an undisciplined soldier. I had been sporadically court-martialed for minor offenses. Once I was reprimanded when I could not salute a disgruntled staff sergeant because I was holding in both my hands piles of soldiers' identification cards. My more serious offenses involved insubordination. The first of these transgressions occurred after I had arrived late to our roll call on January 1, 1964. Out late the previous night celebrating New Year's Eve with Yigal, I decided that since many of the base's soldiers would be late for the same reason, my own absence would go unnoticed. But I had miscalculated.

"What's your story, Private Bakman?" my new superior asked me in the privacy of his office.

"I had a problem waking up on time this morning," I confessed.

"Seriously? And how is this morning different from all other mornings?" he inquired.

"You know the answer to that question."

"I don't. Enlighten me, please."

"I was out late."

"Quite a good reason." His sarcasm was obvious.

"I am probably the only one who is telling you the truth," I said. "I was celebrating New Year's Eve till late and couldn't get up on time." Up until that moment I was not doing all that badly. But then I added an unnecessary sentence. "We both know that everyone else who was absent this morning did the same."

He had had it with my impertinence.

"I see. So you believe that with your truth you are representing everyone who was late this morning?" His smile revealed a triumphant reaction. He gave me no room to answer. "You are right, Private Bakman. You will certainly be able to honorably represent all the others."

And that was it. I was the only one of the latecomers to be summary court-martialed.

By then my personnel file was filled with disciplinary reports, and I was on probation. Another trial could mean a two-week jail term, for which I began preparing myself, though I worried about the way my parents would take it. What I did not know was that my women friends on the base—and I had many—had organized to protest what they thought to be an arbitrary decision. Of all the soldiers who were late for the roll call on that day, they believed, I should not have been singled out. They conspired to have the base's noncommissioned women's corps commander "lose" my personnel file. She refused to do so, as she should have, but my friends coerced her with the threat that each of them would register a complaint against her for an offense she had not committed. When they revealed their mutinous plot to me, I could not agree to be part of it, but I loved them for caring.

I appeared before the regional women's corps officer, who was both sharp and experienced. I could only hope that she did not remember me from previous courts-martial and that she would not dig deep into my file.

"How do you explain your lateness?" she inquired. Having learned a lesson from my conversation with my superior, this time I was not going to be honest. I concocted a story about getting my period on the way to the base.

"When do you usually get it?" the officer-judge asked, not without sarcasm. "Is it the first of each month?"

"No," I replied. "My period is irregular because of being under-weight. I never know when to expect it." That part of my story was true. There was a deep silence in the room as the officer examined her papers and then raised her head to look at me. My heart skipped a beat. If she reads my record, I thought, I am going to jail.

"My skirt was stained with blood." My calm voice surprised even me. "When I got to the base I ran to the barrack to clean myself off, and then I waited for one of my friends to arrive so I could borrow a pair of underwear and a skirt. That's why I was late."

"That's some story," she stated, barely able to hide her amusement before she dismissed me. I heard my heart pounding. The nightmare was over. On my way out of her chamber, she called after me.

"Private Bakman ..."

I stopped.

"I have a small suggestion for you: Find a way not to be late again."

"Yes, ma'am. Thank you, ma'am." I saluted and disappeared as fast as I could.

When my superior saw me back in the office and heard about my acquittal he raised his head and hand up to the sky in a gesture of exas-peration. I was thrilled.

My second case of insubordination occurred when I stopped momentarily at the office of one of my friends. Her superior, a good-natured captain, had asked me to refrain from visiting her during working hours.

"What did I tell you about coming here?" he asked, and then he winked at me.

I was flabbergasted by the wink. Who did he think he was? How dare he show me such disrespect?

Winking in return, I replied, "You told me not to come here during working hours, and I never will again."

As I turned to leave, I saw that my friend's face had gone pale, and her mouth was open wide in disbelief. I did not know that her superior had a permanent tic in his eye. Once again I was summary court-martialed. My punishment was yet another in-barrack confinement, two weeks this time rather than the customary week. One night I snuck out and went home, tired of staying in the base. My parents literally threw me out, demanding that I return to the base before I was caught.

Looking back, I realize how childish and irresponsible my disobedience was. But that was not always true. One night when I was home, my brother-in-law Gershon arrived, quite late, looking anxious. My parents and I were frightened that something had happened to my pregnant sister or their small child. But it was apparent that he was angry with me, and his explanation was quick to come.

"Either I am taking you to your base now, or the military police will come and get you," he hissed at me. "If they do, it will not end well."

I understood then why he was there, but my parents, who had no clue what was going on, turned to me for an explanation. That day I had made my weekly visit to the city-major's office in Jaffa. Needing to get there early in the morning when it first opened, I always went there straight from home, because it was a fifteen-minute bus ride. I would stay there for two or three hours then embark on the long trip to the base. On that particular day, the city-major's office had been busier than usual. By the time I finished my work, it was five in the afternoon. To me, it made little sense to spend two hours traveling to the base, since normal working hours had ended and I would have gone home then anyway. I did what I assumed was most logical: I called my superior to ask for his permission to go home instead of returning to the base. Since he was not in his office, I left a message with his assistant, who agreed that I should go home. But I was in the army, an organization in which an ordinary soldier cannot make her own decisions, however logical.

We did not have a telephone, but my sister did, so my superior had called her home. When my brother-in-law answered, the officer told him in no uncertain terms that either I get to the base on my own or a military police escort would be sent for me.

Gershon brought me to the base. My superior was pleased with himself, and the incident ended there. I was upset about the senselessness of the episode, but I still did not break, then or when a lieutenant colonel from the base retaliated against me for not giving him the movie tickets he had asked for. He had put his name on the list for free tickets, but he was a career officer who earned a respectable salary. Ordinary soldiers, on the other hand, earned a nominal sum each month, barely enough for the sweets or the cigarettes they bought in the canteen. To them, going to the movies was a luxury. The whole idea of dispersing free tickets, as I understood it, was to help those soldiers who could not afford them. Tickets were limited and never guaranteed. I dispersed the small number I had obtained that day to those soldiers whom I knew to have economic hardships. I had no tickets left for the officer, who got angry enough to issue a disciplinary complaint against me because he had to pay a babysitter he had hired. Once again I was confined to the base for a week for my "insubordination." Though I felt I had done the right thing, my disciplinary problems began to bother me. Suddenly, I questioned whether all these episodes could affect the reputation of my boyfriend.

Despite all the challenges I faced during my military service, our life at home went on as usual. My mother's mental condition had been stable for years, except for occasional mood swings and agitation, which weighed heavily on my father and me. Perhaps it was no accident that the only time my father slapped me, when I was nineteen, was related to my mother's behavior. An umbrella belonging to my mother sparked the incident. My sister, married by that time, gave it to her as a birthday gift. Though umbrellas were expensive in those years, it was not the cost that angered my father. Rather, he knew how much my mother adored my sister's present and how much she loved its wooden handle and its pleasing maroon color.

It was pouring one morning when I had to leave for my base. As I had no umbrella of my own, my mother offered me hers. Because the rain had stopped by the end of the day, when I left the base to go home I forgot the umbrella there.

"Where is my umbrella?" my mother asked, when I returned home in the evening. The concern was evident in her voice.

"I forgot it at the base," I replied, perhaps too casually. "I'll bring it back tomorrow." But my mother did not stop complaining.

"I know where I left it. It's in a safe place." I tried to reassure her, but she continued nagging.

"It's just an umbrella," I snapped, raising my voice. "I said I would bring it back tomorrow!"

I had barely finished my sentence when I felt my father's hand on my face. "Did you ever work for an umbrella?" he asked me, smacking me hard. His own face turned ashen because he had raised a hand to me.

I stopped breathing. Then, crying, I yelled, "How dare you raise a hand to me after all I have gone through with the both of you!"

My words were as sharp as a knife. My father's pain was apparent. And yet he wanted me to be precise.

"What exactly are you talking about?" he demanded.

"Among other things," I screamed, my voice quivering, "think about the Saturday you tried to commit suicide with your tie, when I was present. I was only twelve, for heaven's sakes, home alone with the two of you!"

It might have been the first time in my life that I heard the roar of silence. It was as if everything had died: the noises outside the apartment, the noises inside. We fell silent, frozen by the moment. My mother was the first to recover.

"Tzvi, she doesn't know what she's talking about," she said to my father. And that was it. The next day I brought the umbrella back home. The incident was never mentioned in our household again.

———◆———

A month after I was honorably discharged from the military I became the secretary of the department of national events at the prime minister's office in Tel Aviv. I got my job through Lily, the daughter of an old friend of my mother's from her hometown in Lithuania. Seven years my senior, Lily was the public relations person for the department. I first met her when I arrived for the interview she had arranged for me with the department head, who hired me that instant.

My position gave me the opportunity to meet artists, musicians, writers, journalists, and government officials. But for me the highlight of the job was serving as the time monitor and scorekeeper for the International Bible Contest of 1968. A world-renowned event, which in that year was part of Israel's twentieth-birthday celebrations, the competition took place in the Jerusalem's International Convention Center, known as Binyenei HaUma. I shared the stage with a panel of judges that included David Ben Gurion and internationally known Bible scholars, and the competition was broadcast live on the newly introduced Israeli television. For a young woman who had struggled to complete her military service only a few years earlier, it was both rewarding and affirming.

CHAPTER 14

On the Seventh Day

I remained in that job throughout the first year of my all-too-short marriage. It was after my second miscarriage that Yigal and I decided that I would not return to work. We were going to try to have a child, again and again, until we succeeded in becoming parents. It was clear to us that this time I would have to spend most of my pregnancy on bed rest; there was no other way.

After the second miscarriage, I had undergone corrective surgery. My repaired cervix looked strong, the doctor said, and soon I was pregnant again. We were encouraged and hopeful that this time my pregnancy would succeed. But our mood, like that of everyone else in the country, was strained by the rapidly deteriorating political situation.

The tension began on April 7, 1967, when Israel, responding to intensive Syrian shelling, downed six Soviet-made, Syrian MiG-21 fighter jets, rumored to have been flown by Russian pilots who trained the Syrian air force. The episode occurred after three violent months, during which hundreds of incidents near the Syrian border killed scores of Israeli civilians and soldiers alike.

The Cold War was raging, and the Soviet Union, which had been an Arab ally since the 1950s, continued to seek influence in the region. In addition to its diplomatic, economic, and military support, Moscow now added provocation to its tactics, provoking Syrian and Egyptian aggression against Israel.

Caught up in the fury, Egyptian president Gamal Abdel Nasser ordered the United Nations Emergency Force (UNEF) to leave Sinai, on May 18. That peacekeeping force had been stationed there for a decade.

Alarmed, Yitzhak Rabin, Israel's chief of staff, declared a partial mobilization, a move to which Israelis were accustomed. Since independence, the civilian army reserves had served as the backbone of the military in times of need. In the meantime, Nasser and Rabin's acid verbal exchanges further distressed the tense situation. But Yigal—a battalion ordnance officer—had not yet been mobilized.

Five days after ousting the UN forces, Nasser decided to move six army divisions into Sinai and close the Straits of Tiran to Israeli navigation, moves that Israel considered acts of war. In response, Rabin declared a general mobilization. To his disappointment and my relief, Yigal still was not recruited. As my pregnancy progressed, I needed him with me, thankful for every day that passed with him by my side. Like most of my fellow citizens, Yigal included, I hoped that war could be averted, even though it appeared as if a flare-up was imminent. Yigal was torn. He knew how much I needed him, but he also thought that his place was at the front. Perhaps he won't be called at all, I hoped, since he was recovering from a severe case of chicken pox.

We stood side by side on our terrace on the eve of Lag B'Omer—the thirty-third day of the harvest period between the holidays of Passover and Shavuot—which fell on May 28 that year. It is celebrated with the lighting of bonfires, around which children and youths sing and dance, while roasting potatoes until they turn black and crisp. We smiled as we watched the children and their parents around the low bonfire in the small park below us, hoping that next year we would join the celebration with our own child.

On May 30, Jordan joined a defense pact with Egypt and Syria, and all the while Nasser continued to threaten to destroy the Jewish State. In the interim, as critics accused the Israeli government of Prime Minster Levi Eshkol of inaction, Rabin suffered a nervous breakdown. Two days later, General Moshe Dayan joined the cabinet as defense minister. That was the moment when Yigal was called for reserve duty. As if the political situation were not tense enough, on June 4, Iraq joined the military pact that had been signed by its neighbors, sending a large military force to Jordan. With the news getting worse by the hour, as a nation we felt isolated and abandoned. Many of us feared total annihilation, a trepidation that went back to the Jewish experience of the Holocaust. Except that this time, we thought, it would be the Arabs who would try to destroy us.

Our farewell was swift. We hugged and kissed, exchanging hopeful words about Yigal's safe return and the baby. Then he ran downstairs, got in the Jeep that came to pick him up and drove away. I blamed the nausea that came over me on my pregnancy rather than fear. A few hours later the phone rang.

Yigal sounded cheerful. "Hi Zivonet," he said, adding a note of affection to my name, as if to let me know that he was well. "What's up?"

"All is well, Yigal," I said.

"And the young one?"

I put my hand on my stomach, as if I could touch the life that was sprouting within me. "We'll wait for you. What is going on with you?"

He laughed, trying to turn a blunder into something amusing. "You won't believe it," he said. "I forgot my Uzi at home."

"You're joking!"

"It's a fact. I know it sounds silly."

He asked me to deliver the weapon to a nearby intersection, where his unit would be passing through on its way south.

"I'll be there," I promised, happy to have another chance to see him before he left for the front.

———————◆———————

What a sight I must have been: a young, pregnant woman (albeit not yet showing), climbing out of a white Studebaker to wait for a military vehicle full of soldiers, holding an Uzi in my hands.

Yigal looked composed and attractive as he jumped out of the military truck wearing his field uniform. Once again we said our goodbyes, this time more intently. While the truck was waiting, we hugged and kissed, glued to one another for a long time, unwilling to separate. He put his hand on my stomach and held it there as if he wanted to protect his unborn child. I was stirred.

"Don't worry, girl," he said to me, with his reassuring smile. "Everything will be OK."

Was he as anxious and frightened as I was, in spite of his calm appearance? Did he feel, as I did, the looming sensation that perhaps his soft touch on my belly would be sealed in our memory as the last sane moment before the earth started to tremble beneath us? I felt that it was not my heart alone that beat louder and faster when he whispered in my ear, "You know I don't like to be corny, but you'll always be my one and only."

No one on the truck complained or rushed us, but it was time for him to go.

I stood motionless for a long time, watching the truck become smaller and smaller before it disappeared in the distance. I felt as if I were shrinking rather than the departing truck, that I was withering while the distance between us was widening. I thought I heard an animal howling in the distance. It was a frightening sound in the middle of a bright sunny day. I still wonder whether what I felt was a premonition or ordinary fear under extraordinary circumstances.

As the hostility toward Israel mounted, weighing on us like an existential menace, our nation was brought together by the angelic voice of a young singer, who sang the prophetic lyrics of a melodious new song, which she had performed in the country's annual song festival three weeks earlier. "Jerusalem of Gold" became a second national anthem.

I moved my parents into our apartment. In the old Tel Aviv neighborhood where they lived, there was no adequate bomb shelter, as there was in our building. If a war broke out and Tel Aviv were to be bombed, they would have to run to the public shelter at the end of their street, the way we had in the previous two wars, when they were younger and healthier. Worrying about my situation, they welcomed the move, even though it took them farther away from the doctors they depended on.

We were instructed to cover up our windows and color our car lights with dark blue paint. A few days earlier, Egyptian aircraft had been detected near our borders. A blackout was necessary to prevent the enemy from finding their targets by the aid of city lights. Driving in my neighborhood to buy supplies, I hit another moving car. The other driver and I, both civilians, had exchange of information. Our calm did not reflect the national mood.

"I'll call you in a few days, when I have my estimate," the other driver said.

Good, I thought. Things are still pretty normal. Perhaps there will not be a war after all. That he was young and not mobilized gave me reassurance.

But in the morning of June 5, 1967, what would come to be called the Six-Day War broke out, with an Israeli preemptive air attack that obliterated the Egyptian and Syrian air forces, and instantly shifted the balance of forces that Israel's Arab neighbors had sought. Suddenly, the siege on Israel ended; the army now focused on its enemies' ground forces. As soldiers fought soldiers and steel battled steel, the rest of us, worried about our loved ones at the frontlines, followed every scrap of news from the bloody battlefields.

When the navy, the infantry, and the armored corps were still fighting in Sinai, after a fierce and bloody battle Israel's paratroopers captured the Old City of Jerusalem, where the Holy of Holies once stood. No Israeli who listened to the radio on the seventh day of June will ever forget the trembling voice of one of the country's most celebrated commanders shouting, "The Temple Mount is in our hands." In the background the piercing sound of a shofar blown by the chief military rabbi could be heard, together with the sobs of the fighters. After nineteen years of

Jordanian control, Jews were once again allowed to visit and pray by their holiest shrine, the only remnant of the western wall that once surrounded their Temple. It was the first time I saw my father, a truly secular man, cry.

As the country rejoiced I waited to hear from Yigal. Like other civilians who were left in the rear, out of contact with their loved ones, I was terrified about his situation. But I was also hopeful: that a Herculean man like Yigal could not be hurt; that our life would resume the way we had planned it; that my pregnancy would develop without complications; that we would raise our child together. For that, Yigal had to return home, whole or wounded. I pictured him missing a limb, or two. But I did not care, as long as he was alive.

When on Friday, the fifth day of the war, I still had not heard from him, I called his brigade headquarters. If I was anxious before the call, the hesitation I detected in the voice of the secretary after she heard my name alarmed me even more.

"Please hold," she said. "I'll check where he is."

I could hardly breathe. Think about the baby, I reminded myself. Breathe, breathe.

"According to the information we have, Captain Yigal Goren is fine," she said when she returned, after what seemed to me an eternity. But she barely convinced me.

"Are you sure?" I asked her, over and over. The nagging feeling I had had ever since Yigal and I said our second good-bye crept over me again, beginning with the thought that there had to be a reason we had been given that chance to see each other once more. I sensed that even if the war were to end triumphantly, not everyone would rejoice. That one of those excluded would be me. That I would never see Yigal again.

The secretary tried to ease my mind. "You know, it's not unusual in wartime to be unable to communicate. Don't worry, I'm sure you'll hear from him soon."

She was right. A few hours after that conversation my Aunt Esther called me. Her husband, Yaakov, my father's youngest brother, had bumped into Yigal a day earlier in the Sinai Desert. Each promised to call home if they could and send the other's regards.

My aunt transmitted his message. "Yigal wants you to know that he's doing well and that you needn't worry about him. Just take care of yourself. He thinks of you and the baby."

"You know, Esther," I said, a bit calmer than I had been before her call. "Till now I had no idea where Yigal's brigade was situated."

"Yaki said Yigal looks well," my aunt continued.

Her call lifted my mood. But by the time I had received it, unbeknownst to my aunt or me, Yigal no longer looked well.

———————

Two days had passed since my conversation with my aunt. The war was practically over when my doorbell rang, the ring every family dreads, on Sunday, June 11, at two o'clock in the morning. At the door I recognized the city-major I used to see during my military service. I needed no time to grasp the meaning of his visit. Neither did my parents, who had rushed from their bed when they heard the doorbell.

The softened look in the once-arrogant city-major's eyes scared me.

"Where is he?" I blurted, before he had said a word, in a strange, hoarse voice that seemed no longer to be my own. Somehow I knew he was alive—injured, perhaps even gravely, but alive.

"In Haifa," the city-major said. "Rambam Hospital."

I could not understand how it was possible that Yigal was hospitalized in northern Israel though he had been fighting all the way south, in Sinai. Relieved by the confirmation that Yigal was only injured, I became frantic when the city-major urged me to hurry and get dressed.

"A taxi is waiting for you downstairs. There is no time to waste."

"Where are his parents?" I asked.

"We sent them a different taxi," he said, in a tone that alarmed me even more.

I dressed quickly, running down the stairs barefoot, my sandals in my hands. Though my mind was racing in different directions, there was one refrain I kept hearing: "No time to waste." On her terrace on the floor below mine, my neighbor Ora stood crying. She should not be crying, I thought, irritated. Not yet.

To my surprise, the taxi driver was someone I knew well from my days in the prime minister's office. He did not smile at me the way he used to do. Instead, he gave me a somber nod, as if he knew something I did not.

My father, who for the past nine years had suffered from a serious heart condition, felt ill and stayed behind in the apartment, while my mother accompanied me to the hospital. Her face revealed her fright.

Ordinarily, the main roads were quite empty at such a late hour, but that morning they were congested with military and civilian vehicles, mingling together, as if the war were at its peak. The ride, nearly two hours long, seemed endless and the stillness inside the car unbearable. In those days the army did not send a team of doctors or psychologists to assist the families of the wounded or the fallen. We were three in the car: the driver, my mother, and me. Each of us understood that the army's sending a taxi indicated the severity of Yigal's condition, but we hid our thoughts from one another. My head was spinning with thoughts of Yigal and of my ill father left alone in the apartment. I could not fathom losing them both. And the baby. Our baby.

Yigal's doctor was waiting at the hospital. After greeting my mother and me as tenderly as he could, he informed me that Yigal, who had been brought to the hospital some thirty-six hours earlier, was in critical condition.

"I want to see him," I demanded, not recognizing my own voice.

"I can't let you do that. Not in your condition." His voice was soft yet firm.

"I'll decide. I'm here to see him."

"It is your husband who asked me not to let you see him," the doctor continued. "He's concerned about you and the baby."

"But why?"

"His armored vehicle absorbed a direct Syrian hit. He suffered burns over ninety-two percent of his body."

Barely breathing, I could not comprehend what that meant. "If he was able to ask you not to let me see him, then he must be conscious. And if he's conscious, regardless how bad his wounds are, I'm here for him. I must see him now!"

I imagined that Yigal was fighting for his life and that he needed me near him—perhaps then he would recover. I belonged by his side.

Succumbing to my demand, the doctor pointed in the direction of Yigal's room and followed my mother and me as we headed there. On the way, I passed a darkened room from which I could hear a constant, rhythmic noise that sounded like the groans of a dying animal. As I hastened my steps to get to Yigal, I noticed that the doctor was no longer accompanying us. When I turned around I saw that he was standing outside the room from which the horrifying gasps came. Our eyes met. He nodded.

"Do you still want to go in?" he asked, when I approached.

Wasting no time answering him, I walked into the dark room, my mother by my side. There, underneath a tube-like device placed over a bed, lay an unrecognizable, hairless, charred being, desperately gasping for air.

"No!" I wailed. "This man cannot be my husband!"

I screamed at the doctor, pleading with him to tell me that it was a terrible mistake, to release me from the sight that would haunt me for the rest of my life. But the doctor only bowed his head in silence.

I got closer to the injured man, wanting to touch him but fearful of hurting him. I looked for a sign, anything that would confirm that this was the tall, strong, handsome, twenty-eight-year-old redhead I was married to, the man who had so many plans for the future of our growing family. But except for the length of his body, I found none.

The last words I uttered, before I collapsed into my mother's arms and passed out, were, "Don't let his mother see him like this."

I was taken to another room. Coming to, I saw on a bench outside Yigal's room a woman sobbing uncontrollably. I wondered whether she was weeping because she too was unable to recognize her loved one, or whether my screams had made her weep.

Yigal was a battalion ordnance officer in Israel's Eighth Armored Brigade, commanding and controlling combat operations. Two days before his injury, after he and his soldiers had completed their mission in the Sinai Peninsula, he volunteered to join the forces that were brought up north to breach into Syria, replacing an officer who had fallen ill. Before noon on June 9, the armored corps of which he was a part began to cross the armistice line into Syria. It's never been known whether the two navigators who were to direct the force erred in their calculation, sending the corps climbing toward the Golan Heights on the wrong path, or whether in the heat of a tumultuous battle the force chose its own path. Either way, the troops were exposed to the watching eyes of the fortified Syrian army. Facing fierce fire, Yigal's armored vehicle was hit at the bottom of the hill the Israeli force was ascending. Of the six fighters in the vehicle, only the driver would survive. The four other officers in the vehicle died in the horrific inferno. Engulfed in flames, Yigal managed to jump out. Thinking quickly, he rolled on the ground to put out the fire. He then got up and continued to command his force under heavy shelling. Only his military belt was left on his body, its metal buckle melted from the heat of the flames.

I used to wondered whether it was a sheer coincident that his injury occurred at the time I called his brigade headquarters.

In the hospital, after I regained some of my composure, I grasped the enormous challenge I faced: I had to devote myself to saving Yigal. To give him back his human appearance. I understood, too, that to accomplish that I would have to exercise self-control and not succumb to my own pain and sorrow.

"I'll sell our apartment, the car, and everything else we own to get the best plastic surgeons to give Yigal a face," I sobbed on my mother's shoulder. Though it was hard for her too to absorb what she had just seen, she understood the situation better that I did.

"*Mamale*," she replied, as tender as she could be, addressing me with an affectionate Yiddish epithet, "That will be much harder than you think." She shook her head with sorrow.

My head was still on her shoulder when she added, "Mine kind, no one could live like that."

The taxi took us home, together with Yigal's mother, who had seen her dying son briefly. In the roaring silence, I determined that I would sacrifice all other goals and needs except two: to save Yigal and to protect my pregnancy and give birth to his child.

Yigal's father remained in the hospital by his son's side. I will never forget his gray, despondent face when he sat there, watching the shadow of the person who only days earlier had been a vital young man with his whole life ahead of him.

When I left the hospital I did not know that ten minutes later Yigal would be gone. My neighbor Ora was still on her terrace when my mother and I arrived home. My sister, who had come with her father-in-law, was waiting for us there. Her husband, who fought with the Central Command near Jerusalem, was still on reserve duty.

"Yigal is in critical condition," I cried in her arms. Her eyes were covered by dark sunglasses, but I could see her tears. Her father-in-law was sobbing. Moments later the phone rang. It was Gila, my sister-in-law.

"What arrangement is the army making?" she asked.

"What are you talking about?"

"For the funeral."

"What funeral? He is alive!" I was short-tempered and impatient.

"I am sorry, I didn't know that," Gila replied, and hung up the phone. Seconds later it rang again. "Ziva," Gila whispered, "he is not."

Thirty-six hours after he was wounded, Yigal passed away. Like his tiny son a year earlier, who also fought for his life for thirty-six hours.

"He died!" I screamed.

I curled in despair on our green living-room sofa. A solid darkness covered me, thick and crushing.

I am alone, I thought in panic. Not *he is gone*, but *I am alone*. His being gone did not register. Not for a long time.

Suddenly, my life split in two—the before and the after. In the after I was to become a mother to a child I would raise without his father. The thought of that child, our baby, was both agonizing and heartening in the blackness that befell me.

My father sat next to me. "I loved him so," he said weeping.

"So did I," I wailed with him.

We spoke in the past tense, though I still was unable to absorb the actual, bitter meaning of the calamity that had befallen us. When my father, grieved and broken, managed to mutter between his sobs that he should have been the one to die instead of Yigal, I was horrified, fearing that his heart would not withstand his sorrow. An ambulance was called to take my father to the hospital. In the other room, my sister conferred with my doctor, telling him the horrible news.

Soon the apartment was filled with aunts and uncles. A few hours later, Yigal's brother Moshe appeared, having been called from the front. We hugged in silence. In the room, not a dry eye remained. And in the corner grocery store, my neighbors whispered that the silence emanating from our home was worse than a thousand screams.

———•———

A multitude of thoughts clouded my mind in the days that followed. Past events resurfaced as if to spite, bother, hurt, and confuse me. On the one hand, I could not forget the deep insult of being betrayed by Yigal on the eve of our wedding and my distrust of him since, a constant presence during our marriage. On the other, I loved him wholly, savoring the many fine qualities he had. I thought about his last wish while he was still conscious: That his pregnant wife not see him. It was not himself he was worried about, but his child and its mother. His death tormented me.

I wondered whether a new world would spring from the ruins and the ashes—a world in which I could raise my child in a state made safer by his father's sacrifice. We heard this cliché from our leaders after each war. But this time, with the shifted balance of military power peace might come, and it would be a cliché no more, even if my child would know his father only through stories and photographs. But such hopes were soon dashed.

I will always think of Yigal as the emblematic Israeli man, with his brusqueness and gentleness, his frivolity and enormous sense of responsibility. A young man who paid the ultimate price for his country, and the son of decent, loving parents. All the years that have passed have not erased his captivating magnetism.

CHAPTER 15

A Vanished Hope

There was no funeral. As a matter of wartime policy, the army buried its dead in military cemeteries near the areas where they had fallen, giving them a final resting place a year later in the communities where they lived.

Yigal was buried in Afula, a midsize town in the Jezreel Valley. I had passed it many times on trips to the Upper Galilee, sometimes with Yigal, never paying it much attention before the summer of 1967. But in the year following the war, I frequented that sleepy town with my visits to his grave.

His temporary grave, like those of his fallen brethren, was marked with a small white plate attached to a wooden stick, bearing his name, rank, military identification number, and the dates of his birth and death. Neither the sign nor the tiny hillock of sand that covered him told the story of the imposing man who lay six feet below. They did not portray the ambitions that would never materialize, the hopes that were gone forever, his anticipated fatherhood. And yet it was there, by that small pile of sand, that I felt free to express the burning grief that ripped through my guts. It was there that I could let go of my rawest emotions; talk to him about my lonesomeness, which I had not known before. Loneliness for him devoured me in its voracious and unceasing manner, poking my open wounds. Only at Yigal's gravesite could I drift into an illusory universe and speak to him as if we were still three—he, our baby, and me. Only there could I entwine my heart's desires with my grim reality.

Because there was no funeral, I was not required to sit shivah—the customary first seven days of mourning Jews observe after burial. But it felt as if I did. People surrounded me around the clock, my days and nights blending without distinction. From the moment the news of Yigal's death began to circulate on that unbearable Sunday morning in June, a sea of relatives and friends began to arrive at our home to console me and to keep me company. They came in groups. They came in pairs. They came alone.

The first to rush to my side was my old friend Dalia, who came with her parents. We hugged and cried on each other's shoulders. No words had to be spoken. My childhood neighbor Mrs. Slutzky too arrived with her daughters, Gail and Livia, who were Miriam's and my friends. A month earlier Mrs. Slutzky had lost her husband and I had paid her a visit.

"How ironic," she said. "Only Yigal was so much younger than Isaac."

"Who would have guessed that you would be here consoling me in return?" I asked. She held me tight. She had known me since the day I was born.

Elsie, the wife of Yigal's childhood friend, enraged my sister when she called me a *schlimazel*—meaning an unlucky person. "First your miscarriages, and now this!" It was a foolish remark, uttered without much thought, but Elsie, without knowing it, described a belief that haunted me for years to come.

My grandmother came too. Her face expressed her sorrow, and I thought that she was mourning not only Yigal but also her own son Nehemiah, who had fallen nineteen years earlier. She went to console Yigal's mother, as well. "From one bereaved mother to another," she said.

My despair was bottomless. When Yigal's brigade officers came to pay me a visit and told me in horror that one of their men had lost his arm in the war, I burst out, "It was only an arm! He is alive, isn't he?" I remembered Yigal's scorched body and the sound of his last breaths, and wondered how could they not realize the triviality of an arm, compared to the loss of a life. The officers fell silent and soon left.

"How could you be so rude?" my sister scolded me. "You embarrassed these guys, who made an effort to see you."

"I don't have to try to be nice all the time at the expense of truth."

I was reminded of that incident a year later, when a tall, athletic looking man, in his late thirties, arrived at my office, walking with a cane. I do not recall his role in the celebration of Israel's twentieth birthday. But I do remember his depression and his lamenting to me about being half a man because he had lost his leg in that same war. This time I was not as blunt as I had been with the officers. Instead, I spoke with him about how happy his wife and children must be to have him returned home alive. Then I added that I was widowed by that war and that I would have paid any price to have my husband back missing a limb. He began sobbing. The next day he called to thank me for the "lesson I taught him."

When the first week of mourning was over, my gynecologist decided to suture my cervix. He would have been satisfied with the corrective surgery I had had the previous year, he explained, but he was concerned that the shock I suffered could harm my pregnancy. I agreed. Saving our baby was the only thing that kept me going.

I went into the hospital for the procedure, and my parents returned home. Since everyone around me ruled out the idea that I would go back home alone from the hospital, I moved in with my sister's family. But within days I became ill. Miriam and her family were away on a short trip after Gershon had returned home, on a sort of a postwar healing journey. My parents came to stay with me, and within hours after their arrival I began to burn with fever.

As my temperature shot up to 104 degrees Fahrenheit, I heard my mother whisper to my father, "This may be the end."

"Imma!" I scolded her in despair.

"What is it, Zivinka, mine kind?"

"No. It can't happen again," I cried. "I can't lose this baby, not this time!"

By night I was back in the hospital. I was brought into a large room, kicking in the air and screaming my lungs out: "No, no, no. Do something! This baby is the reason I want to stay alive. Do something!"

"Who is this crazy woman?" I heard one patient complaining to another before I sank into a deep void. "She belongs in an asylum, not a maternity ward."

"She is not crazy," another patient sobbed. "She has just been widowed in the war, and she is pregnant."

It was the first time I heard someone refer to me as a war widow; they were the last words I heard before the nurses sedated me with an injection.

I was suffering from an infection that had developed after the suturing procedure I had undergone only days earlier. And so the fight for the lives of the two of us, my unborn child and me, began. Before I closed my eyes I saw the tears in my doctor's eyes. He did not stop hoping and made heroic efforts to save my baby and me.

I was in constant pain. During the days my family was always by my side—my mother, my sister, aunts, and cousins. Their support knew no bounds. Two weeks into my hospital stay, Yigal's mother arrived. It was the first time I had seen her since we had ridden together on that sorrowful journey from Haifa. She tried to smile at me, but she could not mask the pain that had become etched on her face. I tried to smile back at her, to hide my own gnawing pain, but my misery was all too obvious.

"We'll be all right," I told her, meaning the baby and me. My heart went out to her for coming to the hospital during the month of mourning and for worrying so deeply about me and about the child I was carrying.

"The most important thing is you." She stroked my hand.

"I know," I whispered, "for the sake of the baby."

"For your sake first." Her eyes glistened with tears.

"We will survive. The doctor is trying so hard." I could barely finish my sentence.

Her lips trembled. Perhaps she wanted to call me "my child," I thought, or "my beloved." But instead she said the unexpected: "No one can suffer like this for so long. It needs to be over."

I was stunned. She realized that with all of the doctor's attempts to save my pregnancy, my own health had deteriorated. She was ready to lose her son's child for my sake.

I swallowed my tears. What a heroic woman she is, I thought. Where did this bereaved mother find the strength to utter those words? No one but she had the courage to do so. But I decided to fight, not to give up. I wanted that child more than I had wanted anything.

Evening fell. Visiting hours were over, and I was alone. The pain worsened, and I could feel that my body was weakening. By eleven o'clock I felt ill. My head seemed to have separated from my body and float above it. I knew that something awful was happening to me. I alerted the doctor on duty.

"There's nothing wrong with you," she said, her voice full of scorn, when I described to her my scary, surreal experience. "You're depressed. You just lost you husband. What do you expect?" She dismissed my concerns with a hand motion.

"I may well be, but I know the difference between depression and what's happening to me."

"You exaggerate. Try to relax. Take a deep breath. I can assure you that you'll feel better." Her tone was patronizing, pitched as if she were talking to a disturbed person. I begged her to believe me. But the doctor, soon to become the head of the hospital's gynecology department, left my bedside.

I pressed the call bell. No one came. With the little strength I had left I screamed, demanding that the doctor return. She did, her impatience obvious. But then her eyes caught the kidney dish on my night table.

"Why is this dish here?" she asked, alarmed.

"I have been throwing up."

"For how long?"

"Four days, nonstop."

She looked at my chart. "It's not here. Who knows about it?"

"The nurses." Now she looked worried and rang for assistance, ordering emergency lab work.

The tests showed that I was suffering from acute acetone poisoning. Now panicked, the doctor rushed to save me.

"This needle looks as if it's made for a horse," I joked, trying to calm myself, as she began to insert into my right arm a needle so thick that I saw its hole.

"*Motek*," she responded, "if this liquid does not flow into your body within the hour, you won't be here at dawn." The tastelessness of her use of motek, the equivalent of "honey," in such a critical moment, irked me.

She had three more needles, one for my left arm and one for each of my feet. I bit my lips in silence.

Dawn was five hours away.

———————

Later that morning, the distinguished professor who supervised the maternity wing arrived at my bedside, surrounded by a team of medical students.

"Where is the patient who played such a trick on us last night?" he asked in his deep German accent. I was in no mood for his charm. The trick, dear professor, is that I managed to live past dawn, I thought. The trick is that if I hadn't raised hell last night, I wouldn't be here now. You may try to beguile me with your fatherly tone and cavalier humor, but the truth is that you are trying to disguise a terrible bungle. But I did not utter a word.

I stayed in the hospital for a month, to no avail. I had experienced the sadness that came with the unanticipated end of pregnancy. But this time the loss was irrevocable. Yigal and I would never parent a child together. My insides felt dead. My heart went numb.

The miscarriage occurred during the night. I was awake, as I often was, and alone, when I felt an irritation in my nose. As I sneezed, something inside me was torn off and came out of me in spite of the suture that closed my cervix. Oddly I felt no pain. I touched the area and felt a small bulge. This swelling can be explained, I thought, to reassure myself, and I alerted the nurses. My doctor had already left the hospital, they told me, and the two young interns on night duty came instead.

"We have to perform a D and C [dilation and curettage]," one of them said to me.

"I'll prepare the operating room," the other responded.

They must be unaware of how desperately my doctor had been trying to save my child, I thought, in a panic.

"You shouldn't do anything to me until you consult Dr. Livni," I said, distraught. My doctor was one of the leading obstetricians in the hospital, if not in the country. They had to respect him and reconsider, I believed.

"It is not our responsibility to contact him," they said.

"Then I'll contact him myself. Just get me to a phone before we go into the operating room." With no power to resist them, pleading was all I could do. If I could only get out of bed and run away!

"I must talk to him," I repeated with the little strength I had.

"Hospital regulations prohibit direct contact between patients and doctors outside the hospital premises. Only a member of your family can contact Dr. Livni."

"Let me contact my family then!"

"Same thing. Regulations," said the dominant one. With that they wheeled me into the operating room. "At least write down in my chart that I am not giving you permission to invade my body," I demanded.

I was still protesting when they placed an ether mask over my face and began to perform the D and C before I was sedated.

"I am awake," I shrieked. "I feel everything."

"You are ludicrous. You don't know what you're taking about. You are anesthetized."

"How can I talk to you, then?" I wailed in despair.

When I screamed, in unbearable pain, they demanded that I shut up. My screams annoyed them, one of them complained. Alone and power-less, I obeyed. I do not know if there was supposed to be an anesthesi-ologist in the operating room, since anesthesia was nothing more than an ether mask, which the doctors would place on a patient's face. The doctors did that, but they did not wait to ascertain that I was properly anesthetized. Lying awake under their invading hands, I thought of the women who had endured enormous suffering in our nations' recent history. If they survived, so could I.

When I was wheeled back to my room I was despondent—not only because of the medical rape I had just experienced, but also because I had lost the most precious connection I had to Yigal.

In the morning I noticed Yigal's father in the corridor, searching for my room. My heart stood still. Please, God, I prayed, let him not find me.

It was the first day after *shloshim*, the customary thirty days of mourning, and the first time he had left his home after Yigal's death, other than going to his neighborhood synagogue to recite the Kaddish prayer for his son. It was the first time I had seen him since that grim morning at the Haifa hospital. But there he was. He did not know it yet, but his hope that he would soon hold his son's child in his arms was forever faded. The thought of having to tell him that I had lost his grandchild horrified me. I kept wishing that he would not find me, but he did, and so he was the first in our family to learn that I had suf-fered a miscarriage. So wretched was his expression when he heard the news that I almost could not bear to look at him. But I did. Intently. Compassionately.

"The most important thing is that you're healthy," he said. He looked at me as if he meant to say more, things he did not dare to voice. He did not stay long.

The profound remorse and accountability I felt for losing the child, as if I had transgressed or not done enough to save it remains among the most painful of my memories. I ached with the desperate sense that I had failed in my responsibility to immortalize Yigal through his child and that I owed his parents their grandchild.

"This is the first time I have seen some color in your face in a long time," my mother said to me, when she arrived at the hospital after Yigal's father had left. She sounded pleased. She sat by my side and took a closer look at me. "This is also the first time you don't seem to be in pain," she further observed.

"No… it's over," I mumbled.

"What are you saying?"

"The baby is gone," I whispered. "It happened at midnight."

She looked at me with disbelief, her green eyes fogged with tears. She leaned down and kissed my forehead, then praised God for ending my ordeal—the physical one, that is. Like me, she knew that my emotional torment had just begun. She held my hand and did not let go, and yet I felt as if I were drowning in a deep dark ocean, with no horizon in sight.

———————

From the hospital I returned to my sister's house. By then Yigal's business partner had purchased the Studebaker he used for driving lessons. After I had regained some strength, I looked for a smaller car, and with the guidance of my brother-in-law I bought a used Volkswagen Beetle. I hesitated to buy a car so closely associated with the Nazi regime, but it was the safest used car available for what I could afford to spend. So I made a bargain with myself, letting go of one dilemma, anticipating the many others I would face each coming day.

I returned to my old job at the prime minister's office. The timing was right. With the planning of events celebrating Israel's upcoming twentieth birthday amidst its stunning war victory, the office was frenzied. I dove into work as if there were no tomorrow. Though work and the traveling it required were therapeutic, there were brutal moments. The first occurred when Oscar, a pyro-technician who had known Yigal since their days at the air force, appeared in the office.

"How is the redhead?" he asked me, with his usual gusto. Unable to answer, I shook my head as if to say *no*. No to what, I did not know. Was it a "no" to Yigal's burnt-red hair? A "no" to Yigal's life? A "no" to the ruins of my life after he was gone?

"He is gone," I managed to finally say. I had no strength to say more.

There followed the silence I had become used to, then the "I am so sorry. I didn't know." Oscar's eyes and mouth were wide open; his hands grasped his face, and he moved away to hide his sobbing. I escorted him out, numb when we parted.

My boss bombarded me with assignments he believed to be healing. As Israel's twentieth Independence Day neared, he asked me to type excerpts from *Gvilei Esh* ("Parchments of Fire"). Containing many volumes, it is a collection of stories and letters, diaries, and short memoirs left behind by the fallen soldiers of Israel's wars. These mementos included their music and poems, paintings and drawings. My tears rolled down my cheeks and neck as I typed those entries, barely able to see the words. Whole, youthful lives, full of hopes, were folded in those pages. "Continue to type," my boss would insist, when I felt that I could not. Sometimes I had to type excerpts from another commemorating series, *Yizkor*. If there was virtue in the work I had been asked to do, I did not recognized it then. My loss was new and raw and real, and I mourned it every day, all day, trapped in the chains of grief.

Before the autumn of 1967 was over, accompanied by family and friends, I visited the spot where Yigal's armored vehicle had been hit. Next to the charred steel skeleton of the half-track I found a shoe, a fork, and a tin mess dish. I picked up those items and held them close to my chest, trying to attach a person to each of them. Who wore the boot for the last time in his life? Whose lips touched the fork? Whose mess tin was it? I wanted to keep them for myself, as if I had a right to own those things, but I left them. They are long gone, but the burnt vehicle remains in that same spot, rusted yet soundlessly proud.

On our way back, we stopped at Migdal Shams, a deserted Syrian town on the Golan Heights. It was carpeted in apple orchards and from the trees hung an infinity of ripe apples. Amazed by the sight, everyone began to run to the trees, joyously grabbing for the juicy-looking fruits. Dismayed, I remained behind and watched, thinking not of the apples but of the fork, the dish, and the shoe I had just held. Those who ran to the trees looked to me not like the family and friends who had stood by my side from the day I was widowed, but like strangers on an ordinary trip, enjoying a peaceful orchard on a beautiful fall day. Then it hit me: This was life after war. For those who had not paid as high a price, life quickly returned to normal. For the others, normalcy was a relative term, filled with trivialities.

A picture I have from that trip, of me standing next to a Syrian bunker, attests to the bitter battles that took place on the Golan Heights. My ashen face and frail figure portray grief and sorrow. My pain over Yigal's death did not subside, nor did the memory of our life together.

———————

Yigal's brigade commander wrote me a personal letter after the war. In it he praised Yigal for his courage, his leadership, his decision-making abilities in the heat of battle, his composure and camaraderie, and for being a role model till the end. The letter is gone, along with the rest of the documents and pictures my mother destroyed. But its memory remains intact in my mind, as if I still hold it in my hands.

There were other reminders of loss: a place, a food, a smell, a song. At times I felt him sleeping by my side, stroking me softly. One night, when I moved closer to him, I banged my head on the wall. The blow woke me up into grim reality, the shock overpowering, the cruelty of the moment profound. In the morning, still traumatized, I told my sister what had happened at night, and she laughed. At that moment, four months after Yigal's death and three months after losing our child, engrossed in my shuttered life, I came to a decision. Grateful for the warm shelter and love my sister and her husband had unconditionally given me, I felt the time had come for me to move back to my home and face the world on my own terms.

CHAPTER 16

Tossed between Darkness and Light

One evening I went to my parents' apartment, as I often did. I knew they worried about me.

"What are you up to these days?" my father inquired.

"Nothing new," I muttered.

He exchanged glances with my mother and sighed. "The world continues to turn," he said, sipping his cold drink. "Nothing new, you say, ah?"

"I get up, drink my coffee, drive to work and go home. My Beetle too is the same." I did not try to hide my sarcasm.

They smiled. We were each playing our part in a game. I assumed the conversation would end with their usual remarks, but I had something else coming.

"And how's Lily?" My mother often asked about her friend's daughter and my coworker, thankful for Lily's help in getting me a job after my military service. By then Lily and I became best of friends.

"No news there, either."

"You know, mamale," she said, "we never hear from you about your life, other than work."

"What do you mean?" I narrowed my eyes at her, suspicious.

"You know the answer. I want to know that you have a social life like any other young person."

"Imma!"

"We worry about your social life."

"Stop it," I begged.

She smoothed her hair with her pretty hand. "I won't. A month passes by, then another. Before you know it, a year goes by. It has been a year already, and you..."

My father added his own observation. "Facts are facts." Pensive, he lit a cigarette. "Life might have its own path, but you should try to affect it. Do things."

"That's why I returned to work," I protested.

"It's not enough," my mother said.

"And I paint, you might recall." I have always painted or decorated things, but I have started to do so earnestly when I quit my job after my second miscarriage.

Though their love for Yigal was irrefutable, my parents wanted to see me resume my life and move on. They knew I was till grieving for Yigal and for our unborn child. But there were issues, they insisted, that I could not avoid, potential problems that needed resolution. The hurdle that worried them most was the *halitza*—meaning "removal of a shoe." This humiliating religious ceremony, which takes place in front of three rabbis and two additional witnesses, would absolve me from my Halachic duty to wed my married brother-in-law. As rendered by the dictate of levirate marriage, a childless widow must marry her deceased husband's brother and produce a child in order to immortalize her lost husband and carry on his name. Unless her brother-in-law agrees to release her from that obligation, the widow is forbidden to marry another man. The release is granted to her in a ceremonial procedure, the *halitza*.

"You must go through with this," my mother said. "There is no way out of it."

"There is," I said. "You don't go through it. You already made me go to the *mikveh*. No more of that stuff!"

"Then there is no marriage." She looked worried.

"Who's thinking about marriage?" I snapped, now angry.

"You may not think of it today, but you don't know how you will feel in the future." It was my father's turn.

"And your relationship with Yigal's family is wonderful," my mother added. "That helps." She was thinking of a story that had been printed in the newspaper that morning about a family that had refused to grant "their" widow the necessary release, because "she belonged to them forever." It was one account among many that circulated in the press as the first year of mourning ended, and widows of the Six-Day War began to think of rebuilding their lives. In many cases families extorted large sums of money from the widows; in one case the brother-in-law was a young boy, and the widow was required to wait years until he became a "man" at thirteen. Such stories were behind my parents' efforts to influence me.

"These day you can get married in a civil ceremony," I said, building my case.

My father cleared his throat. He lit another cigarette, took a drag, and exhaled the smoke in a wide stream.

"Not exactly," he said after a pause. "The state doesn't really recognize it. Besides, we live in a society that doesn't necessarily see things your way."

He managed to agitate me. "But Abba, civil law in this wonderful land of ours forbids polygamy, and our chief rabbis have outlawed levirate marriage. You have no case. Now leave me alone!"

"You must think of tomorrow," my mother continued.

"Tomorrow? What kind of tomorrow? It's not enough that my life is in ruins? Now I have to go through this shameful ceremony that has no place in our modern lives? Not this time." The rebel in me was ignited. "I think of my yesterdays. That is what is left for me to do now. Whatever the future may bring my way, I refuse to succumb to this ugly religious subordination."

I looked at my father, wondering how an intelligent man like him, a man who despised religious coercion—the man who had once prepared for the two of us a bacon sandwich on the holiest day of the Jewish calendar—could think that I should deny my principles and succumb to the demands of a small, albeit powerful, group of people who sought to inflict their fundamentalist beliefs on the rest of us. My cherished father, who was not always able to demonstrate his love, was showing it by worrying about my future. When I realized how much anxiety my refusal to go through the ceremony was causing my parents, I gave in.

———◆———

On the day of the ceremony, I arrived at the Chief Rabbinate building in Tel Aviv before my brother-in-law, Moshe. I walked into the rabbinical courtroom; the three rabbis were already there.

"Where's the brother?" they wanted to know.

"On his way." I knew I sounded nervous.

"And your in-laws?"

I was shocked. "They are not coming."

"We need them, as witnesses."

"Don't you think they have gone through enough pain, without this?" I did not hide my anger. "They will not be here. Not if it depends on me!"

They gave up. Moshe arrived, and the ceremony began.

In the *halitza*, the rabbis "sell" the brother an oversize leather sandal that has long straps. He puts the sandal on his right foot, ties the straps around his leg in an elaborate way, and walks a few paces to prove the sandal belongs to him. My part as the widow was to take a few steps toward him, bend down, and hold his foot in my left hand, after I ascertained its cleanliness. I had to untie the straps with my right hand, remove the sandal, and cast it aside in a way that demonstrated disdain. I then had to spit in front of his face and recite the Deuteronomic declaration, "So shall be done to the man who will not build up his brother's house." Only after we had performed all of these acts correctly would I be considered free to marry another man.

After Moshe had put on, tied, and walked in the shoe, my turn arrived, and I walked toward him. One of the rabbis stopped me.

"Go back and start from the beginning," he commanded. "You started with the wrong foot."

I do not recall with which foot I began to walk. What I do remember is that the rabbi asked me whether I had served in the army and then suggested that if I was able to march as a soldier, I could do it correctly in the rabbinical courtroom. I started again, this time with the "correct" foot.

After I untied Moshe's sandal and threw it on the floor, I spit in front of him.

"Not enough saliva," the rabbis determined, after examining my spit on the floor. "Spit again. Take your time. We have all day."

Nervousness made my mouth drier still. I produced more saliva by sucking on my tongue and inner cheeks as hard as I could. I spit for the second time.

Another inspection.

"Still not enough!"

I produced more and spit for the third time. The rabbis were satisfied.

If the ceremony were not disturbing enough, at the end the chief of the three rabbis, an elderly man with a snow-white beard, walked toward me. I expected some words of sympathy. But instead, without shame, he asked me to donate money to a religious charity. His audacity made me so furious that I went to slap him. But Moshe, who saw me raising my hand, ran over and grabbed my arm, then led me backward, away from the scene.

Afterward, I sat alone in an outdoor café not far from the court. Sipping coffee, I watched the passersby. On the street, traffic was heavy. Life went on. I felt Yigal's presence, not sure whether he was pleased or not. I stayed there for a long time.

As stories continued to circulate in the press, the military rabbinate revoked the need for remaining war widows to go through that ritual. I was delighted by the change, but I also felt deceived. Not by the military rabbinate, but by myself, for have given in and taken part in that degrading ceremony.

I have always believed in the separation of religion and state and in one's personal freedom to practice his or her beliefs. That is why I accept the choice of those widows who embrace the custom as a symbolic severance from their past, and that of observant widows who view the *halitza* as a form of protection. A choice: that is what such ritual should be. Not an obligation.

———◆———

At roughly the same time the Defense Ministry—the governmental arm responsible for the rehabilitation of war casualties and their families—came up with its own form of discrimination, decreeing that childless widows of the Six-Day War were no longer eligible for their monthly death benefit. Instead, it offered to subsidize schooling for all widows, so that they could attain new skills of their choice, to help them "rehabilitate," or adjust, mostly financially, to their new life. While I embraced the opportunity for professional training, the government's distinction between childless widows and widows who had children did not sit well with me.

I chose a newly introduced, four-year cartography program in the Technion's Tel Aviv branch. The curriculum would have trained me to plan and design geographical maps. Because of my painting ability and my love for geography, I believed it was a perfect profession for me to pursue. But low enrollment forced the program's cancellation. I was disappointed, but I had an alternative. Having been painting for a number of years, I yearned to become a professional artist. I enrolled in an art academy that had recently been established by the influential artist and professor Arieh Margoshilsky and had quickly become reputed for its excellence. Professor Margoshilsky himself accepted me into the program, allowing me to forgo the entry exams, after he had seen a few of my paintings. Two of them had just won an amateur competition and were shown at a respected Tel Aviv institution.

To my chagrin, the Defense Ministry refused to subsidize my studies at the academy, stating that becoming an artist was not a viable profession that could sustain me financially, and therefore was not rehabilitating. I fought the decision on the grounds that the government's definition of rehabilitation was rigid, limited, and irrational, and insisted on my right to choose my own path to rehabilitation. I prevailed.

My teacher thought I had a promising future, and my offer to mount a show of my own, dedicated to Yigal's memory, was accepted by the Ramat Gan branch of Beit Yad Le'banim, the association of the families of fallen soldiers of the Israeli Defense Forces. But the show never opened. Life had other plans for me.

———◆———

The government's agreement to subsidize my art studies did not abate my anger over the planned termination of the death benefits of childless war widows. Funding our schooling was a positive step, but as the only element of our "rehabilitation" it was, to my mind, insufficient. I believed that by terminating our allowance, the government acted unjustifiably and arbitrarily, with no consideration given to our changed economic condition, childless or not. And so I fought the government, trusting that I was acting not only on my own behalf but also for widows who were discriminated against by the same powers that were supposed to protect them.

"You remind me of your grandmother," my father said to me one day. "When you fight for something you believe in, you are just as stubborn as she was."

"Is that good or bad?" I asked.

He laughed. "It's an important tool to have." He turned earnest. "You're in the right. If you think you can withstand the pressure, don't give up."

I did not. I wrote letters to the responsible ministers, arranged meetings with Knesset members, conducted interviews, and made known my intention to take the case to the Israeli High Courts of Justice if necessary.

The replies I received, including one from Defense Minister Moshe Dayan, were sympathetic, but sympathy alone would not reverse the new law. Knesset members (MKs) to whom I had written encouraged my activism but offered no help, with one exception. In late spring 1969, I met with the Labor Party MK Shoshana Arbeli-Almoslino, then chair of the Knesset Labor Committee, known to care about women's issues. She enlightened me with her rich political experience, and promised to introduce a bill in the fall, when the Knesset reconvened, that would call for the reinstitution of the death benefits to childless war widows.

In response to my campaign, the Defense Ministry offered me psychological help to deal with my grief, as if that were the problem rather than its discriminatory policy. Because in those years the government did not yet offer mental help treatment to bereaved families, as it would much later, the proposition was unusual. Through all my dealings as an activist, I made sure I was poised and dignified, leaving my emotions aside, and that was in part why I found the offer of psychological help so offensive. I felt I was being treated as a woman crazed by sorrow. I declined the offer, as an insult and an improper substitute for what I felt to be a justified benefit.

MK Almoslino had advised me to get the press on my side, and I began to call reporters. Most were either too busy or had more pressing issues to report. Only one, who worked for the widely distributed *Yidiot Aharonot*, wrote a short entry about my cause.

My campaign had other disappointments. The biggest was my futile attempt to mobilize opposition to the changed policy among the other childless widows of the Six-Day War. We were 128 to my recollection. For days I traced their names, addresses, and telephone numbers, and called them or traveled to their homes to meet them face-to-face. Some had moved back in with their parents, as the government suggested we do. Most of the widows were reluctant to campaign against a government that was still enjoying the glory of an unprecedented military victory. The widows of the Israeli Air Force pilots considered themselves exclusive, as the air force took care of its own "family." Many of the rest of those 128 women were emotionally incapable of becoming involved in my efforts. But even those who refused to join me expressed their admiration of my strength and my decisiveness. I respected their choices. I was disappointed but not discouraged.

It was time for exposure. With the help of my friend Lily, I was able to meet Bruria Barir-Avidan, the senior reporter of the most popular women's magazine in Israel. She is a well-known, energetic, and talented writer, five years my senior, and her sensitivity was welcoming.

For the interview, which took place in my apartment, I managed to recruit five childless widows. Two were air force widows, who had no demands of the government but, like the others, came to offer moral support. The third attendee felt uncomfortable speaking against the government, whose suggestion she had accepted and moved back in with her parents. The fourth widow had tried to conceive for most of her twelve-year marriage and felt that having no children because of conception problems emphasized the arbitrariness of the government's decision. But she too refused to criticize the government. The fifth told me that she had "moved on" with her life, and felt that becoming involved in my campaign would set her back.

We sat for hours, during which time I poured my heart out to that talented reporter, answering each of her questions with honesty and candor, describing the indifference and apathy with which childless widows of the Six-Day War had been treated. A week later the interview was published. It resonated widely, and the issue began to be debated in the press.

During my campaign I forged close relations with several people in the Defense Ministry who were privately sympathetic to my cause yet remained steadfast publicly. From them I learned that the changed policy was in part a deliberate tactic geared to compel young childless widows to "rehabilitate" themselves by remarrying because of financial pressure. But with the increased media attention, the government decided to extend the payments for an additional year.

By 1970, with the active involvement of MK Shulamit Aloni, who headed Israel's civil-rights movement, the Knesset passed a law reinstating the pension until those widows remarried. The law has gone through many changes since. In 2010, an amendment pertaining to compensation for war widows who had remarried went into effect. Once again, I became a recipient of death benefits.

As my fight turned more public, other widows, both with and without children, began to seek my advice. It was not my intention to turn into a "therapist" whose sympathies were also sought by bereaved parents and disabled soldiers. When I recognized that my deeper involvement was setting me back emotionally, I stopped my interactions with the latter two groups, maintaining that I lacked the background to help them. But I did not abandon my sisters in grief.

After my photograph had been printed with the magazine article, I began to receive enthusiastic, if unwanted, marriage offers from strange men. Most were harmless, but a man who called himself John Buchholtz began to stalk and harass me. At first I did not pay much attention to the intruder, but my boss became alarmed and involved his connections in the police.

"Your life is in danger," the police told me, after weighing everything I told them about the man. They were adamant. "This is not a kid's game. The stalker knows what he's doing. He knows who you are, where you live, whom you are with, and when you are home alone. His actions indicate that he is a pervert, who calculates his steps carefully. He may be violent. We must catch him."

They recommended a variety of steps that would have protected me and helped them capture the stalker, but those techniques would have disrupted my life and deprived me of my privacy. I decided against the idea, opting for a life change instead. Having a stalker was only one of my problems.

CHAPTER 17
Transition

When I returned to work after Yigal and the baby were gone, my coworker Lily, with whom I had only a professional relationship, attempted to befriend me. For a long time I was indifferent to her efforts. This was not because she had shown envy of me in the past or because I judged her for the tempestuous life she had maintained soon after her husband had died of cancer. Mostly it was because of my growing cynicism. Now that she too is a widow, I thought, she needs my friendship.

One day, when my Beetle was being serviced, she offered me a ride home.

"It's nice of you," I said. I was grateful.

She laughed. Her laugh was a bit husky, at times sounding real and genuine, other times artificial and forced. This time it sounded sincere.

"Who knows," she teased. "Today I offer you a ride, tomorrow it may be you offering me one."

At the time she was a thirty-one-year-old mother of two, attractive, even blooming, in spite of the difficult year she had experienced.

"Can I ask you a question?" She turned to me as we approached my apartment building. Lily was both direct and unpredictable. I hesitated. "Fine," she said, after a short pause. "One *tiny* question then. Why are you so averse to me?"

My answer was as blunt as her question. "It's because of your bossiness."

She burst out laughing. "The two of us are more similar than you think," she said. "But I didn't ask you that question out of nowhere. I too have had a terrible experience, and I'm a bit older than you."

"What does that have to do with anything?"

"I can help you get out of the dark." She was no longer smiling. Feeling a slight quiver in my stomach, I shrugged.

"Listen, Ziva," she said, looking into my eyes. "Life cannot be endless mourning. You didn't see me do that when I lost Meir. The way he slipped through my fingers. I smiled and I laughed, even when I didn't feel like it. I had two young kids. Do you understand?"

I was silent. I knew about her infidelities during her marriage, which could perhaps be explained by her mother having forced her to wed when she was eighteen rather than fulfill her military duty as her friends did. But I also knew the enormity of the loss Lily felt after her husband's death.

"I know what you want to say," she said. "That your situation is different. That you don't have children to come home to at the end of the day. It's all true. For now. But you can't let it persist. There will be other chapters in your life. So get out of the dark before it blinds you."

"Easy to say," I muttered. Though I knew she was right, I was not ready to admit it.

"It might look hard now, but one day you'll wake up and ask yourself whether you're still a woman—a living and breathing human being who has urges and needs." Now it was I who looked into her eyes. She was not kidding. "One night you'll wake up wishing that something other than your memories will hug you," she finished.

"What does *that* mean?"

"It will scream from within you that you are waking up." She was smiling again. "You haven't learned yet the enormous force life has. The desire to be loved." Her smile turned into a chuckle. "I know. You must think I'm some kind of unprincipled woman. It's OK. You're allowed. But one day you'll say that Lily was right."

We parted. I got out of the car, as she needed to get home to her children. Before I closed the car door, I bent to look at her through the passenger window. "Thank you," I said. "For everything."

"Don't forget what I said," she called, and she drove away.

I had never lived alone before I left Miriam and Gershon's house and moved back to the apartment where I had lived with Yigal, now an empty fortress in which I could seclude myself in my ample free time.

I knew the move would be agonizing, and that I would feel lost without Yigal. But I also understood that it was an important step, one that demanded courage and determination. My strength had been tested before, I reminded myself, many times. I compared my move to a baby's first strides, putting one foot in front of the other. I would open the door. Would I walk in without hesitation, or would I take a moment? Should someone be waiting for me there—my mother, my sister, a friend, someone with whom I could communicate in silence? Would our apartment feel like a home? Would I be able to sleep alone in our bed?

But all those thoughts did not prepare me for the subtleties of my new situation: For the lonely evenings, when twilight began to blend with the darkening shadows of night. For when I wanted to curl up in Yigal's chair and feel as if his strong arms embraced me still. For the riveting, gripping nightmares that were repeated night after night. In those terrible dreams, I was standing alone in a dark space on the edge of a round crater, the ground of which was a shadowy desert. From the center, a huge hand slowly emerged, fingertips first, getting larger and larger as it moved upward, stopping when the hand was fully visible atop its wrist, its fingers straight, its color a murky bluish gray that I imagined was the shade of dark, gloomy death. Its swollen veins looked as if they were full to bursting. It was badly injured. When it threatened to grab me I woke up, terrorized.

Though I recall almost every minute detail from the period following Yigal's death, I do not remember the first time I walked through the door when I returned home. Was my neighbor Ora standing on her terrace like a watchdog, as usual, signifying a sort of normalcy, as if nothing had changed? Did I buy my first bouquet of flowers on my way home, or did I wait a day or two? I made it a habit to always have flowers, not just to bring a hint of color into my new existence, but also to symbolize my resolve to turn a new page in my life.

The first time I returned to our grocery store, the grocer and his wife greeted me with a bewildered silence, followed by sad smiles and then genuine tears. For the first time in my life I bought food for a single person. I brought my laundry to our cleaners and went to my beauty parlor. The proximity of these shops was comforting, the familiarity reassuring, as my world remained trapped between past and present.

One evening, collapsing in Yigal's chair, I thought of Lily's speech. I recalled the painful path she had walked when her husband was dying. It was a long road that readied her for its tragic conclusion. By contrast, nothing had prepared me for Yigal's sudden death. The shock I experienced when I saw him last and my powerlessness ripped me to pieces. That instance when I stood by his bedside, his face erased, his body scorched, and he no longer looking human, haunts me to this day.

———————

A photo on a shelf captured the two of us in a joyous moment. A miraculous picture: In it he looked whole and healthy and radiant. It ignited in me time and again a yearning that tore at my heart.

I did not have to close my eyes to smell him or see his image as if he was standing before me—alive. As if I were able to touch him. To hear his calm and confident voice, his laughter. To dream with him: colorful dreams, springtime dreams, enchanting dreams.

At times I wondered, as I still do, how our lives would have turned out if he had lived and was alive now. There are things I cannot forget, though I wish I could: His pride in his manhood, and the occasional crudeness that contradicted his grace and maturity. The French woman he met on the beach and my nagging suspicions that she was not the only one of his escapades, even though I had no evidence of him being unfaithful after our marriage.

Yigal had his faults, but I had mine. I was immature; too unaware of basic things a woman should know, like the need for a pregnancy test when in doubt. I did not realize how much he loved me; and I was too suspicious of his supposed infidelity.

But those blunders, which time might have healed, did not reflect our marriage in its entirety and the many loving, happy moments we had had. Sitting in the apartment we had shared, I did not want to give up that which was taken from me so cruelly. I was not ready yet to turn to a new page, as Lily had suggested, though I recognized that there was more than a seed of truth to her words. That, in and of itself, was progress enough.

I kept Yigal's clothes hanging in the bedroom closet as if he might return home any minute and choose a change of clothing, after he showered, at the end of yet another workday. Then we would have a bite, meet friends, and return home to weave more dreams. And I, as always, would rest my head on his shoulder and gaze at his beautiful hands. I loved looking at those long hands, with their perfectly coordinated joints, each finger full of life.

One day one of his ties dropped to the floor. Rina, my old neighbor and friend, still reminds me how I ran to her apartment next door, sobbing. The sudden falling of the tie, which he had worn when he was alive and would never wear again, made his death so painfully vivid.

I visited Yigal's grave often, usually driving back when night began to drape the hills around me. One evening, as I drove through Wadi Ara in northern Israel, I spotted two young soldiers hitchhiking. I stopped my car and offered them a lift. They warned me that the road was dangerous, and that I should be careful, especially at night.

"This is the quickest road from Afula," I told them, "and I know the way."

"Are you from Afula?"

"No, but my husband is buried in the military cemetery there."

They fell silent but not for long.

"Still, I would be careful if I were you," the soldier sitting on the passenger side resumed. "What if we weren't Israeli soldiers, just dressed like ones? People get killed because of mistakes like these. That you are a young pretty widow for sure doesn't help you."

Yes, I was a widow, and I had to get used to it. The uncoupling hit me time an again. I was shaken when Yigal's aunt and her husband asked me to return the wedding gift they had given us. It was not the rudeness of their demand that bothered me as much as its symbolism of my new societal status.

Another insulting incident occurred when my friends Elsie and Michael invited me to join them for a Friday night gathering at their friends' home. Yigal and Michael had known each other since childhood, and their friendship had grown throughout the years. Elsie was a good-hearted woman who was known for her straight talk. Michael always impressed me with his decent and proper behavior and his sincere, sweet smile. Yigal and I saw them often, and after the war their concern for my well being seemed genuine.

That evening their friends received me with open arms. But, after a while, to my astonishment, our hosts began to show pornographic movies, which the guests, all married couples, were expecting. I was revolted. I was not a prude, but I believed it was inappropriate and tasteless to show those films in the presence of a young widow, the only single person in the group. Disappointed at my friends' insensitivity, I resolved never to be trapped in a similar situation again. I would accept fewer social invitations and drive my own car.

Despite the awkwardness of that evening, I considered Michael, who was in the construction business, to be a good friend. He often stopped at my apartment to see whether anything needed fixing and to offer any other help I might need. I was grateful to have him and Elsie as such devoted friends—until the evening they invited me to go bowling, a game just introduced in Israel.

Michael called me to make the arrangements. I thanked him and said I would meet them at the alley, true to my resolve.

"Nonsense, we'll pick you up at eight," he insisted.

"I'd rather drive myself. I may want to leave before you."

"No problem, Ziva. We'll take you home whenever you want, OK?"

I went along, not wanting to be difficult. When I got downstairs that evening, Michael was alone in his car.

"Where's Elsie?" I asked.

"She doesn't feel well," he said, starting the car.

"That's a pity. We should go another night."

"You're right. That's what I told her, too." He threw a friendly look at me, but in my head a warning light began to flash.

"You know Elsie. She insisted that we go without her because it's important to get you out of the house."

I got in the car and we drove off. Throughout the evening Michael behaved like a perfect gentleman, pleasant and cordial.

"It was nice to see you smile again," he said when he dropped me off, and I felt ashamed for the alarm that had flickered in my head earlier.

A week or so later Michael appeared at my door, wearing his dusty work clothes, as he was on his way home from a construction site. He had come to check that everything if my apartment was in working order.

"Thank you, Michael," I said, assuring him that all was fine. "Do you want a glass of ice water before you leave?"

It was a hot and humid day, and he was sweating. As I readied to step into my kitchen to get the cold drink, he grabbed me and began to kiss me. Bewildered, I pushed him away as forcefully as I could.

"What is wrong with you?!" I shrieked.

He did not let go. "Can't you see that I have fallen in love with you?"

"Michael, stop!"

"I am in love with you. I can't take it anymore." While he paused, panting, I took control of the situation.

"Leave my apartment," I commanded, in the coldest voice I could summon, "and never come back!"

Aside from the shock and the insult, I was upset because of Elsie. For years I have wondered what lies Michael told her to explain my sudden disappearance from their lives.

I did not know that he would be the first among a community of men who would "fall in love" with me. It must have been widowhood that made me so "beautiful." How else could I explain the sudden interest expressed by so many men in the "greenness of my eyes," the "olive color of my skin," and the "blackness" of my hair, in my "petite figure" and my "femininity"? Had I been less "stunning," "unique," or "special," when I was a married woman? All that attention puzzled me. I knew myself as a woman who kept alive the memory of her man, who was no more. And suddenly, I found myself discovered and exposed to the lust of hunters seeking new conquests.

I often wondered whether other widows had to cope with such improper behavior from men. And sometimes I wondered whether Yigal was capable of behaving so coarsely. I thought not. A gentleman like he was would not harass a woman he desired. He would not have to—women fell for him.

One evening, I received a phone call. "Hallo, Ziva?" a woman on the other end of the line said. I was home alone, mournful and vulnerable. My heart skipped a beat.

"Yes?"

After a pause she hung up. But I recognized her voice as that of one of Yigal's driving students. A bit older than he and married, she had, for some reason, never been able to pass her driving test, and her lessons with him went on and on. They developed a close relationship. She did not hide her admiration for him, and he talked about her often. Occasionally I became suspicious about the nature of their relationship, but I remained silent. Aside from the incident with the French woman prior to our marriage, which made me wonder about Yigal's ability to be faithful, there was no evidence for my apprehension.

And yet, I could not stop but wondering why this woman had called now. What did she want to say to me? Did she mean to console me? Did she want to tell me how heartbroken *she* was?

A year or so after the war I ran into a woman who had served with me in the army. She had heard about Yigal's death from Drora, a mutual friend from our army days.

"Drora saw Yigal before he went to battle," she told me, guilelessly. She had no clue that her words sliced through my chest and into my heart.

"It's impossible ..." I began, before suspicion silenced me. I will never know whether my Uncle Yaakov was the last person I knew to have seen Yigal alive, or whether it was Drora. I will never know whether, when he stroked my pregnant belly while we said our last good-bye by the waiting truck, I was the one to receive his last caresses. That sense of not knowing still remains with me today.

———◆———

Just then, as I was drowning in bewilderment, salvation, however dubious, came from an unexpected quarter.

Henri was my gynecologist. I had continued to bleed since my miscarriage, and he continued to treat me and monitor my health. Kindhearted and sensitive, my devoted physician became an attentive and supportive friend, one I began to count on for sound advice beyond medical matters.

"Henri is an angel who was sent to me from heaven at such an awful time in my life," I told my sister.

"You need a friend like that by your side," she agreed. Though Yigal continued to fill my life as if he were present, I began to grieve for him differently. I was beginning to accept that his being gone was irrevocable, final.

After six months of treatments, the bleeding still continued, and Henri prescribed medication. I brought the prescription to the pharmacy across the street from my apartment building.

"Do you know what kind of pills these are?" the pharmacist asked me.

"To stop my bleeding," I answered, matter-of-factly.

"These are birth-control pills," she corrected me.

"With me, they'll have a different result." Though I remained calm, I imagined my neighbors gossiping about the merry widow sleeping with men so soon after her husband had died. The pharmacist, like everyone else in my neighborhood, knew what had happened to Yigal.

"I wish you had told me that the pills you had prescribed for my bleeding are birth-control pills," I told Henri on my next visit, hesitating because I did not want to appear ungrateful. "I would have bought them in a pharmacy far away from home."

His smile was as warm and kind as it had always been, his affection evident.

"You have no reason to worry," he assured me. "The pills will help your bleeding. I'm a physician, your neighbor is a pharmacist, and that's where the story begins and ends." Then he added, "Besides, it would be only natural for you to be intimate with a man, if it's your reputation that you're concerned about. You have been alone for many months. You are only human."

His remark sounded to me like a recommendation a doctor gives a patient who does not know what is best for her. In truth, I felt no need for intimacy. Since Yigal's death I was sexually numb.

The fact that Henri was married was not paramount to me. He was my dedicated physician and I felt fortunate to have him as a friend in times of need.

That was the situation until Henri scheduled me for an evening appointment, after he had finished his rounds at the ward. Given his position in the hospital, it was not unusual for him to see patients after regular office hours, but this was my first appointment that deviated from our regular timetable. When we were at his office, Henri suddenly suggested we go out. "It's time you see my private residence, where I sleep when I'm on night shift."

I felt my heart quivering. If I suspected that going along would alter our relationship, I pushed that thought aside.

On that first night, Henri merely showed me his modest, sparsely furnished room. A week later, he read some poetry to me. I do not recall what poems they were, except that they were love poems. He recited them with both passion and composure. When he noticed how entranced I was, he kissed me—first hesitantly and then fervently. I succumbed. The man who had won my trust now won my body, too.

———

Henri was neither good-looking, nor bad. He was fairly tall and slender, and had black, thick hair and strong facial features. His dark eyes adapted to my moods, filling up with tears when I talked about my grief. That was the secret of Henri's charm—his ability to identify with the other. He was brilliant and cultured, and he had a sharp sense of humor and a tender if sarcastic smile. Above all, he always looked dependable in his white physician's coat, and I trusted him immensely. The more I saw him, the more dependent I became on our rendezvous, and on the encouragement I got from our conversations.

Henri did not talk about his family life. I had briefly seen his tall, attractive wife when after my miscarriage I had an appointment at his private office in their spacious home in the outskirts of Tel Aviv. He was an art connoisseur, and to my surprise, a painting I had given him as an appreciation for his efforts to save my pregnancy was hanging on his wall all by itself. There, without words, was proof of his praise of my work.

There is little doubt that my sense of gratitude toward Henri contributed to our bond. He had not swept me away as the man of my dreams, but nevertheless we forged a deep intimacy, based on a flawless balance between a wounded woman and a tender and affectionate man.

A gentle, experienced lover, Henri taught me things about my body I had not known. With him, I could escape into a tempest of passion and desire. He strummed its strings like a skilled musician and led me down enchanted paths that brought my sexuality to unfamiliar heights and ecstatic crests. I had had a good, gratifying love life with Yigal, but lovemaking with Henri was different. He approached it like an anatomist, one who had mastered the human body with grace and awe and considered a woman as a masterpiece. He was Pygmalion, I his Galatea.

———◆———

One day I confessed to my suitor, Ehud, that I was involved with another man. When he persisted, I told him it was my gynecologist.

"He's a charlatan," Ehud responded, unable to conceal his anger. "He took advantage of you as your doctor."

"You're jealous."

"His use and abuse are appalling," Ehud insisted, but I remained blinded to Henri's ploy.

All the signs of my doctor exploiting me by taking advantage of my grief and despair were there. But because the affair was a pleasing episode at my time of need, and because it was a healthy reawakening of my dormant life, it was easy for me to think of my relationship with Henry as a pure love story.

I remembered what Lily had told me about the kind of loneliness that ends with a sudden storm. That was how I viewed my relationship with Henri. He helped me navigate the long months of sorrow, leading me to a place where I could forget the reality in which I lived, and deny the facts of my somber existence. Our needs were mutual.

Henry and I met weekly. Neither sickness, nor social obligations, nor bad weather prevented me from going to see him. I would leave a big family event, rushing to Henri, who waited for me eagerly. One time a bus missed my car by an inch or two when I skidded while on my way to him on a torrential night. The driver got off the bus to check how I was.

"I hope you don't have an emergency being on the road at this hour on a night like this" he said. His words and the near head on collision shook me to the core. The storm inside of me mirrored the storm outside.

I felt as if I were giving up control over my life. As if I had relinquished my independence. I was suffocating. I needed to set myself free. Shape my future on my own terms. Change my surroundings. Take charge of my life. Get away, if only for a while.

———◆———

Henry was not happy. "You are evading me." His voice was sorrowful.

"More or less," I admitted. "I have to think. Bring order to my life. I feel like a leaf in a river, floating with no direction."

In the heat of summer there was no better solution than a trip to distant lands. I left in July for a six-week organized tour of Europe. My pregnant sister and her husband drove me to the port city of Haifa to catch my boat to Greece. We hugged and cried as if we would never see each other again.

"Promise me one thing," Miriam said.

I laughed. "I'll have a good time, I promise."

"That's right," Gershon agreed.

I tried. In spite of our dark history there, I embraced the European culture and the new atmosphere the trip had afforded me. What I had learned from history books came to life. The sites in Greece, Italy, Switzerland, Monaco, Lichtenstein, Luxemburg, France, and England were all fascinating for a young woman who left her small country for the first time.

I made new friends who were excited to see the world; others were ready to leave a broken heart behind and start a new life. But the trip failed.

On the boat that sailed us back to Haifa, I was chosen the beauty queen of the ship. As ironies go, I had to dance to the tunes of "The Merry Widow Waltz," from Franz Lehár's operetta of that name. While I waltzed with the man chosen the ship's most handsome, I held back my tears.

On the last night onboard, my roommate, also named Ziva, was awakened by my sobs. She soon joined me. Her life was not a happy one either. "Two miserable Zivas," we said to one another, trying to laugh away our gloom.

I returned home from my tour on August 28, Yigal's birthday. My sister and her husband picked me up. Did you meet anyone? Her eyes begged, but she did not ask. I slept at their house that night, awakened early in the morning when Miriam went into labor. On August 29, her twin daughters, Michal and Yael, were born, sisters to Orit and Gil. Their birth was the confirmation of a new beginning.

Henri was anxiously awaiting my return, and I went back to his arms.

CHAPTER 18

Caught in a Storm

I was searching for my Archimedean point. I thought that if I found it I could toss away my weary world. Less then seven months into our love affair my relationship with Henri had all but collapsed, in spite of the respect and fondness I still felt for him. The passage of time had given me a wiser and more mature perspective, and I no longer depended on him as I once had. As his role in my life was dissipating, so was my love for him. But the change was a bitter pill for Henri to swallow.

As I pondered whether I should cut our ties gradually or do it abruptly and let us both move on with our lives, I remembered Stefan Zweig's *Beware of Pity*, which I had read in my youth. It was one of the books my father had brought home for me, and the lesson I learned from it was that in matters of love, commiseration was a dangerous thing. When I could bear my hesitation no longer, I decided to seek Lily's advice. We were sitting in a small restaurant near our office, but Lily looked so stressed, I was reluctant to talk about my own problems.

"What's up, Lily?"

"Don't ask."

"What does that mean?" I suspected that she was upset with one of her pursuers. Coquettish, she attracted men like bees to honey.

I could see on her face the stress she was under, as if she were going to explode.

"Talk, Lily." My tone was encouraging.

"My life's a mess," she declared, so engrossed in her thoughts that her cigarette nearly burned her fingers.

"Can you elaborate? You're speaking to me in codes I have to work too hard to break. Let me in."

She burst out laughing, the way she always did when someone tried to appeal to her better nature. She lit another cigarette.

"There's someone," she then confessed, "who is complicating my life. It's been going on for some time now."

"Who is he?"

"You know him…"

"He has a name, doesn't he?"

"I'll tell you, but you must promise not to say a word."

"I promise."

"Monty," she said. She then waved a warning finger at me. "You promised not to say anything!"

"I didn't!"

"But your eyes! You do know that your eyes talk, don't you?"

My surprise was genuine. Monty was the nickname of one of Israel's top generals. At that time he was the military aide to the prime minister on the subject of warfare. Lily had met him at one of our department's events, but I had had no idea they had developed such a relationship—although I had noticed she had been looking happier than she had in a long time.

When Lily mentioned the general's name, it hit me that I had seen him at her apartment after her husband's death, acting like a caring old friend. I remembered too that after she and I had had that conversation in her car, Lily had asked me if she could use my apartment during the day. Because of her duties, she spent considerable time outside the office, and was able to disappear for a few hours at a time without raising suspicion. Though I had found it a curious request, I had not refused her. Now I filled in the missing pieces.

"You and Monty in my apartment," I mumbled in disbelief.

"Stop shaking your head," she said, still pointing her finger at me.

"Fine, Lily. But why the stress?"

"Oh, Ziva, Ziva," she sighed. "Now you are asking a good question." She made an effort to smile, but it looked more like a painful spasm. "This is the thing: I am in love, but the relationship won't lead anywhere. I'm going through a tough time ... uncertainty... Do you understand?" She lit another cigarette, exhaling the smoke in a slow and deliberate motion. She looked pensive. "I haven't heard from him for a few days—almost a week, to be exact. It's not like him," she said, revealing at last what was bothering her.

"You've no idea what a mistake it is to be erotically involved with a married man," she added. I noticed that she said "erotically," and not "romantically," and wondered whether eroticism was all that Monty offered her.

In September, with the Jewish high holidays behind us, Lily's mood improved. Monty had called to apologize for his neglect and reassured her that their relationship was important to him. He had valid explanations for his silence, she told me, which she accepted. Once again, we could hear her husky laughter rolling through the office.

"Ziva, *you* need a bond like this," she told me. "It gives you the feeling that you are on top of Mount Everest."

It was the right moment to tell her about Henri.

"Wow!" Lily exclaimed, her eyes wide with surprise. "This is the last thing I expected to hear from you." There was satisfaction in her voice. "So, you learned something from my babble that day, didn't you?"

———◆———

Autumn was at its peak. Its first rains brought along winter's gray shades and evening chills. The safety summer had bestowed on me since I was a child was gone. I felt trapped.

Lily got used to Monty's erratic schedule. The unpredictability kept her tense, if prepared. Whenever he asked to see her, she would run to meet him, anytime, anywhere. When Lily asked me one day to drive her to Jerusalem, I agreed, against my better judgment. Monty was waiting for Lily in a Jerusalem hotel, but her car was in the repair shop. How could I refuse her?

"These are bad driving conditions, Lily, especially for going up the Jerusalem hills," I reasoned. "Not to mention that I have never driven to Jerusalem, and I don't know the city's streets." Though the weather was not as stormy, I recalled the close call on the night I drove to see Henry.

"Don't worry," she urged me. "We'll manage."

"I wish I had your confidence."

"Do me this favor, Ziva, I beg you. This is so important to me."

We got into my Fiat 600, which had replaced my Beetle awhile back, and started to drive. We made good time until Sha'ar Hagai (Gate of the Valley), where the highway begins its rise through the Jerusalem hills, about fourteen miles west of the city. At that point the engine began to sputter, and the strong wind began pushing the car backward.

"What should we do?" Lily asked. I tried to ignore her anxiety.

"We'll let her rest. The climbing is choking her."

I ascended to a spot where we could stop. I did not need to shut off the engine, because it died on its own. By now Lily was distraught. She had told Monty she would meet him at eight and it was almost seven-thirty.

"I promised him I'd be on time," she grumbled.

"So? Things happen. Why are you so worried? He's not waiting for you on a street corner, is he?"

"You don't understand, Ziva. It has been awhile since we saw each other. Besides, he doesn't react well when people are late. I don't want to ruin the evening. It's supposed to be special."

"What's so special?"

She shrugged. "Every meeting with him is special."

"Lucky you, Lily," I snapped. I had little patience for her whining. I turned the key, and the car started. It made the steep slope and glided up the next hill as if it had wings. Lily was elated. Each additional inch got her closer to her Monty.

But five minutes later the Fiat began to cough again, bucking heavily. I had no choice but to stop on the road's shoulder.

"I'm afraid this is it, Lily."

"What shall we do?"

"Look for a ride."

I expected to be able to find a solution to dealing with my car once we got to Jerusalem. Maybe the mighty general himself would be able to help. I turned off the lights, and then the ignition, and got out of the car. Lily remained seated, looking half-numb.

"Get out of the car, Lily." I opened her door and pointed to the sky. "Maybe someone up there decided you're not to see you boyfriend tonight."

"Don't be a defeatist," she reprimanded.

While standing there, stranded, I recalled the last time I had been on that road, months earlier, when my father and I had taken a cab to Jerusalem to watch the Independence Day Parade. Due to my status as a war widow, along with other guests, the government had invited me to attend the parade. At first I had hesitated, but then I asked my father to join me. It was with mixed emotions that I had watched the impressive display of military power. For most spectators, it had been a glorious day.

But there was nothing glorious about being stuck on a gusty night near the capital city, dependent on the help of passing drivers. We waited awhile before a truck driver stopped and tried to start my car. Unsuccessful, he offered us instead a lift to the hotel, which we accepted, though the back of his truck was stuffed with crates packed with cackling chickens.

I could not contain my laughter as I took note of the surreal picture we created: two well-dressed women, one of them on her way to spend a passionate evening with her lover, in a truck stuffed with stinking, squawking chickens. Grateful in spite of the noise and pungent smell, Lily and I arrived at the Jerusalem hotel at last.

"Make sure you don't smell like one of those chickens," I joked. "It'll be much worse than just being late." If a look could kill, I would be dead. Lily had no patience for my sarcasm.

I told Lily that I would wait for her in the lobby and call around for a mechanic while she spent time with Monty. First she vacillated, and then she called Monty's room to tell him she had arrived. "OK, Monty," I heard her say, after she explained her lateness. She hung up the phone and told me that the general would take care of the car later.

"Monty wants you to come up for a cup of coffee," she added.

"Thanks, but no thanks," I said. "I am not part of this drama."

Lily looked disappointed. "I am not going up without you."

"I prefer to stay in the lobby."

"Out of the question," Lily persisted.

Something about the situation bothered me all of a sudden, as if a scenario of which I was a part was unfolding without my knowledge. Though Lily was capable of concocting strange plans, I suspected that it was not she who was trying to embroil me in some bizarre episode, but Monty. He had a reputation as a cunning schemer and a womanizer.

Lily would not let it go. "What are you worried about?" she laughed.

"You and your boyfriend and the schemes you are capable of. I am not doing so badly that I need to be a third wheel."

Once again her laughter cut me off. "A third you won't be, for sure, but a fourth maybe!"

The secret was out. I was angry with Lily for the plot to fix me up with one of Monty's cronies, though I knew she meant well. We agreed that I would go up for a quick cup of coffee and leave without making a scene.

When we entered the room I saw a man in a uniform standing in the far corner facing the window. Unable to see his face, I did not recognize him.

———◆———

Monty was known not only for his skills in military organization but also as an intellectual. A biblical expert who applied the wisdom of ancient tactics to modern warfare, he wrote on the tactical maneuvers of Joshua Ben Nun—the strategist who led the Israelites in their conquest of the land of Canaan. When I had seen Monty at Lily's home, I thought he resembled a biblical warrior himself. His sharp-angled face looked as if a sculptor had carved it. Now, at the hotel room, that aura was gone.

Greeting us politely, he suggested we "feel at home," which Lily did. She prodded me to greet the man at the window.

"Come, Ziva, meet Mano," she said, as if she had known him for a long time. Before I could digest the name Lily had uttered, the man turned to face us. Though we had never met before, he nodded and smiled at me as if we were old friends. I felt as if my heart would stop beating. Curious about my reaction, Lily looked at me, her eyes dazzling with pride. She was satisfied.

———◆———

Major-General Emanuel Castel, as I shall call him, known widely as Mano, was a living legend in my country. He had garnered acclaim for finalizing Israel's victory in the Six-Day War and his brilliant strategy in fighting the War of Attrition with Israel's archenemies and combatting terrorism.

His ancestors were rooted in the land he fought for, having come to the Ottoman Empire from Castile, Spain, after the 1492 Jewish expulsion. In his youth he had joined Haganah, and naturally advanced to its elite fighting force, Palmach. His talents as a warrior were first recognized when he commanded the regiment that broke the siege of Jerusalem in the 1948 War of Independence. He soon became one of the youngest officers in the military's Artillery Corps. After the 1956 Sinai War, Chief of Staff Moshe Dayan selected Mano as the right man to rebuild Israel's Paratroopers Brigade. It was a turning point that led Mano to become the commander of special operations far from Israel's borders. He would eventually climb to the top of the country's security echelon.

On his swift path to the top, Mano had acquired the title "the quiet man." He never raised his voice and he kept his cool even in the heat of battle. For his actions in the Six-Day War he gained further distinction and became one of the most admired figures in the military and among the public at large. During the period between the Six-Day War and the 1973 Yom Kippur War, Israel's military elite had become the state's "nobility," its officers as popular as rock stars. We Israelis viewed them as the best among us: leaders capable of steering the military and the country as a whole to a war-free existence and a safer future. Mano Castel was prominent among those admired figures. There was hardly a day his picture did not appear in the newspapers, and it decorated houses and terraces on national holidays. Esteemed and venerated, he was believed by many to be the most natural heir to Defense Minister Moshe Dayan.

He was the last man I expected to find in the hotel room. For a moment, forgetting the situation I was in, I was delighted to meet him.

A knock on the door brought me back to reality. A room-service waiter entered, wheeling a cart with a coffee service and platters of small sandwiches and cookies. A perplexed look passed over the waiter's face when he spotted Lily and me. An eerie silence ensued after his departure. To break it, I turned to Lily.

"Did you see how the waiter looked at us? What did he think we are, some kind of Bouboulinas?" I referred to the nickname given to the old French widow and hotel owner in Nikos Kazantzakis's novel *Zorba the Greek*. Thanks to the movie adaptation, the character's image had gained popularity at the time.

Lily burst out laughing, and the men followed. I did not think my remark was that funny, but it did break the ice. The laughter in the room did not comfort me, however. I understood that Mano Castel was there by design rather than by chance. I tried to relax, sipping some coffee and tasting a cookie. I even contributed to the conversation. But I could not hide the tension I felt.

Mano turned to me, suddenly. "You feel uncomfortable here, don't you?" His manner was direct, as if we had known each other for a long time.

"Yes, I do," I said. "Not only am I not supposed to be here, but I am tired after fulfilling my duty as my friend's driver. My car is dead, and I want to take care of it so I can get home. Is there any reason for me *not* to feel uncomfortable?"

He was smiling, but he still emitted a sense of undisputed authority, although he was only in his forties.

"I promise you, you'll get home tonight. If your car isn't drivable, we'll take care of it."

I thanked him, inclined, because of his calm demeanor, to trust him.

I was still standing, when there was another knock on the door. It was the waiter, returning with two bottles of wine.

"This is for you, to brighten your dark mood," Monty said. His sly smile and the way he offered the food and drinks, which I suspected had been ordered before Lily and I had arrived, made me feel uneasy.

"I don't mean to ruin everyone's plans," I said, "but I prefer to do my own thing and pick up Lily later this evening."

I detected that Lily felt uncomfortable too, but I could not curb my anger at the "surprise" she had prepared for me: a gathering of two married generals—the highest ranking in the Israeli army, both household names—and two young widows, one of whom had lost her husband to the recent war they had planned and executed. There was something distasteful with that arrangement.

"It's your loss," Monty said, still grinning, in response to my desire to leave. "We should get out of our routine," he then suggested, "and make love in a foursome and then switch partners. Not a bad idea, ah?"

I felt the blood drain from my face and the hair on the back of my neck stand up. I had never heard of such things. My anger at Lily became an inferno, though I knew she could not have planned that part of the scheme. Monty's suggestion, I suspected, both hurt and embarrassed her. The last thing she wanted, I supposed, was to share the bed with another couple, and she did not want him to sleep with another woman.

I got my coat and made my way to the door. Monty stretched his long legs in front of it to block my way.

Mano was still standing, at a distance, next to the window. I did not know what he was thinking about Monty's suggestion, but it did not matter. Horrified, I ran across the room seeking his protection, though he was a perfect stranger to me, relying on the instinctive trust I had felt in him.

"Don't let that man touch me," I pleaded with him. In response to my terror, he held my arms with both his hands and gave me a look that seemed to say, "You are safe."

"It's just one of Monty's mischievous ideas," he said to me in his reassuring voice. "A very bad one."

In spite of the oddness ugliness of the situation, I could not help but notice Mano's tall, strong, muscular body and his powerful yet pleasant face.

But it was time to put an end to the evening.

The two generals drove us back to my dead Fiat. After working on it for a while, they managed to start the engine. We all smiled with relief, and when the car began its descent toward Tel Aviv, they drove behind us to make sure we continued safely along the hilly road. Only when we reached Sha'ar Hagai did they increase their speed, waving good-bye while passing us.

Lily was silent all the way home. As if by an unspoken agreement, she and I never mentioned that awkward evening throughout our long friendship, and I have never found out how it came about.

When I arrived home and began to comprehend how bizarre the evening had been, I remembered that among my pictures was a historic photograph Yigal had loved, one of the few from the period before we met that I had kept. The rest I had given to his parents. The photo was taken in Israel's war room, known as "the pit." In it, Mano is seated at the head of a conference table, lighting a cigarette. He is flanked by such notable figures as Prime Minister Levi Eshkol, who also served as defense minister; Deputy Defense Minister Shimon Peres, who would later become prime minister and president of Israel; Tzvi Tzur, then the chief of military staff; Yitzhak Rabin, then the deputy chief of staff and head of military intelligence, later prime minister, who was assassinated by an Israeli extremist in 1995; Moshe Kashti, then general manager of the Defense Ministry; and three other officers whom I could not identify. Yigal is seated at the end of the table next to a wall map. He was a young, promising officer already then.

———————

I told one person about my Jerusalem escapade, Henri. Still appalled by the event, I related the story to him the next day. Henri, who knew how to calm and console me, remained silent at first. When he recuperated, he said few words.

"You shouldn't have gone."

"I realize that," I said, and in my heart I knew that I had erred in telling him the story.

Unsettled. That was how I saw my life. I wanted to change direction. To start a new page that I alone would compose. To stop drifting away in life's uncertainties. To surrender the feeling of emptiness and allow new things to cross my path. My sister Miriam noticed the change.

"You are returning to life." She stated. It was an accurate description of the state I was in.

———◆———

One evening, a month after the Jerusalem episode, my phone rang.

"Hello, Ziva?" My heart skipped a beat. It was the voice of Mano Castel. Till that moment I had been able to put him out of my mind.

"Speaking."

"I hope I am not disturbing you."

"It's fine," I answered, hoping that my stern tone covered up my excitement.

"I owe you an apology for that night," he said.

"I never expected one," I replied. "It was a hiccup. A bad evening."

I heard the smile in his voice when he replied. "You make life complicated," he said, "but it's good to hear your voice."

"OK, officer, sir," I said, my voice softened. "Your apology is accepted, and I thank you for it."

He laughed. "How about dropping the 'officer, sir' nonsense?"

"What do you suggest, then?"

"Simply 'Mano.'" There was a pause. "I didn't plan to call you," he then continued. "But I haven't stop thinking of you since that night. Next time I'm in Tel Aviv, we should meet for a good cup of coffee."

"Yes, si—, oops, sorry. Certainly, Mano."

The conversation ended on a pleasant note, but I did not put too much weight in it. Mano could have the most beautiful women in Israel, and could not find me especially desirable. Rumors circulated about his relationships with a known actress and an attractive Knesset member.

Besides, I was not in the state of mind to think of him seriously, as I had not yet ended my relationship with Henri.

A week or so later, Mano called again and asked whether I could meet him for coffee the following afternoon. "I have a break between meetings," he explained, "and I think we should seal a renewed acquaintance with that good cup of coffee I promised you."

His straight talk and his familiar, appealing voice did not delude me. He was a married man looking for a fling. I hesitated.

"What's troubling you?" he asked.

"I can count ten reasons…"

He laughed. "Let's talk about them face to face over that cup of coffee, and if you like, we'll have something else."

"If you mean Monty, then, no thanks." I laughed too then, loosening up.

Mano's ability to be captivating was well known. Now I experienced it myself. I was unable to refuse him. The following day I went to the sidewalk café, as we had planned. Terribly appealing in his crisp uniform, he looked younger and more attractive than I remembered him from our Jerusalem encounter. It did not take long for me to tingle all over with anticipation.

He had thick, shiny brown hair, and bushy eyebrows protecting a pair of vivacious dark eyes that could sooth yet penetrate. His stare was almost too intense to bear, and his smile seized my heart. Deep lines that etched across his forehead and from his nose down to his jawline hardened his face, but the deep dimple that adorned his chin softened it.

Sitting so close to him in bright daylight, I discovered an imposing man who did not have to make an effort to look calm, or make those around him feel at ease. Cool and composed, he reflected eloquence and clarity, charisma and authority, all sealed with an enchanting smile. It did not take long for the tension I felt to vanish, as if by magic.

"I heard that you paint," he said, during our conversation.

"You have done your homework." He laughed, and I continued. "Perhaps you also know that I lost my husband in the last war?"

His eyebrows furrowed and his facial wrinkles deepened as he frowned. He looked at me intensely, as if his penetrating brown eyes were seeing me for the first time. His earnestness convinced me that he would be respectful.

We were seated on the sidewalk in view of every passerby. Mano ignored the inquisitive looks directed at him and concentrated on me. It was a good feeling.

"How's the coffee?" he asked.

"The truth? I haven't thought of it. But now that you've asked, it's as good as you promised."

I do not know why I blurted, "I heard you are separated from your wife."

"You did your homework too," he said. "There is some truth to that, but it's not entirely accurate. Are you curious about it?"

"One doesn't have to do homework about you to know these things. Rumors are in abundance. But yes. I want to understand what you mean when you invite a young single woman to have coffee with you."

His stare was penetrating.

"Your cynicism is intriguing." He smiled.

The separation from Henri turned out to be more complicated than I had anticipated. The more I tried to pull away, the more clinging he became. Unwilling to let me go, he tried to lure me back into seeing him in any way he could. When I realized that reducing our meetings was not the answer, I knew I had to stop seeing him altogether. Our last rendezvous took place in my apartment, where he had never been before. It was a sorrowful encounter.

"Is this the end?" Henri asked, his sadness contagious.

I nodded in silence.

"It's Mano, isn't it?" The break in his voice attested to his misery.

He had not forgotten the story I had told him about the Jerusalem incident, and he linked the episode to my diminished interest in him. "He must have contacted you," he grunted.

I understood his distress, but my lessening interest in Henri had little to do with Mano, and much to do with my own growth and my ability to learn to live with my losses. I felt indebted to Henri for being part of that change in me, but I could not go back in time.

Henri interpreted my silence as a confirmation of his suspicions about Mano.

"I'll go to the press. They'll be happy to publicize your relationship," he said, as if he had nothing to lose.

His words shocked me. "What are you saying, Henri? It sounds like a threat."

"These generals do not like negative publicity. It hurts their reputation," he grumbled. "I am not prepared to give you up. You mean everything to me. So I suggest that you don't get involved with him."

"I am not involved, Henri, and I have no such intention."

"Then don't leave me."

It was a disheartening moment, seeing my good-hearted, sensitive friend—a smart, noble, and witty person with a wonderful sense of humor—degrade himself in order to keep our relationship alive.

"Our situation is unhealthy, Henri, and you know it."

"If you leave me for Mano Castel, the press will have a field day. It's not everyday they get a story about such a high-ranking general having a love affair with a widow whose husband died under his watch."

I was repulsed and yet saddened. I had esteemed Henri, and I did not like to see him reach such a low point. Our once beautiful story was now tainted with bitterness, and there was no way back. Seeing me freeze, Henri realized he had faltered.

"Ziva, I'll do anything you want," he softened his voice. "The terms are all yours. Tell me what you want and I'll do it. Just don't leave me."

He left my apartment sobbing.

I will always be grateful to Henri for his gallant attempts to save my pregnancy after Yigal's death, for the things he taught me, for the love he showed me, for helping me survive the dark period after the war, for helping me grow.

———◆———

I did not plan to swap one love affair for another or to get involved again with a married man. I tried to erase Mano from my mind, but I found it impossible not to think of him when I saw his picture in the press. I was certain that he had all but forgotten me, when his call came.

"Good evening, Ziva." The voice was unmistakable.

"Good evening, Mano."

"I thought about your paintings," he continued.

I could not contain my laughter. "My paintings?"

"I want to see them."

I hesitated, afraid of what might come next. But Mano was patient. Pauses between sentences were part of his speech manner. Silence did not discourage him.

"OK," I finally uttered. "When is a good time for you?"

"Now." He was serious.

"I just came home. How about another night?"

I heard him chuckle. "Ziva, with my schedule I don't know what's going to happen a minute from now, let alone tomorrow."

He convinced me, and I found myself swept away in a frenzied, thundering love adventure, and a breathtaking and tumultuous chapter in my young life. Unaware of the degree to which the affair would consume me, I crossed all the red lines I had set for myself when I left Henri. I lost my resolve, as the charismatic general, in his quiet way, conquered me wholly. If Henri brought me back to life, Mano gave me the lust for living.

I assumed then, as I do now, that the effect of constant war and uncertainty was the force that brought Mano and me, and other people like us, together. It led us into a miraculous tunnel, secluded from the world around us, though I was not certain that we would come out together.

Mano often stayed the night at my apartment. For the first time, I shared my bedroom with a man other than Yigal. In my bathroom, once again, there were two toothbrushes.

During one of Mano's first visits, I showed him the photograph with him and Yigal. He held the picture for a long moment. Watching him examine it, I felt that one circle closed and another opened, though I had no clue where that new circle would lead.

"I remember this lad," Mano said, in his quiet, low voice, still looking at the photograph. That is what he called Yigal, "lad." If only he had said "young man" or "man" or "young officer." I wanted to say to him that "lad" did not describe the man Yigal had been. But then Mano remembered the bloody battle that erupted as Israel's armored corps began to ascent toward the Golan Heights, and the legendary burnt armored vehicle, which symbolized that suicidal encounter that led to Yigal's death. I was sitting close enough to see the turmoil that overtook him. So instead of saying what I thought, I froze in a tormented silence. I hoped he would not add something banal about how sorry he was for my loss. He did not, as if he read my mind, his facial expression showing what he felt.

"You can't imagine what happens to a commanding officer when he loses his soldiers," he said then, almost whispering, to himself as much as to me. He looked tender when handed me the photo, and I was thankful for my restraint, as well as his. At that moment I knew that the man I most wanted was sitting right next to me.

———◆———

From the moment Mano and I first made love, we shared stolen hours of exquisite intimacy. At times we made love throughout the night, and he would scream with carnal satisfaction. He knew well how to love a woman. Sometimes we talked endlessly. In the mornings we behaved like irresponsible young lovers, disregarding any neighbors who might hear us laugh or see us naked through my windows.

Though Mano never mentioned the need for discretion, it was an unspoken condition I accepted from the start. Only a handful of close friends knew about the marital crisis he and his wife were undergoing. There were also his twin teenage daughters, with whom he tried to spend as much time as he could. And now I too was added to the picture, my existence in his life kept secret, or so I thought.

His faithful driver would drop him off by my apartment building, or Mano would drive himself, parking around the corner, believing that my neighbors would not notice his official car. I too assumed that none of my neighbors noticed him climbing the stairs to my apartment during his frequent visits. At first he was strict about arriving after evening had fallen and leaving before dawn, making sure his beret covered his rank on one shoulder, his tilted head over the other. I used to make fun of him about that attempt to hide his identity when his face was so widely known.

A few months after we had been together, he had enough confidence in me to give my telephone number to the general chief of staff, so he could call Mano when needed. Except Mano did not warn me about such phone calls. The first time I heard the voice of Chief of Staff Haim Bar-Lev asking for Mano when I answered my phone, I almost dropped the receiver. I was stunned that the highest military officer in the country had my telephone number and called my home so casually, looking for my lover, to discuss military emergencies. Israel's fierce war on terrorism had begun. The Palestine Liberation Organization had infiltrated Israel from neighboring Arab states, and had been committing indiscriminate, brutal acts of terror against men, women, and children. Mano was among the few who were responsible for planning and executing Israel's response to those attacks. Though he never asked me to do so, I always left the room when those calls arrived, giving him the confidentiality I thought he needed.

One morning when Mano did not have his car, we decided that he would leave my apartment and begin walking down the road I drove to work, and then I would come along, as if by happenstance, and pick him up ten minutes later. As he passed a bus station, a young woman waved to him enthusiastically, calling, "Good morning, Commander!" He waved back and continued to walk.

I picked him up a few meters down the road from the bus stop. The waving woman was my childhood friend Livia, who once again lived near me. She had admired Mano since the days when he had commanded the frontier region where she had lived during her military years. Whenever I saw Livia waiting for the bus on my way to work, I offered her a ride. That morning, seeing my car, she began to run toward it as she always did. Except this time I continued to drive, waving to her in a motion that suggested "not today." Baffled, she walked back to the bus station, to see Mano climb into my car a moment later. Livia never asked me about that bizarre incident, not even when I mentioned it decades later, trying to offer an explanation at last. For her, as for others who knew him, Mano remained a legend.

———————

One evening I mentioned to Mano the rumors about him being a charming womanizer.

"Gossip, it's all gossip. Don't believe those tales about me. I'd need time to be the Casanova I'm accused of being, and you know how limited my free time is. You should know it's mostly yours."

We were seated on my living room sofa, munching on meat-filled puff pastry and an eggplant dish I had prepared. Does he tell his wife the same thing after returning home from my arms? I wondered. But I did not care if he did, for no one knew better than Mano Castel how to shower me with love and attention and give me the feeling that I was the only woman on earth.

Mano's regular telephone calls were sweet; his calls on Sabbath afternoons to find out how my beach days had been, or whether I had eaten, were precious. Remembering the sarcastic comment I had made in the Jerusalem hotel room, he used to call me Bouboulina when he wanted to make me laugh. Other times he called me Starshine, from his favorite song in the new Broadway musical *Hair*.

In quiet times after our lovemaking, he opened up, sharing with me his doubts, dreams, and aspirations. We listened to music and relished our conversations on current events, literature, and theater. If there was one thing he regretted he could not share with me in public, it was our love for the theater. Sometimes he would call to tell me that he could not see me on a particular night because he was going to the theater, and I knew he was in his wife's company, in spite of the rift in their marriage. Hemda, to whom he had been married for almost twenty years, had gained her own reputation as a commentator in the field of Hebrew literature. She was impressive and attractive, and although something had broken between them, Mano found it difficult to separate from her.

One evening I had a chance to see Hemda Castel in Mano's company. After seeing a movie, Lily and I decided to go to the Elephant, a popular restaurant in Tel Aviv. It was not far from the neighborhood where the Castels lived, but because I knew Mano was going to the theater that night, I was certain there was no chance of bumping into him.

After the theater, he and Hemda often went to the famous Café Kasit on Dizengoff Street.

To my astonishment, when Lily and I walked in I saw Mano sitting at a corner table in the company of other people. He and Hemda were side by side, their profiles to the entrance. My body stiffening from the surprise and my heart racing, I wanted to leave the restaurant at once. But before I was able to think of an excuse that Lily might accept, Mano turned his head and saw me standing there, hesitating. Self-assured and composed, he nodded and smiled at me. I acknowledged him with my own nod and found a table in a different part of the restaurant. Lily, who noticed our greeting, remained silent. Since the Jerusalem incident his name had not come up in our conversations. Mano stopped by our table when his party was leaving the restaurant. Afterward I learned that he had told them he wanted to greet a former soldier who had served under his command.

"Good evening, Ziva," he said. "How are you enjoying your meal?"

"Good evening," I replied, as calmly as I could, without saying his name. "The food is as good as always. Thanks for asking."

"And how are you, madam?" He turned to Lily, barely waiting for her answer.

"It's good seeing you, Ziva. I hope to see you again sometime soon." Then he nodded to Lily and left.

Lily got it.

"I am furious at you," she said. "How could you keep this from me, your closest friend?"

I was too enthralled with Mano's cool manner to pay attention to her reprimand. And I felt no compunction to tell her about my affair with Mano, since she had figured it out. I asked her to drop the subject, and she acquiesced. Her ability to accept boundaries even between us was a side of Lily I loved.

"Just one thing," she said. "Nothing will come of it."

———

Glancing at Hemda Castel, who I knew to be ten years older than me, I saw an attractive woman of maturing beauty. Her auburn hair was styled in a French twist, its dark color emphasizing her light skin. I knew from Mano that she had gray eyes, which must have been accentuated by the color of her hair. She looked like a woman no man would give up without difficulty, a woman no other could easily compete with. But I had no intention of competing with her. All I wanted was to hold onto the joy Mano's presence bestowed on me in the privacy of our secret romance.

Mano was eighteen years older than me. I brought out the youth in him, and he behaved like a teenager discovering the thrill of a new love. Ecstatic, I would jump into his arms as he walked through my door, and he would hold me tight. We then slow-danced to popular love tunes, and he would seem exquisitely happy, able to free himself from the heavy burdens of being Major-General Mano Castel. Occasionally the metal rank insignia on his shoulders scratched my face, and he would kiss the scratch over and over again, and then move his lips to every feature on my face, and I would feel complete.

Slowly I realized what the true situation was between Mano and his wife. This man, who had the reputation of being the ultimate military strategist, vacillated when it came to making a choice about his own life. But beguiled by his allure, I too would do nothing about my situation, precarious as it was. I was a woman who lived for her lover, needing to fill the missing pieces in my life while I ascertained who I was and where I was heading. It took time and disappointment for me to realize what a cliché my affair with Mano Castel was, in spite of the love with which he showered me.

I was not the only one swept up in that enticing existence. Mano too needed the digression, as did his contemporaries in the military. Perhaps this was the common thread between him and Yigal—the need to validate their masculinity by having as many women as they wanted, without equating their behavior with betrayal of their wives or fiancées or viewing their acts as an aberration from the love they felt for them.

One evening when Mano returned from a trip to the United States, he surprised me with a thoughtful gift. In addition to a pair of elegant leather gloves, he presented me with a first-rate transistor radio, so we could listen to music in bed. That night, relaxing after lovemaking, we heard Simon and Garfunkel's "Bridge Over Troubled Waters." At the end of the song he promised to be such a bridge for me, from ocean to ocean. It was the first time I heard him say anything about the future. A week later, during the verse "I love you" in another song we heard, he nodded his head, smiling, pointing his finger at his heart, then at me, as if to say "my heart is yours." Throughout all those long months, neither one of us ever uttered the word "love" to the other. We did not need to.

That night I asked him what I meant in his life. He gave me one of his famous pensive stares.

"To ask this is like walking with an arrow to a target and sticking it in its center," he said at last, dodging my question.

"You are evading me."

"Yes, Ziva, I am," he said, nodding in agreement, "because our situation isn't simple, and neither is the answer."

"I am listening," I said.

His discomfort was evident. "I wouldn't want any of my words to be misinterpreted by you," he uttered. "But I can tell you that when we are together, or when I think of you, and by now you know that I often do, you are the most important person in my life."

"This evasion is insulting."

"I was afraid of such a response."

"I want to understand what my place is in your world, outside of here."

I knew the answer, and in fact I had from the start, walking into this affair with open eyes. And I did not intend to break up his family. But I expected an answer.

"You know that outside of this place I am a different man, a fact I never hide." He articulated his words in his usual way, pausing between them. "When I come here I am loaded with a tremendous responsibility, but with you my stress vanishes like a dissipating cloud."

He then took me in his arms, holding me for a long time before whispering, "I do not like to use clichés, but you are extremely dear to me. More than you know."

One night I revealed to Mano that I had consulted with a psychic I had met through a friend.

"Are you interested in such amusements?" he wondered.

"Not usually," I admitted, never having spoken to a psychic before.

"So what did that fortune-teller predict for you?"

"He was certain that I'd live abroad for many years, married to a diplomat."

"Good," he said smiling. "I will replace Yitzhak Rabin as Israel's ambassador in Washington, and...."

My forced, nervous laughter interrupted his sentence. It was a careless comment, I thought. If it dawned on me that the remark could be a test not a tease, I ignored it.

——◆——

Friends who knew nothing about Mano thought I should start dating. But single young men did not interest me. Because of my experience, I considered these youths too childish to grasp or handle my situation. When I managed to meet a particular suitable man, it did not work out. When my romance with Henri ended, I had dated a childless divorced man who, seven years older than me, seemed like a perfect match. But when in an intimate moment I called him "Yigal," he broke up with me, unable to "compete" with a dead man.

On another occasion, deep into my relationship with Mano, I went on a blind date with a young man who came from Jerusalem to meet me. But as long as I was under Mano's spell, that handsome, bright, and seemingly kind young man had no chance of developing a relationship with me.

When I arrived home from my date that evening, my phone rang. It was Mano, raging. "Where were you? I have been calling you all evening. I came from the other end of the country to see you, and you were not home."

It was the first time I got furious with him.

"I had a blind date with a single man," I said. I cared little if I sounded emphatic.

He was silent for a few seconds, but then continued. "I had arranged for a special helicopter to take me to Tel Aviv to surprise you, but you weren't there!" He did not bother to suppress the disapproval in his voice. It was the first time he was angry with me.

"You are a married man," I replied, equally annoyed, "feeling free to live your life the way you want. I cannot sit home waiting for your unannounced visits."

There was a silence again, and then an apology. He would see me the next day, he asserted; I would be waiting, I promised. We spent that night as if nothing had happened.

Months passed, our affair continuing as ever. One afternoon, Lily's cousin Susana and I went to a trendy Tel Aviv restaurant not far from my office for lunch. My heart began to race when I saw Mano with three high-ranking officers. As befitted a discreet lover, I did not acknowledge him.

"Ziva, look who's here!" Susanna whispered. "It's Mano Castel. I'm crazy about him!"

She laughed like a child, and I smiled casually, hoping he would not approach me as he had in the other restaurant. But after Susanna and I were seated, Jacky, the restaurant owner, brought me a dish that

I had not ordered. It was a delicacy made of chicken-livers and mushrooms placed over phyllo dough. Bending over, Jacky whispered, "The Major-General sent the lady my specialty of the day, of which I'm very proud."

"Please thank the Major-General for me. But I don't eat liver. Please don't be insulted," I added. "I'm sure that my friend will enjoy this dish, which looks sumptuous."

I found Mano's gesture unsettling. How would he know that I do not eat liver, I thought, we have never dined out together.

Composing myself, I nodded to him, showing appreciation, and he nodded back, flashing his notorious warm smile.

"What's going on?" Susanna asked, sounding suspicious. "I'm sensing a flame between you and the general, the passion that can light a fire. How do you know him?"

I used his lie. "We have know each other for a long time. I worked under his command when I was in the army."

"Ah!" she sighed, the envy in her voice unmistakable.

A year into our relationship, Mano and I were again in a restaurant at the same time. He did not nod when he saw me coming in, nor did he look in my direction throughout the meal. As he continued to ignore me, I longed for one glance, a tiny sign of recognition. He is immersed in a serious conversation, I thought, trying to console myself. He will surely call me later today. That he might have had reason for this discretion was irrelevant to me.

I panicked when no call was forthcoming. It is over! Our enchanted journey is no more. He is no longer interested in me. Such thoughts set my head spinning. Time had stopped. My misery was as deep and dark as a well, my agony profound.

"Hallo, Ziva" he said, his voice as affectionate as always, when he called the following day.

"Yes, Mano." I was ready to hug the world, heat radiating through my chest.

He apologized for being unable to pay attention to me in the restaurant and promised to make up for it that evening. "I can't wait," I assured him, not certain that I wanted him to hear my breathlessness.

He lived up to his promise. He was loving and passionate, gentle and thoughtful. But something had broken in me the day before, and I could not fix it. Like a vase my mother used to talk about in my youth—the cracked one that can never be whole again once it had broken, even if glued back together.

Mano was fast asleep when I made my decision, lying motionless next to him, feeling as if my lungs were collapsing, my hands cupping my mouth lest I begin to cry: I could no longer be enslaved to Mano Castel's love or allow myself to suffer such misery as I had endured the previous day. Not for a married man. I had to leave him if I did not want to grow old as his lover and be rejected by him when he no longer desired me. Yet, bonded to him by my love, I knew I did not have the strength to leave, not with him so near. I would take another trip abroad, I resolved, though I was flooded with apprehension.

On my turntable I played Miriam Makeba's heart-wrenching "Forbidden Games," her gentle voice and lyrics giving expression to my predicament.

CHAPTER 19

Doubts

Turbulent days followed as, filled with qualms, I agonized about how to escape the undertow into which I had been so breathlessly swept. It was a painful decision, but I was determined to end my relationship with Mano.

Though his role in the mess I was in was undeniable, I blamed myself. I could have abided by my resolution not to get involved with another married man after Henri, but I did not. Besides, Mano had never made any promises to me. An occasional hint perhaps, inspired by a tender moment, but nothing I could take seriously. We stood on shifting sands, on which every footprint was erasable by a passing wind.

I did not tell Mano that I wanted to end our relationship. I knew that he would try to change my mind and that I would succumb.

———

"You behaved despicably," Miriam scolded me. Gershon, by her side, nodded in agreement. They were standing a few feet away, looking down at my slouching figure on their living-room sofa.

I had barely said hello to the man who had walked into their house and introduced himself. I had remained slumped on the couch, sitting gracelessly next to him, showing not an iota of interest, though he appeared to be a well-dressed, gentle, educated man.

"You could at least have been courteous," my sister nagged. "But instead you chose to embarrass Gershon and me."

Weeks earlier, on the same sofa, I could not stop sobbing while Gershon preached to me about the predicaments, both moral and practical, of having a love affair with a married man—let alone a man like Mano.

I had shared my secret with my sister, and, unable to keep it to herself, she had revealed it to her husband. Angered by her betrayal and disappointed at her self-righteousness, I could not forgive her. She had inherited her sanctimonious attitude from our mother, who would have been scandalized by my forbidden love affair. Though disturbed, I was relieved that my sister had not involved my parents, too.

Gershon did not try to hide his contempt and disapproval of my involvement with Mano, whom he viewed as an older man who had deceived me. Me, he saw as an unscrupulous adventuress.

"Somewhere there must be a young man who meets your expectations," Gershon said, concluding his discourse, and Miriam agreed.

"Don't be so judgmental!" I shouted, tears gushing down my cheeks.

"You don't know what loneliness is, and you have no idea how single men behave when they meet a young widow." Three years later my sister herself would be widowed; in time, her priggishness would vanish with life's lessons.

Though disparaging, Gershon was correct. I had often wondered how I, a person with an otherwise unquestionable sense of decency and integrity, could permit myself to carry on affairs with married men. I would answer my own question with a great deal of sarcasm. You still have your principles, I would think. You would never sleep with a man whose wife you knew, and you are faithful to your lovers.

But even now, I do not regret my experiences, for I have known great love, and I learned great lessons about the meaning of dignity, independence, and determination.

Soon the next suitor appeared, and I discovered that Miriam and Gershon had hired a matchmaker for me.

"We meant well," she said, using that old mantra when I confronted her. But when I saw her tears I could be nothing but forgiving. Holding her hands, I reassured her that when I was ready I would meet the right man on my own. Then it dawned on me that my sister not only wanted me to meet a man, but she wanted me to meet one immediately. Unable to bear the thought that we would be separated, she had sought to prevent me from leaving the country, as I planned to do.

———

It was with haste and trepidation that I left the home I knew, the family I loved, and the life I lived, after receiving a sudden offer from the Defense Ministry. This episode began at my grandparents' home on a summer evening in 1969.

I visited my grandparents regularly, but that particular evening I went to their home to see my cousin Tzvika and his wife, Havi, who had immigrated to the United States more than a decade earlier and were making one of their rather infrequent visits to Israel.

Theirs was the first condolence cable I had received after Yigal's death, sent as soon as my Aunt Sarah, Tzvika's mother, had informed them. They remembered me the way I had been the last time they had seen me: an insecure teenager, not yet fifteen, too shy to speak.

When they received the news, they had been aghast not only by the death of a young man, whom they had never met, but by the thought that the timid young girl they remembered had been left alone and pregnant. It was thus not surprising that our meeting at my grandparents' home was emotional.

"*Vous hertzech*, Zivkale?" my grandfather asked in Yiddish, using one of his nicknames for me and asking how I was doing. My grandmother stood by his side, waiting for my reply.

"I'm planning to go on a trip abroad," I answered. "But I'm not sure yet where I'll go."

"You are coming to America to stay with us," Havi exclaimed. Her enthusiasm was reflected in her wide grin and the gleam in her eyes.

"America?" I asked, with much less zeal than that with which the offer had been made.

"At least consider the option. Our home will be open to you for as long as you want."

I was thinking of a three-month trip that would provide me the space to reflect and the time to gather the strength I needed to leave Mano. After giving it some thought, I accepted my cousins' offer. But airline tickets to New York were expensive. I was getting by financially, and when in need, I supplemented my income with typing jobs. But after Yigal's parents, with whom I maintained a close relationship, had taken the share of our savings they were entitled to, using it, they said, for a memorial in their synagogue; and after I had paid for my journey to Europe the previous year, my savings were depleted. Besides, the Defense Ministry was still planning to stop its death benefits to child-less war widows after a yearlong extension.

Considering my options, I came up with the idea of flying on one of the Defense Ministry's freight flights to the United States, which by then was Israel's sole arms supplier.

I had a mixed relationship with the Defense Ministry. Although I was still fighting its discriminatory policy, through my activities I had developed a cordial and mutually respectful relationship with Arieh Fink, head of the ministry's Rehabilitation Bureau, who welcomed my idea with enthusiasm.

"For how long do you want to stay there?" he asked.

"Three months, if I find a place I can afford; one month if I don't. I don't want to be a burden on my cousins for longer than that, which is too long to begin with." I told him that I needed some time on my own and that the trip was important to me. He surprised me with another question.

"Tell me, Ziva. Are you ready for a real change in your life?"

I had no idea what he was leading up to.

"If you want to live abroad for a longer period, I can make you two offers—a position in Paris or one in London."

It was much more than I had expected.

"How long of a period are we talking about?" I asked.

"Not months," he explained. "You would have to make a two-year commitment. I think it'll be good for you for a variety of reasons, even though right now it may sound like too long an obligation."

It would do the ministry good, too, I thought, with a degree of cynicism, defusing my pending threat to take the benefits case to the High Court of Justice.

"You want to get rid of me?" I asked. I was not joking.

"An interesting idea," he admitted. "But we're not there yet. I'll make some inquiries, and let's see where it gets us."

I agreed, but did not take the plan too seriously, having little confidence in the bureaucratic process it would require. I was shocked when I received a call two weeks later from a lieutenant colonel who was in charge of my excursion. Fink and he had wanted to send me to Europe, he said. But the London mission had no openings, and the one in Paris was too inhospitable for the colonel's taste. They chose New York instead. I should be ready to leave in a week. Not only do they want to get rid of me, but they want me to be far, I thought with mixed emotions. My head was spinning.

Because I did not consider the initial offer as being serious, I had not discussed the matter with anyone, let alone made plans to leave. If I was to go overseas, I needed at least a month, I told them, and the ministry agreed. But I still hesitated. Leaving behind my whole world for years rather than months was not something I could do in a casual manner.

First, there was my family to consider. My mother and my sister could not bear the thought of me leaving, even for two years, and it was almost incomprehensible to think about parting from my sick father.

"Go," he said, without hesitation. "It may be the chance of your life." It was not his style to tell me that he would miss me. But for years after his death, time and again my mother would tell me that each day my father would remark that there was nothing he wanted more than to see me. To this day I wonder whether she knew that she pierced my heart each time she told me that.

Then there was my work on behalf of childless war widows, which put me in a real dilemma of having to choose between what I considered my moral duty to stay the course of what I had started and my need to put my life in order. By the time I had to make the decision, the benefits issue had gained publicity and assumed a life of its own, and I could get away.

———————————

I gave notice at work, even though only weeks earlier my job had gained permanent status, thanks to the tireless efforts of the head of the main office in Jerusalem. Needless to say, he was angry about my leaving. I also had to rent out my apartment and store my belongings. Except for saying my good-byes, dispensing my things was the hardest part of my departure. Those that were from my life with Yigal, I sent to New York. I kept them for decades, until some broke, and others got lost, and a few were stolen. Among the precious stolen items were Yigal's and my wedding rings and the small diamond ring he had given me for our first anniversary, after my first miscarriage.

And there was Mano Castel. I kept my plan a secret from him, fearing that he could sabotage it with a single phone call he did not even have to make himself. I will forever remember his facial expression when I told him I was leaving for New York for two years. White as a ghost, he seemed to go numb at first.

"When did *this* come about?" he wanted to know, when he recovered from the initial shock.

"A couple of weeks ago." My heart was racing.

"And you didn't find it necessary to tell me earlier?" Not used to that kind of behavior on my part, he gave me a bitter smile. I did not think it necessary to explain to him why I wanted to leave.

"Don't go," he said. If he realized that he was the reason for my leaving, he did not show it.

"It's too late for that, Mano."

"New York is not for you," he tried to persuade me. "It's too big; it can be cruel. Stay here, this is your home."

"I promise you, I won't get lost," I said, not sure where my confidence came from.

He sensed my tenacity.

"Then I'll come visit you," he said, after another pause. "And we will continue to see each other on your visits back home."

He seemed unable to face the fact that I was leaving him. The gloom on the face I loved made my body shiver, but I was also satisfied by my resolve.

The following day he called, his voice longing.

"We only have a month left till you leave. I must see you often."

With those simple words I questioned my resolve to leave.

———◆———

I was given a diplomatic passport and a one-way ticket to New York. My salary would be manageable, if modest, and the Defense Ministry would add one hundred dollars each month toward my rent, the equivalent of the death benefits I had received. In addition, the ministry would secure a room for a month in a hotel near where I would be working, while I looked for an apartment.

"Let me repack your suitcase," Mano said, the night we parted, looking at the red-and-black-checkered luggage I had bought for that trip. He thought he could do a better job than I had done. We were sitting on my living room couch, the bag resting on the floor, ready for my trip the following day. With a certainty symbolic of my newfound independence, I declined. That night we hardly slept.

A week earlier, at my parents' apartment, about forty of my aunts, uncles, and cousins had come to say their good-byes. It was a bitter-sweet farewell party. I still have the tiny pocketknife my Uncle Yossef, owner of a cutlery shop, gave me as a gift, to use for self-defense in a city that was then notorious for its crime rate.

On September 29, 1969, I departed for London, where I would spend two days with a young couple, Mano's acquaintances, who were warm and hospitable. It had been my decision to stop in London, but Mano insisted that I not stay alone in a hotel, and I acquiesced.

My mother, my sister and brother-in-law, and my Aunt Sarah escorted me to the airport. I wore an elegant suit that had been made for my trip by the seamstress who had sewn my wedding dress five years earlier, and a pair of long earrings my sister had given me as a farewell gift. In the airport, she took off the earrings she was wearing, and gave those to me as well. Photos of my departure reveal my nervous yet smiling face next to the somber faces of my mother, my sister, and my aunt. After our tearful good-byes, I walked to the gate without looking back, for I knew if I did, I would not find the strength to leave.

———

"I must ask you something," the pretty young woman walking by my side said to me thirty-seven years later. Her big eyes were as blue as the sea before us.

"Go on."

"How could you leave all this?"

The "this" she referred to meant the world to me.

The woman was my daughter, Odellia. Though she knew many of the stories of my past, I appreciated her sudden need to know more about how I had said good-bye to my country almost four decades earlier.

The two of us were walking on Tel Aviv's waterfront esplanade with her toddler, my granddaughter Gabriella. It was a hot summer afternoon. To the east, new high-rises had changed the skyline I once knew. To the west, the Mediterranean sprawled as it always had, glittering with the warm sun.

Odellia did not allude only to the sweet scent of the Mediterranean summer emanating from the transparent powder-blue sea and the scorching golden sand. Nor was she talking only of the scenery, of the rows of persimmon orange, hunter green, and ultramarine blue umbrellas protecting beach-goers; or of the beach-front cafés or the hip urban shops and restaurants.

Nor was she referring just to the old and new sections of Tel Aviv, the history and art museums, the theaters and concert halls, all telling the story of a vibrant society and a rich culture. She did not mean just the neighborhood and home where I grew up, our visit there with her own daughter being the highlight of her trip. The thrill she felt when we entered my childhood house, her daughter in her arms, consumed me as well. It was a unique moment that would never repeat itself, like the moment my father put in my hands the silver cup that had been in our family for generations.

No. What Odellia referred to when she asked me her question was also the deep love and warmth that family and friends bestowed on us wherever we went, as they always do when I visit the place of my birth. She referred to the intense shared feelings I left behind when I gave up all that was so dear to me and I moved to a far and unknown place across the oceans.

Odellia had visited Israel many times before. But it was the first time she was there with her own child, her motherhood revealing to her a real and painful picture of the day I left everything I loved: home, family, and country.

"Life can take you to places you had not planned to be, and force upon you decisions you never thought you would have to make," I answered, hoping that I had experienced enough of life's uncertainties for her and her children, too.

CHAPTER 20

New York, a New World

I arrived in New York City on the first of October 1969, three months shy of my twenty-sixth birthday. My cousin Tzvika met me at Kennedy Airport.

"There were two fellows here from the Defense Ministry expecting to take you to your hotel," he said. "They left after I told them that I was taking you home."

Home was in the Jewish section of Flatbush, where every neighbor knew the others. It was not unlike the sociable lifestyle I had come from. So warm was the welcome bestowed on me by my cousins and their three young daughters that moving to the Manhattan hotel my government provided me for the first month of my stay was not an option I considered—even though I would spend three hours a day commuting from Flatbush to Manhattan and back.

Nothing that awaited me the following day was familiar to me. I was on my way back to Brooklyn, after a short visit to the office where I would work for the next three and a half years. Something must have happened, I thought, alarmed, as I walked to the subway station at Lexington Avenue and Fifty-first Street. Why were so many people running in the same direction, looking as if they were in frenzy?

It was my first encounter with Manhattan on a Friday afternoon. The tumult, I soon learned, was the usual rush before the start of a weekend.

That morning I had joined my cousin's tenant on the commute from Brooklyn to Manhattan so that I could learn my route.

"Remember, do not make eye contact with anyone on the train," my cousin's neighbor, a thin, pale, frightened-looking man, warned me. Lucky to find a seat on the packed subway during the morning rush hour, I sat motionless, scared to look at any of my fellow commuters. But I could not avoid the big, tall man standing in front of the passenger on my left, holding a half-opened newspaper in one hand over the middle of his body, with his other hand hidden underneath. Curious, but unsuspicious, I craned forward to look under the newspaper, for the man was not reading it.

"LOOK WHAT HE IS DOING!" I yelled, in my fresh foreign accent, when I saw that the man was masturbating. To my amazement, no one reacted, not even after the man ran out when the train stopped at the next station. No doubt, in the city I had come from only days earlier such an episode would have stirred a huge commotion.

"Are you insane?" my companion asked when we got off the train, even paler than usual. "You could have gotten yourself killed with your screaming. You're lucky the man ran off the train instead of stabbing you."

Mano was right, I thought, troubled. He had warned me about New York's madness when he tried to persuade me to stay home.

———◆———

On Monday, October 6, I started my regular work schedule at the Defense Ministry Mission in New York. Seated in my office, with the door open, I noticed to my utter annoyance a trickle of coworkers parading by, stealing glances at the new arrival.

"You were all too obvious," I would remind my friend Batya through the years.

"What did you expect?" she asked, recounting the story. "We heard that a war widow was arriving from Israel. We anticipated a middle-aged, matronly looking woman. Instead, the news spread that a young, glamorous, well-dressed woman with nice legs and high heels had arrived."

I had smashed a stereotype. That characterization of how a widow was expected to look was not the full extent of the socially constructed image of women who had lost their husbands, especially those husbands whose death in war was glorified by society. For widows were expected not only to look their part but also to *behave* it, and act far more righteously than widowers were permitted to act.

Within a short time of my arrival, I began to receive offers from wealthy New Yorkers to be kept as a mistress. Those men were unable to understand why a young woman of moderate means would refuse a most affluent lifestyle. "Sugar daddies," who treated women as tradable property, were in abundance on the city scene. Being an Israeli war widow made me more attractive, because of the way Americans, Jews in particular, romanticized it.

But of all the incidents during those first days in my new environment, probably none typified the experience of newcomers to a foreign country more than the following episode. On my second day at the office, having made no friends, I went alone to lunch at the nearest restaurant I could find. It was Chock Full o'Nuts on Lexington Avenue and Fifty-first Street.

"A haamboorger, please," I said to the waitress behind the counter, in my foreign accent, sounding out the syllables. Hamburger was not my favorite food, but it was familiar enough for me to order. The waitress's response sounded to me like a bark, no part of which I was able to understand.

"A haam-boor-ger," I said, slower this time, but the waitress again barked impatiently.

"A h-aa-m-b-oo-r-g-e-r," I repeated, for the third time, enunciating each syllable. I was by now close to tears, less because of the humiliating experience than because it reminded me of what I missed: the comfort and familiarity of home.

"For heaven's sake," a man seated at the counter next to me scolded the waitress. "Stop being so dense and give the kid a burger already."

He explained to me that the waitress had wanted to know how I wanted the patty to be made.

———◆———

After a month in the city, I found a tiny ground-level studio in a brownstone building on Manhattan's Upper East Side. A rather tall window facing the street gave it the aura of space, but the iron bars I had installed for safety imparted a cage-like ambience.

I remember with fondness the evenings I spent in my small studio with my girlfriends I made in New York, lamenting about being single in our late twenties. Although I did not quite fit in the same category, having been widowed, I was single nonetheless.

I recall the troubled looks my cousins had on their faces when they first saw my place. So proud was I to invite them to see my new home that they dared not voice their concerns. Only after I had moved to a safer apartment following two frightening incidents did they confess to me that they had regretted allowing me to sign a lease without their seeing the apartment first. Their concerns were just, stemming from the steady rise in violent crime in New York City in the 1960s and 1970s, a trend that began to subside in the early 1990s. Today, there is a luxury high-rise in place of that small, ivy-covered building in which I first settled.

I made friends and assumed a rich cultural life. But I missed home. Because overseas telephone calls were costly then, I corresponded with family and friends through letters written longhand (an art that has all but disappeared), limiting my overseas telephone use to speaking with my parents and sister.

Less than six months after my arrival in New York, I was ready to leave.

"Give it one more month, and see another doctor," Ezra, head of personnel, urged, when I was prepared to break my commitment and make arrangements to return home. "That is how long people say it takes to adjust to New York City. By then, I am sure your condition will improve."

My "condition" was facial swelling and a bad rash covering my entire body. A doctor had diagnosed it, after probing into my background, as a condition caused by stress, resulting from my longing for home. He suggested that I return home at once, if I cared about my health. Though prepared to make plans to act on his recommendation, I sought a second medical opinion. This time, my condition was diagnosed as adult rubella, or German measles. I waited the month, as Ezra had advised. It did not take much longer for me to fall in love with the city and what it had to offer: its rivers and parks; museums; music, theater, ballet, and opera; foods and restaurants. It was a culture, or cultures, new to me, and the famous anonymity seemed a luxury to someone coming from a society that did not respect privacy the way other societies would.

But leaving Israel and adjusting to New York did not end my relationship with Mano, although that was the reason I had left my home in the first place. Some months after my departure, he came to my new city on a fund-raising trip as a guest of a prominent Jewish organization. Missing him and too weak to refuse him, I joined Mano in his suite at the Essex House Hotel. Freedom and anonymity turned the few days we spent together into magic, as intense as if our romance had never been interrupted. Though we frequented Broadway and dined out openly, the meals I recall most were the private, elegant breakfasts served in his hotel room. I have often wondered what he did with the many photos he took of me that week, including the intimate ones.

He left me alone to attend one or two important meetings. One was at the Waldorf Astoria with Prime Minister Golda Meir, who had stopped in New York while on an unpublicized trip to Washington. The Nixon administration was trying to broker Israeli-Arab peace negotiations, talks Prime Minister Meir and her cabinet opposed.

When the time came to say good-bye, the separation was harder than I expected.

The last time Mano and I spent together was in June 1970, when I returned for a visit to Israel.

"A man was calling for you," my father said, when I arrived at my parents' apartment.

"From work?" I inquired.

My father raised his shoulders. "He wanted to know if you had arrived yet."

"Did he tell you his name, Abba?"

"He didn't leave his name, but his voice was familiar. It sounded like Mano Castel."

My father could not have been mistaken. Mano's voice was too distinctive and widely recognized.

"It could have been him." I tried to keep my voice steady. I was surprised Mano had called my parents' house. For a moment I felt important in his life, wondering whether he missed me so much that he could not wait for me to arrive.

———◆———

A few weeks after I returned to New York from that visit, I found out that I was pregnant. It felt surreal, being with child, alone, after all I had gone through trying to have a baby with Yigal. At first I wanted to see the pregnancy through, but given my past miscarriages, doing so while living alone so far from home was irrational. I toyed with the idea of going back to Israel and staying with my parents through the pregnancy, perhaps making up a story of a quick marriage and divorce to override the embarrassment it might cause them. But my mother was taking care of my sick father, and the living conditions in my parents' home had not changed for the better. My sister had four young children to take care of, and I was sure her husband would not approve of the situation. Agonized, in August 1970 I had an abortion, without Mano's knowledge. But I shared my secret with Lily, who insisted that Mano must be told.

"He has to know," Lily kept saying to me over long-distance phone calls.

"He doesn't," I would reply, to no avail.

And so, against my wishes, Monty told Mano about my abortion. Though Lily's and Monty were no longer romantically involved, they remained close friends.

In contrast to my illegal abortion in Israel, I had this abortion in Mount Sinai Hospital, months after New York State had decriminalized the procedure. Dr. Kaplan, the physician performing the procedure, recognized the extent of the damage caused to my cervix the night I lost Yigal's and my baby. In all his years of practice, he said, he had never seen a case like mine.

"What happened, and who did that to you?" he wanted to know.

"I can't go there," I answered, refusing to speak of it.

"When you are married and ready for a child, come see me," he said. "You'll need very special care."

During the abortion procedure, though I was fully anesthetized, my body shook violently. Dr. Kaplan ordered neurological tests afterward, but they showed no epilepsy or other brain disorders, which he wanted to rule out. With the help of a neurologist, he determined that the uncontrollable shaking was the result of profound fear, which I could not control even while unconscious.

My friend Aviva waited in the hospital throughout the procedure, and took me home when it was over, a kind gesture that both of us still remember.

After the abortion I never heard from Mano again. Perhaps he could not forgive me for aborting his child without his knowledge, or else he thought it was not his. I knew him to be unforgiving when he thought his honor was compromised. Though ignoring me was a dishonorable act, I wanted closure on my own terms and called him on my next visit home, in the spring of 1971.

"Ahuva, he can't talk right now," his secretary told me, returning to the phone after she had put me on hold. This is Ziva, not Ahuva, I wanted to correct her, but I did not. About a year later he came to New York, visiting the Defense Ministry mission, where I still worked. Because Bundy, the head of the mission, thought me to be "the most respected and most elegant woman in the mission," he occasionally asked me to guide Israeli dignitaries around to cultural events or shopping venues of New York. My past relationship with Mano was unknown to him, and he asked me to help Mano with his shopping. I agreed, for seeing Mano one last time would have given me the closure I never had. But it was not to be. Appearing distraught, Bundy entered my office and released me of that chore. It was clear that Mano did not want to see me.

For years I imagined bumping into him on the streets of Tel Aviv or New York, confronting him with questions about the disrespectful way in which he dropped me after he had learned about the abortion. But that, too, was not to happen. Rapid illness took his life six years after I had seen him last.

CHAPTER 21

The Rape

O nce I decided to stay in New York, I enrolled in the School of Visual Arts to further develop my painting skills. When my instructor compared my brushstrokes with those of the Spanish Renaissance painter El Greco, I thought he was flaky. But when he insisted that I adhere to my unique style, I recalled that my former teacher, Professor Arieh Margoshilsky, had given me the same counsel. And though I doubted my ability to become the artist I aspired to be, I continued to study. I produced numerous paintings but kept none, succumbing to self-criticism and dissatisfaction with my mediocre work.

But I excelled at my job. I became the purchasing agent for one of Israel's most important defense industries, a position I sought when it became vacant. At first my immediate boss rejected my proposal because I was a woman, a reason I could not accept. Only after I reassured him that I would be the first to admit to him that I had overreached in my ambitions, should I fail to do the job "like a man," was he persuaded to support me. I worked independently, outshining any of my male predecessors.

I felt worthy in my new position and enjoyed the cultural richness my adopted city had to offer. Most important, I got over the bad ending of my relationship with Mano. Hurt, but not ruined, I knew my worth and came to see that a man who esteemed his honor beyond reason, who could treat a woman he loved as he had, deserved neither my love nor my pain. It was time to mend my life and move on, meet a serious single man, and build a family. My father's words—"Go, it might be the chance of your life"—echoed in my mind with both encouragement and hope. Just then, when a new vitality shot through me with invigorating strength, I was numbed by another blow.

Aaron, a military man, had been Yigal's best friend, and he and his wife, Rachel, became my trusted friends. Aside from the relationship between our husbands, Rachel and I became dear to one another, and I saw in our closeness the quality that makes everlasting friendships.

Aaron and Rachel were the first couple to whom Yigal had introduced me: "Meet Ziva, the woman I chose." Throughout our courtship and marriage, we saw them at least once every week. After Aaron had been relocated and with his family had left Tel Aviv, we spent most weekends together, alternately staying in each other's homes.

I remember with both pain and melancholy a particular Friday evening the four of us spent at the ballroom of the Dan Hotel in the mountainous area that overlooked Haifa's glittering bay. I sat at our table with Aaron, watching Rachel and Yigal dance. When the singer started in on Frank Sinatra's "Strangers in the Night," Yigal stopped dancing with Rachel and fetched me to the dance floor. For the rest of our friendship, Rachel used to remind me of that night in Haifa. With tears in her eyes, she would repeat Yigal's words to her: "Forgive me, Rachel, but this dance is Ziva's. This is her song." The song still moves me.

Soon Aaron was promoted, and he and his family moved back to the suburbs of Tel Aviv, and we saw each other even more. Loyal friends that they were, Aaron and Rachel were distraught over Yigal's death. Before I left for the United States, I spent countless evenings in their home, mourning Yigal together. Short of Miriam and Gershon, they were the couple closest to me. Aaron treated me the way a brother would and was always kind and respectful. Once I accepted the offer from the Defense Ministry to move to New York, he was instrumental in helping me secure the terms I desired.

Defense Minister Moshe Dayan came to New York for a visit in October 1970, and Aaron, who by then had a high position in the defense establishment, joined Dayan's team. We arranged that after dinner with Dayan's group, I would sleep in a spare room in Aaron's spacious suite at the Carlyle Hotel, for the following morning we were to be picked up early for a trip arranged for him by the United Jewish Appeal. I was to be his interpreter.

I felt it was natural for Bundy, the head of the defense mission where I worked, to invite me to be part of the small group that joined Dayan for dinner, more so after he had asked me to rush to a nearby store to buy ties for Dayan, who had no proper attire, informal man that he was. It seemed to me just as natural for Bundy, who was aware of our familial relationship, to ask me to be Aaron's translator.

The evening with Dayan was extraordinary and memorable. Following dinner, Bundy had arranged for the group to see the new Broadway musical *The Rothschilds*. For security reasons, we arrived at the theater a bit late, when the musical was already in motion. As we took our seats, a whisper passed through the theater like a wave. When the word had spread that Moshe Dayan, the legendary general with the eye patch, was among the latecomers, the entire audience stood up and together with the actors on stage began to sing the Israeli national anthem, "Hatikva."

Israel's stunning victory in the Six-Day War three years earlier was still a source of great pride for world Jewry in general and American Jews in particular, for it was the United States that had become the Jewish State's main ally after that war. Never before had so many mainstream Diaspora Jews identified with the State of Israel, which was still caught in the midst of the War of Attrition waged against it by Egypt and Syria. Dayan, the admired hero, was at the peak of his glory.

To this day I can feel the rush of emotions that overtook everyone in our group. I was so captivated during those enchanting moments at the Lunt-Fontanne Theatre that I did not bother to wipe the tears off my face. Somehow able to compartmentalize that experience from what followed that night, I still marvel at that embracing audience and cast.

We left the theater early, once more for security reasons. On the way out, Aaron whispered to me that Dayan had asked him who I was, and that my story had moved the general. Aaron then told me that he did not know what time he and Dayan would be back at the hotel, emphasizing Dayan's unpredictability, and suggested that I go to sleep, for we had a long day ahead of us.

A friend named Michael walked me to the hotel. "This plan doesn't sound good to me," he said. "It's a foolish decision that could end in a way you do not anticipate." But I did not listen to him. With a key to Aaron's suite in my possession, I entered one of the bedrooms at half past eleven, locked its door, and got ready to go to sleep.

At two in the morning, I was awakened by Aaron's banging on the suite door. When I opened the door he was angered by the time it had taken me.

Sleepy, I went back to my room. But Aaron followed close behind me and stopped the door with his foot. There was a strange smile on his face, of a kind I had never seen before.

This cannot happen, I thought, Michael's warning hitting me with full force. To hide my fear I decided to be firm and show self-control.

"Aaron, what are you doing?" I asked, pretending to be calm, though my heart was pounding with fear.

"You know," he said, blocking the door with his tall body.

"Please let go of the door," I said, "and let me close it. I'm tired. I want to go to sleep. We have a long day tomorrow."

My appeal to his common sense did not work.

"I'm coming to your bed to sleep with you," he said.

Stay cool, I told myself, terrified. Perhaps he is drunk, unaware of what he is doing. I will order some coffee for him. But he pushed me into the room and then onto the bed and started to kiss me.

"Stop it!" I screamed. I struggled to get away, but he kept at it.

"I want you," he moaned, in a voice I had never heard him use before.

Please, God, I pleaded. Answer my prayers now. Do not let this happen. But God had nothing to do with what followed.

"Get off me," I shrieked. "You're hurting me."

He did not heed my cries. I tried to push him off with all the strength I had, but he fought back like a vicious animal. With the sound of my heartbeat thrashing in my ears, I screamed, hoping that my shrieks would penetrate his head before he did something he would regret for the rest of his life. But he continued, and so did I, hitting him with my fists and kicking as hard as I could. He was a tall, strong man who weighed twice as much as I, and my violent struggle seemed to arouse him more. He managed to pull his pants down with one hand while holding me down with the other. Cruel and terrifying, he was a rapist like all other rapists, whether in hotel rooms or in dark alleys.

"No," I screamed, at the top of my lungs, hoping someone would hear me and call for help. Perhaps *he* would. But he was brutal.

Change strategy, I thought. Plead with him; maybe he will come to his senses.

"Rachel—what about Rachel?" I cried.

"She said that with you it was all right."

"Yigal, remember Yigal. He was your best friend!" I pleaded, as if Yigal were in the next room. As if I were calling him to save me from his friend, who had turned into a beast.

"He's dead," I heard the devil say.

At that moment the reality of Yigal's death became crueler than ever before. It was as if he died all over again, and his death had left me too vulnerable. He was dead, and I was a piece of meat, no longer his widow but merchandise that exchanged hands. Beastly hands. Inhuman hands.

I could hardly breathe, but I continued to fight until he suddenly let go of me. He had climaxed, only partially penetrated inside of me. I managed to push him off and ran to the bathroom. More than anything I felt dirty. I washed frantically, sobbing.

When I came out of the bathroom I saw my rapist sleeping, as if nothing had happened, while I was shattered into pieces. Though the room was heated and I was dressed for the October chill, my body was shaking. All I wanted was to leave the room, to get away from the place I would never forget. New York City taxis were on strike, and I walked home in a daze, caring little whether anything happened to me. My world had crumbled.

I arrived at my apartment at dawn, mentally and physically exhausted, my body aching from my fight with the villain. In the entranceway to my tiny apartment, Yigal's framed photograph glanced at me, and I hated him with all my heart. A scary hatred. One I had not felt before. I hated him for leaving me alone and for having the friends that he did. I smashed his picture into the wall with as much force as I had used fighting Aaron a short while earlier. The glass on the frame shattered into as many pieces as my broken heart, but that was insufficient. I also tore the photo into small pieces, as many as I could. I then fell on my bed and began to cry.

Not trusting myself to be alone, I called my friend Nira, but I could not utter a word. Only strange sounds, those of a wounded animal, came out of my throat. Nira, thinking there was a pervert on the other side of the line, kept hanging up her telephone each time I called, until I managed to whisper, in a voice that did not belong to me, "He raped me."

"Ziva, is that you?" she screamed, not recognizing my voice. It did not take long for her to get to my apartment. We stood together for a long time, silent except for the sound of my sobs.

Before seven my telephone rang. "Where are you? Why aren't you here?" Aaron asked, as if nothing had happened. "The driver and I have been waiting for you." I hung up, and he did not call again.

For the following two weeks, I isolated myself at home. Bundy was looking for me on that Monday. When I returned to work he did not ask questions, but he never asked me again to usher visitors around the city.

I considered charging Aaron with rape but refrained from doing so. My first concern was that the publicity of the case would crush my parents, and that they would not survive the knowledge of what had happened to me. And the whole idea frightened me. Like other rape survivors, I feared that I would be accused of provoking my own rape. No one would believe me, I thought in panic. What was I doing in his hotel room to begin with, they would ask.

I was also certain that Aaron, holding a high position in the military and defense establishments, would abuse his power even further. Nothing was beneath him, I presumed, my mind running wild imagining an army of false witnesses he would be able to recruit, who would assassinate my character. I feared he might know about my past relationship with Mano and would use it against me in a trial. If I had had an affair with one married man, people would suppose I had slept with him, too.

My fears were not irrational. It was not until the late 1970s and early 1980s that so-called rape shield laws were adopted by various jurisdictions in the United States, limiting the ability of defense attorneys to cross-examine rape complainants about their past sexual behavior.

I was also thinking of Rachel and her children. Tormented, I would look at the latest photos of the children she had sent me, asking myself not how their father could do what he had done to me, but what my pressing charges would do to them.

Four months after the rape, after a visit to Israel, I received a letter from Aaron in which he reprimanded me for the pain I had caused Rachel by avoiding her during my stay. She had learned about my visit from a mutual friend.

The cynicism notwithstanding, I felt uneasy about hurting Rachel and wrote her a letter, explaining that I had come to Israel at the spur of the moment to be with my sister while my brother-in-law had undergone an operation. Rachel understood. We met a year later under the most awkward of circumstance, which, to my regret, I allowed to ensue. Afterward, unable to pretend any longer, I stopped all contact with her. Another year passed, and on a visit to New York she reached out to me, but I could bear my silence no more. In the privacy of her hotel room, I explained to her why I had severed our relations. It mattered little to me that she did not believe me. It mattered even less a few weeks later when, calling me from Israel, she related to me Aaron's version of events: I was waiting for him, naked, in his bed, seducing him.

I refused to lower myself to that level of discussion or dignify his accusation with an answer. It made no difference to me whose version Rachel believed, and I did not expect to hear from her again. But a few weeks later she called.

"Ziva," she said, "I know you told me the truth." My wounds remained so deep that I cared little about how she had discovered that truth. It was the last time we spoke for forty-five years, until the summer of 2016, when we met fortuitously in Tel Aviv. It was a bittersweet encounter, followed by an overseas conversation or two. Whether we would be able to rebuild a friendship, as she hopes we do, I do not know.

Nearly thirty years after the rape, when attitudes toward sexual harassment and rape had changed in many parts of the world, I was able at last to share that experience within the framework of my lectures on women and war. I looked into whether I could still press criminal charges against Aaron, but he soon died a dreadful death from bone cancer.

Changes in sexual harassment laws and attitudes have transformed the lives of American women, and to my satisfaction Israel's Knesset also passed a law making sexual harassment a criminal offense. For decades, rumors had been circulating in the country about the commonality of sex offenses carried out by high-level officials and military officers, but the truth had always been swept under the rug, and none of the offenders were charged. That changed in 1999, when the new law passed. Since then numerous officials have been sent to jail for rape and sexual harassment, including high officers in the military and the police force, cabinet ministers, and a president. On the international scene, the 1998 Rome Statute, which created the Permanent International Criminal Court, determined that rape used as an instrument in times of war, was a war crime.

Since then support for victimized women grew considerably. The changes in this area have been made to a large extent because of brave women who did not hesitate to declare, "We have been victimized and we will be wronged no more."

CHAPTER 22

Stephen

The rape was a deep emotional setback at a time when I was ready to rebuild my life. For a time, instead of moving forward with persistence and determination, as I had planned, I withdrew, seeking instead solace in isolation. Even though I anticipated that I would not forget that horrific night soon, I did not expect the brutality inflicted by a friend I had trusted to haunt me to this day.

Still, I was determined to put it behind me. After two weeks of seclusion I decided that I would not allow the experience to paralyze me any longer. You will fight the demon that tries to tell you that misery is your lot, I told myself.

I resumed my painting classes. The act of expressing myself in strokes and color felt right. I was fortunate to have the friends that I had. On weekdays I worked, took classes, and spent time with a small circle of these supportive friends; on weekends with them I resumed quenching my thirst for the rich cultural life the city offered. We saw plays and visited galleries and museums. We discussed books and took long walks in Central Park and on the East River promenade. At times I traveled to Washington or Philadelphia to be with other friends and visit museums there. My friends knew to leave me alone when I craved solitude. But when I needed comfort, their support was invaluable.

Among my New York friends was an Israeli woman my age named Danna. She and her husband, Misha, surrounded themselves with a group of Israeli friends. Among them was a man whose name, coincidentally, was Yigal, a charming and outgoing fellow. When we first met, he smiled at me and said, "Mark my words. I'll marry you off soon."

Though I did not take him seriously—he was not only a kibitzer, he also liked to drink and play around with women other than his wife—I agreed to a blind date he arranged for me. But when I learned that the man was married, I decided not to date any of Yigal's pals in the future.

———————

"My name is Steve," a caller with a mature and commanding voice introduced himself one Saturday morning in November 1970. When he told me that he had received my telephone number from Yigal, I was about to hang up. But my instincts made me hesitate.

"I have just picked up my curtains from the dry cleaner," he said in a serious manner. "And I have no idea how to hang them. How about coming to my apartment and helping me do that?" Amused by his strange invitation, I burst out laughing.

When he mentioned his address, I noticed that he lived in the same apartment complex as Danna and Misha, and decided to check him out. So instead of rejecting his eccentric request straight off, I told him I was busy at the moment and asked him to call back in an hour.

I phoned Danna to ask her whether she knew an acquaintance of Yigal's named Steve, who lived a building away from her and Misha. She did not, but she promised to check him out. Within minutes she called back, agitated. She did know Steve, she said, and he was married.

"What else could one expect from Yigal?" I asked Danna before I hung up the phone. But she called back. She had made a mistake. "It's another Steve," she said. "The Steve who called you is single, and he's a great guy. In fact, Misha wanted to introduce him to his sister, but Steve wasn't interested. "Believe me Ziva, you have nothing to lose. Go help him hang his curtains. If you don't, Misha will not speak to you again, and I'm with him on that."

True to his word, Steve called back. "So what about the curtains—are you coming?"

As it turned out, Steve and Yigal knew each other through soccer, a sport to which Steve has devoted a great part of his life as a player, representing the United States in the Pan American games, and as a life-long supporter dedicated to promoting the game in the United States. Convinced that Steve and Yigal were not close friends, I saw his invitation to help with the curtains in a different light. To my surprise, Steve later told me that when Yigal gave him my telephone number, without disclosing that I was a war widow, he presented me as a special woman he should call only if he sought a serious relationship. That was Yigal, too.

When I arrived at Steve's building, the doorman directed me to an elevator without ringing upstairs to announce me. When I rang the doorbell, an attractive guy opened the door. He looked at me, puzzled.

"The curtains?" I said, but the guy at the door had no idea what I was talking about.

"I'm sorry, I don't have any. But now that you're here, I wish I did." He smiled.

"You are not Steve?" I laughed.

"You're in the wrong side of the building," he said, after I showed him the address.

What a great story that could be, I thought, once he had redirected me, my zeal to meet Steve diminishing. But when I arrived at the right apartment an even better-looking guy opened the door. He looked athletic and masculine, though a little too short, and was quite handsome, with light brown hair and the bluest of eyes underneath thick eyebrows. His apartment was tastefully furnished for a man who could not hang his curtains. I soon learned that he had bought the apartment's refined items, curtains included, from the former tenant. He had little patience for selecting furnishing, though I later learned he spent a great deal of time choosing his fine clothes.

It felt natural hanging the curtains and talking with Steve, and the more we talked the more comfortable I became. That is, until Steve started to be a man like all other men.

"Is that what you usually do with the help?" I asked.

I threatened to leave, but he suggested we go to the movies, and so we did. The movie depicted a Jewish American lifestyle that was foreign to me, and I made a point of saying so. It turned out his parents lived that way: In winters they rented a small apartment in Florida and in summers they stayed in a bungalow colony in the Catskill Mountains.

In the movie theater Steve took my hand, and I submitted. I felt connected and secure, in a way I had not felt with a man who was single and available since Yigal had died. We ended the evening at Ginkgo Tree, a popular Chinese restaurant in his West Side neighborhood, which has long gone. We read our fortunes. Mine was unremarkable, but his said, "Your ideal person is here." We laughed.

Though it had been an extraordinary day, I decided I would not date him. Not only did I find him too short, he was an American, and I was planning to return to Israel a year later, when my term with the government was to expire. But he continued to call, and I continued to see him. Over time, I discovered his radiant personality and fine inner qualities. He was wholesome, generous, interesting, smart, and funny. He was a man who loved to live, even though his income was modest, as he was a Brooklyn Assistant District Attorney. Above all, he treated me with a maturity that had been lacking in any other young man who had sought my company.

"I will disconnect the phone," I offered, when Steve stopped at my apartment during the beginning of our relationship. My phone never stopped ringing.

"I don't mind the phone," he said, smiling, while sorting through my eclectic record collection. "In fact, one of the things I love about you is your laughter when you talk on the phone." He was fascinated by the number of friends I had. "What happens when you enter a room is incredible. The way your friends surround you with so much warmth. I'm not used to that. I had a girlfriend for two years who had no friends at all." He then mentioned some other unflattering traits she had.

"And yet you stayed with her a long time," I commented.

"She is very pretty," he confessed, "and I was attracted to her beauty. But I wasn't committed to that relationship." Then he corrected himself, befitting an attorney. "But her beauty is not as delicate as yours; her skin is not as smooth." He smiled and touched my face.

"Lucky you," I said, mocking him.

There was a whole list of other compliments he bestowed on me, from my "vivaciousness and sense of freedom" to my "sense of humor," but no less important was my strong connection to our common heritage.

For a person I later found to be quite reserved, he revealed a lot to me. His girlfriend had wanted to marry him. But their relationship was devoid of meaning, he said. He had either broken up with her already or was breaking up with her when he met me. The details were unimportant to me, but I was troubled by the fact that he had been with her for a long time in spite of the way he seemed to feel about her. He gave me the impression—a wrong one, as I would learn—that he was an indecisive man. Being a bachelor at thirty-two was not the norm then, either.

My hesitation notwithstanding, Steve and I began seeing each other regularly, except, at his insistence, on Friday nights, an arrangement I neither understood nor appreciated.

"What would happen if I insisted that we go out tonight?" I called to ask him one Friday evening.

"What if I said no?"

"Try."

I went to his apartment that night and found him there, wearing a pair of exercise shorts and a T-shirt, resting in an armchair and watching a basketball game. It was one of his old habits. But he had another habit of going with a bachelor friend of his to Friday night parties. My daring paid off. That practice ended that night, and we began to see each other on Friday nights.

Three months into our courtship I sprained my ankle—as ironies go, on a Friday. That evening Steve hurried me to the St. Vincent's Hospital emergency room, where an orthopedist friend of his awaited us. When the doctor instructed me to stay off my feet for three days, Steve insisted that I stay with him. He took care of me the way a caring man should. I alternated between pain and laughter, for Steve was blessed with a sharp, if unusual, sense of humor. Because cooking was not his strong suit, he ordered food from nearby restaurants. By the end of the weekend we had dined on dishes from the finest eateries on the Upper West Side.

"What should I get us for lunch?" he asked me on Sunday.

"Gourmet food, of course," I kidded.

"Only the best for you," he announced when he returned. With fanfare and pomp he served me a huge chopped-liver sandwich he had bought at Fine and Shapiro, the most popular kosher restaurant in the neighborhood. Thankful for his effort and enthusiasm, I did not tell him about my aversion to liver. I ate the sandwich at a snail's pace, taking tiny bites and rolling up my tongue so I would not taste the liver. After what seemed like an eternity, I had managed to eat less than a quarter of the sandwich.

"What's the matter, don't you like chopped liver?" Steve looked at me, puzzled, as if I had deserted my heritage.

"I hate liver!" I screamed, half-gagging. We could not stop laughing.

My thoughts took me back to the Tel Aviv restaurant where, three years earlier, Mano had sent over to my table the chef's special, also made of chicken livers. I could not help but reflect how far I had come from that moment, when I had had to hide my relationship, forbidden to be the free-spirited woman I was. And so, my spontaneous if discourteous divulgence at Steve's apartment was a liberating moment for me, the importance of which was not evident to me in that moment.

Before long, I rushed off to Israel—arriving, by coincidence, the day before my brother-in-law was to be operated on his Melanoma cancer. Steve received my postcard, in which I mentioned sickness in my family, he called my sister's house and offered to come to Israel to be with me during those difficult days. He found me there through the return address on the postcard. I declined his kindhearted offer, but I was beginning to understand that I had met a decent man.

———◆———

Not long after I returned from my trip, I was shocked to discover a young man masturbating in between the two doors at the entrance to my small apartment house. Two weeks later another man entered the building in the middle of the night and began pounding on my door so hard I was sure he would break it. I called the police, but they showed up more than half an hour later and by then the man had left. I was petrified, and I do not know why I stayed in my apartment that night, but when I told Steve the story the next day he was adamant that I leave my ground-floor studio and move into his apartment that night. I did. But I was still not sure about our relationship, and was resolute about having my own place. I found a spacious one-bedroom apartment that I shared with a friend who spent most of his time abroad.

Six months into our relationship, at a dinner-dance the Defense Ministry organized to celebrate Israel's twenty-third birthday, Steve confessed that he had fallen in love with me. I still remember what I wore that night: It was a long maroon dress I had bought that morning.

It had a small, exotic print, a Chinese collar that accentuated my neck the way I wanted; my arms were bare, and my legs were visible through the flowing gauzy fabric. And I had a new hairdo that heightened my face. None of those details escaped Steve's sharp eyes. He was impressed when Bundy, the mission's head, approached and asked me to make a plea to the assembled guests for donations for Israel's security needs. He apologized to Steve for taking me away from him for part of the evening, but no one else in the room, Bundy said, had my ability to persuade the crowd. If I suspected that Bundy was using my widowhood, I did not protest.

And yet, not long after that night, I broke up with Steve. A chain of misunderstandings irritated me to the point that I supposed I would be happier without him. During that time, Steve called to tell me that his father had suffered a stroke. Though sympathetic, I refused to see him. But I missed him, and after several weeks had passed, I agreed to meet him for a brief coffee in my neighborhood. The minutes turned into hours. We resumed dating, and soon I moved in with him.

In September 1971, ten months after we first met, Steve went with his closest friend on a two-week trip to Prague and Budapest. A week after his return, while we stood under the shower, he asked me if I wanted to get married. Not "Would you marry me?" but "Do you want to get married?"

"To whom?" I asked, as if I did not understand.

"To me," he smiled, and I gave a big "yes," because I loved him and he was the right man for me, at the right time in my life. He was the man I had promised my sister I would meet, without the help of a professional matchmaker.

We planned a small reception at the St. Regis Hotel in Manhattan. Together we bought my wedding dress, a striking, long Victorian style, with a skirt of blue velvet and a white organza silk top. Its long sleeves were delicately embroidered, and the low décolleté was square. A maroon satin ribbon separated the upper part from the lower, emphasizing my thin waist. But the wedding we desired and the dress we chose did not satisfy my future mother-in-law, Pearl, with whom I had a difficult relationship. She sent Steve a harsh letter, in which she demanded a big wedding for her son. She did not decline to express her disappointment in my dress. Though she did not say so, her displeasure about the small reception and the uncharacteristic wedding dress stemmed from her concern that both things insinuated that her son's bride had been married, a fact neither Steve nor I hid.

There is an endearing tale about Steve's mother's antipathy toward my marital status. One day, while walking with her granddaughter (and my future niece) Elizabeth, she met a friend on the street.

"What's new?" the friend asked.

"I have great news," Steve's mother rejoiced. "My Stephen is getting married!"

"*Mazel tov.* You should have a lot of *naches*. And the bride," the friend whispered, "Is she Jewish, or is Stephen too, like my son, is marrying a…"

"An Israeli, no less!" Steve's mother interrupted her friend, unable to hide her pride.

"Did she get her bridal dress already, your future Israeli *shnur?*" The friend continued to probe.

The joyful mother tried to evade that question, but her friend was quick-witted. Listening to Steve's mother's sputtered description of the dress, she grasped the truth.

"Was she married before?" she inquired.

"Of course not!" Steve's mother said in a steady tone that could fool her prying friend.

At that moment, young Elizabeth interrupted. "But Grandma, she was, too. Don't you remember that her husband died?"

No one was more delighted about that story than Steve's father, whose nine-year-old granddaughter had put his wife in her place.

In spite of my efforts to ignore Steve's mother's interference, there were times I felt I should rethink our nuptial plans. But with his father's poor health and my brother-in-law's deteriorating condition, Steve and I decided to hasten our wedding date. The event would give Miriam a pretext for bringing her husband to New York, and from there she would take him for a consultation at the Dana-Farber Cancer Institute in Boston. I made a gesture to Steve's mother and asked her, to her delight, to help me choose a different dress. Together we went to B. Altman's department store, where I selected a simple long, white dress. She was pleased, even though it was not a bridal gown.

———

The wedding was set for the twenty-third of December, three months after we had decided to marry. But I got cold feet about our relationship one more time. First Steve told me that he had met his former girlfriend for lunch to tell her that he was getting married. "It was a decent thing to do," he explained.

I did not see it that way. "No," I exclaimed. "The honorable thing to have done was to ask me if I would mind you doing that."

Afterward, one of our friends phoned to warn me that Steve's friends, her husband included, intended to surprise the groom with a call girl at the bachelor party they planned for him. By the time Steve called to remind me about the blood tests we were to have that afternoon in order to obtain our marriage license, I had made up my mind.

"No blood tests are necessary," I declared. "There will be no wedding."

His silence was piercing.

"Steve," I said, keeping my voice as steady as I could, "too much has happened." I alluded to his meeting with his old girlfriend and to a blunder during the early part of our relationship, but I could not mention the surprise that was awaiting him, having promised our friend that I would not repeat what she had told me. So I mentioned the bachelor party, which was foreign to my culture.

"Don't worry about the party. It's a long-established American custom that means nothing to me."

"You are not marrying an American woman," I reminded him. "Perhaps you should."

Minutes later, one of my coworkers rushed into my office to tell me that Steve was in the lobby, having a heated argument with a security guard, who refused to permit him to come upstairs to my office.

"Steve is going crazy," my friend alerted me. "You'd better run downstairs."

A pale and distraught Steve took me aside. "I am a sure thing," he pleaded. "I dedicate my life to you. Do not cancel the wedding!"

My heart went out to him, and the wedding took place on the date it was planned.

Gershon died on that same day at home in Israel. His death was kept a secret from us until we returned from our honeymoon in the Swiss Alps. My parents did not make it to our wedding either, my father being too ill to travel. Instead, they sent a poignantly worded telegram, which Steve read out loud at the wedding.

Losing two sons-in-law within four and a half years broke my parents' hearts. How strange it was that on the day they lost one son-in-law, they gained another far across the ocean.

———◆———

Steve proved himself a *mensch*. A criminal attorney, he is both sharp and tolerant. His decency as a husband was first tested when Rachel arrived in New York with Aaron and their children. She could not be happier for me, she said, and when she insisted on visiting Steve and me with her family, I did not know how to refuse her. It was a year later that I revealed to her that her husband had raped me.

Steve and I had no secrets, and his reaction to my torment about whether to have them in our home was measured and discreet.

"It's your decision and I'll respect it, even though I despise the man," Steve said.

I agreed to the visit, a decision I still regret. In hindsight I know that I should have saved both of us from the horrifying experience of hosting the man who raped me. But at the time I still chose to hide the truth from Rachel. I hoped that Aaron would have the civility to stay away, but he joined his wife, shameless man that he was. All I could do was ignore him and attend to Rachel and the children. Steve was ice cold to him. Later I learned that Aaron expressed to Yigal's and my friends his disappointment in my choice. His audacity knew no bounds.

———————

Steve turned out to be a most adoring partner and a committed family man. His love for our daughter, Odellia, is endless. He loves and respects our son-in-law, Richard. Our two grandchildren, Gabriella and Jacob, bask in his infinite love. He has been generous to my family in Israel.

Our marriage has been successful by most measures, with its share of the usual ups and downs, satisfactions and disappointments, crises and resolutions. I would like to close this chapter with two memorable episodes.

I always visited Yigal's parents on my trips back home, and when Odellia was eleven months old, I brought her to meet them. They greeted me with their usual warmth, although they could not conceal the pain on their faces. While we sat at the table sipping cold drinks, Yigal's father stood up, took Odellia from my arms, and lifted her up and down in the air the way any grandfather would do.

"Where's Grandpa? Say hello and smile to Grandpa," he said with each lift, and each time my heart broke to pieces. My mind wandered back to the hospital, six years earlier, when I told him that I had lost the grandchild he so wanted.

He then took Odellia through the glass door that separated their living room from their terrace. By then they had moved from the single-family home they had lived in for most of their lives to a second-floor apartment. He held Odellia outside the terrace railing, with both his hands beneath her tiny armpits, swinging her from side to side.

As I watched them from the living room, I became so terrified it felt as if my heart stopped beating. Yet I could not bring myself to run to the terrace to grab my child from his arms, lest the gentle man who had once been my father-in-law think I did not trust him. My sister, who was there with me, seemed as horrified as I was.

"Do something," my eyes pleaded with her, as we exchanged looks. At long last, Miriam stood up and walked toward Yigal's father. Gently, she took Odellia from his arms, explaining to him that the height might scare the baby (who seemed to be enjoying the ride).

I continued to bring Odellia with me whenever I visited them. Yigal's mother never could hide her agony and tears, and I believe being a witness to that has made Odellia a more compassionate human being. She still remembers the clothes Yigal's mother wore the last time she saw her.

The second episode occurred six years into my marriage to Steve, during my nephew Gil's bar mitzvah in Israel. Yigal's parents were among the numerous guests invited to the celebration, which took place at my sister's house. They accepted the invitation, though they knew I would be there with my husband, whom they had not met. Many of the guests, family and old friends, were aware of the imminent meeting, and we all awaited Yigal's parents' arrival.

The room went quiet and everyone watched as I, with Steve a close distance behind me, walked to my former in-laws. I greeted them with the usual tenderness I reserved for them. Then I took Steve's hand and walked him toward them, and in a voice as steady as I could manage, I introduced my husband.

"It is a pleasure to meet you," they said to him in Hebrew, and I translated.

"It is an honor for me to meet you," he replied in English, and I translated. The moment was over.

I never told them that during our first year of marriage, at a fundraising breakfast for the UJA, when attendees announced their donations in honor of their loved ones, Steve donated money in honor of his wife's fallen husband. I was not there to hear it, and it was not he who told me.

I met my husband, Steve, in 1970, when he asked me to help him hang curtains. I felt connected to him from the moment we met, and he has been an adoring partner and committed family man. It's a sign of his character that a year after our marriage, without me knowing, he donated money to the United Jewish Appeal in memory of Yigal, my first husband

AFTERWORD: MOVING ON

Four months into our marriage, Steve left his position at the Brooklyn District Attorney's office and started a criminal-defense practice with one of his colleagues.

In 1973 we were blessed with a little girl, a miracle baby, as my gynecologist referred to her. We named her Odellia, meaning "I will thank God" in Hebrew. I had a difficult, bedridden pregnancy, and Odellia was born eight weeks premature. She weighed two pounds twelve ounces.

"Your baby has little chance of surviving," the doctor who treated me that night in the hospital said. "It's you we are worried about."

"This baby *will* survive!" I told him, feeling assured. When I heard her cry the moment she came out of my womb, I *knew* she would. Nothing bad would happen to her. Not my baby girl. Not this time.

My precious Odellia spent six weeks in an incubator at Mount Sinai Hospital's premature infant ward. I watched her from morning till night, every day. After work, Steve would join me, and together we watched her put on weight, ounce by ounce, and grow stronger.

She was five weeks old when I was allowed to hold her for the first time. My baby girl felt so tiny and vulnerable in my arms. "Trust me," I whispered to her. "I'll protect you from now until I am no more." Holding her close to my chest after all those months of anxiety and anticipation felt like nothing less than a miracle.

"Be careful when you feed her," the nurse told me when we were taking her home. "She doesn't know yet how to breathe and swallow at the same time, and she might at times turn blue." I was terrified, but she and I managed. It took ninety minutes to feed her, every three hours. First two ounces, then three, four, and so forth. At three months old, my daughter looked like a healthy newborn.

But it was at that age that she had to endure two surgeries that could have been related to my need to take hormone shots during my pregnancy. What was supposed to be a routine pediatric hernia operation, lasting no more than half an hour, turned into a three-hour surgery when her surgeon discovered that her tiny ovary was cystic, twisted, and gangrenous. He removed that ovary, and called it a miracle, saying she would not have lasted another day because of the gangrene. In spite of her swollen groin and heartbreaking cries, her pediatrician had misdiagnosed the symptoms.

Ten days after that first surgery, on New Year's Day, 1974, we rushed her to the hospital with a bowel obstruction, the result of abdominal adhesions from scar tissue. Our poor baby was operated on again.

At eighteen months she had to undergo yet another surgery, this time to fix a heart murmur. For three weeks I watched her day and night. Her every breath, her every move. For three weeks, until she was declared to be in perfect health, I kept my strength. Then my strength gave out, as now I saw danger everywhere. Fear took over my entire life. That old demon came back, except that now it was after the being dearest to me, my precious daughter. I had to defeat that fiend for good, and so I did.

When my daughter was four and five, I suffered two miscarriages. Though Steve and I yearned for another child, I decided to end the abuse to my body, and we stopped trying. Odellia, who grew into a beautiful, charming, witty, compassionate and sensitive woman, has more than made up for that disappointment. In 2001 she married Richard, her perfect match. Their daughter, Gabriella, was born in 2004, and their son, Jacob, in 2007. They are an immeasurable source of happiness to us.

———————

Odellia, my beautiful daughter, shown here on her 40th birthday and with her husband, Richard, and their children Gabriella and Jacob. Odellia, means "I will thank God" in Hebrew. Despite my many miscarriages and the fact she was born eight weeks premature, I always knew my precious baby girl would survive

This book would be unfinished without mention of the passing of my parents.

My father, who could never visit me in New York because of his heart condition, passed on at the age of sixty-five from a heart attack. On July 4, 1976, alone at home while my mother was watching my nieces and nephew, he must have gotten too excited when he watched a television report on the hostage-rescue operation carried out by Israeli commandos at Entebbe Airport in Uganda. A week earlier, members of the Popular Front for the Liberation of Palestine hijacked an Air France plane with 248 passengers, 94 of whom were Israelis. Thirty years later, the astonishing mission is still the subject of movies and documentaries.

When my father died, I was in Washington, D.C., with my husband and daughter, celebrating America's bicentennial. My sister could not reach me until late Monday night, upon my return to New York. Because Orthodox Judaism does not permit a woman to recite the Kaddish prayer for the dead, the Israeli burial society did not wait for my arrival from New York, insisting on proceeding with my father's funeral "on time"—within twenty-four hours of his death. Had I been a son, they would have waited. Needless to say, it took many years for me to get over such shameful discrimination. Hevra Kadisha, Israel's orthodox burial society, has since become a little less stringent in this matter and would have postponed the burial until my arrival.

My mother passed on May 4, 1993, while recovering from a successful removal of a benign meningioma. Ten days after her surgery her heart gave out, perhaps the result of a blood clot that traveled from her brain.

I was by my mother's side a week before her surgery, alleviating her fears, and a week after, attending to all her needs, as if she were a baby. When I left her, she was recovering well, ready to return to the assisted living facility where she lived. Three days after my return to New York, I had to fly back to Israel to attend her funeral.

As satisfied and fulfilling as motherhood has been for me, I still yearned to widen my horizons. In 1977, I enrolled in the City University of New York (CUNY). I intended to pursue a bachelor's degree in art history but soon opted for political science instead, earning my BA in 1980. In 1992 I earned my doctorate from CUNY. In between, in 1986, I began to teach political science at CUNY's Queens College campus. While concentrating in international relations and comparative politics, I keep a focus on the subject of women and war, which has remained close to my heart.

I was fortunate to obtain a Fulbright-Hays scholarship, which enabled me to spend part of 1995 and 1996 in Israel, researching the Israeli-Palestinian conflict from the viewpoint of a particular group of women. In that period, I interviewed thirty-two Israeli women—bereaved mothers, sisters, daughters, and widows. They also included mothers and wives who had cared for their wounded sons and husbands, the mother of a soldier missing in action, a handicapped woman who had been wounded in a Syrian attack while in national service, and other women who had suffered the consequences of war and its aftermath. Salwa, my Palestinian assistant, interviewed on my behalf eight Palestinian widows from the West Bank whose husbands had been killed in the first *intifada*—the Palestinian uprising that lasted from 1987 to 1992. I wrote about my findings and have presented them in academic conferences and other forums.

My experience as an interviewer of bereaved and aggrieved women is too detailed to burden my readers with here. Perhaps needless to say, beholding the tragedies of the women I interviewed was difficult and emotional. I witnessed their heartbreak, and relived mine, over and over again. Some of their descriptions, the words they used, were so gut-wrenching I sometimes felt I could take no more. But the experience was rewarding too, as together we cried and laughed and broke bread in the small hours of the morning. I was moved by the confidence and trust these women had in me and the stories they shared that went far beyond the needs of my research. Most satisfying was the knowledge that I empowered many of the women I touched. And so, close to a quarter century after I had become one of them, I closed the circle.

Currently I live in New York with my husband, Steve, and continue to teach political science at Queens College. My passion for writing has not stopped with this book, and I am now working on my first work of fiction.